Ontario
Two Hundred Years in Pictures

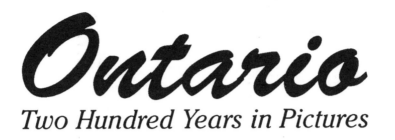

W9-DCF-879

Roger Hall and Gordon Dodds

Dundurn Press
Toronto and Oxford
1991

Design and Production: JAQ
Copy Editor: Mark Fenton
Printing and Binding: Gagné Printing Ltd., Louiseville, Quebec, Canada

Dundurn Press wishes to acknowledge the generous assistance and ongoing support of
**The Canada Council, The Book Publishing Industry Development Programme of the
Department of Communications** and **The Ontario Arts Council.**
     Care has been taken to trace the ownership of copyright material used in the text,
including the illustrations. The author and publisher welcome any information enabling
them to rectify any reference or credit in subsequent editions.

                                                            J. Kirk Howard, Publisher

Canadian Cataloguing in Publication Data

Hall, Roger, 1945–
     Ontario : 200 years in pictures

Rev. ed.
First ed. published under title: A picture history of Ontario.
Includes bibliographical references and index.
ISBN 1-55002-077-3

1. Ontario – History. 2. Ontario – Description and
travel – Views. I. Dodds, Gordon. II. Title.
III. Title: A picture history of Ontario.

FC3061.H34 1990   971.3   C90-095729-8
F1058.H34 1990

Dundurn Press Limited   Dundurn Distribution
2181 Queen Street East   73 Lime Walk
Suite 301   Headington
Toronto, Canada   Oxford, England
M4E 1E5   OX3 7AD

Cover illustration: *The Jackes Residence, "The Elms", Toronto*; c. 1875, artist unknown
(Canadian School, 19th century), oil on canvas, 81.3 x 61.0 cm. Used by permission of
the Art Gallery of Ontario.

Ontario

Two Hundred Years in Pictures

For Sandra and Marietta

Contents

Preface

❖

Ontario is the subject of this book, but in a way Ontario is also the object. Our purpose has been to come to terms with Ontario, something we have found easier to do in pictures than in words. Ontario's identity is more show than tell.

We make no claims to have been comprehensive. It would be presumptuous and impossible to relate the collective history of eight million people and their predecessors over two centuries in a couple of hundred pages. We are convinced Ontario's story is rich, unique, and exciting and we hope some of the flavour is shown here. Increasingly, we have come to realize that the Ontarian experience is wrapped around two or three themes: first, a fundamental and ongoing sense of "loyalty"; then the maintenance of a healthy balance – between city and country, between region and province, and province and nation; and finally, the maintenance of tory attitudes (that's small "t" tory) which argue for cautious, purposeful, and moderate change in all things – government, religion, education, society, and, of course, Ontario's provincial pastime and pleasure, politics.

Some will accuse us of a certain preoccupation with Toronto and the royal family. For this we don't apologize, nor do we suggest that only Torontonians took photos, and took them only when royalty came to town. Royal occasions are benchmarks for much of Ontario's history, and the monarchy was the living embodiment of loyalty. A royal visit was an opportunity to recharge emotional and imperial batteries. Toronto's pre-eminence and domination of provincial affairs, while frequently undesirable, has been and remains irresistible.

Others might feel our efforts have been inadequate because we have largely ignored the con-

temporary scene, the newest manifestation of Ontario since the Second World War. This has been a deliberate choice. Too many picture histories give the readers an impression, when they come to "the end," that the millennium has been reached, and so they reveal the grand and glorious present as the logical outcome of the past. We have tried to avoid that impression. Besides, our opinion is that the factors that explained and unified much of Ontario's past have been buffeted and largely dismantled since 1945 by massive immigration, continuous urban growth, and the cumulative effects of modern technology.

We have also been forced to turn aside a good many photographs and illustrations concerning a vast range of topics that we should like to have included. But this is a bare-bones account, and our ambition was to present pictorial matter rather than simply illustrative material; that is, we wanted portraits of people and places rather than things. In this quest we have received a great deal of help. John Mezaks and Alex Ross of the Archives of Ontario should be singled out, as should Scott James and Linda Price at the City of Toronto Archives. We are grateful also to other staff members at these institutions as well as at the Public Archives of Canada in Ottawa (especially Denyse Caron), the Metropolitan Toronto Central Library, the Toronto Harbour Commission, the Regional Collection at the University of Western Ontario, the University of Toronto Archives, Wayne State University Archives in Detroit, and the Eaton's of Canada Archives. We are particularly grateful to Sandra Martin for her editorial advice. Thanks are due as well to Mel Hurtig, who suggested the book to us.

Preface to the 1991 Edition

A dozen years have passed since the first publication of this book. We are now on the eve of the bicentenary of the Constitutional – or Canada – Act of 1791, the Act of the British Imperial Parliament that brought the parliamentary nucleus of modern Ontario (and modern Québec, for that matter) into being. With the recent failure of the Meech Lake Accord and an accompanying resurgence of nationalism in Québec, it seems likely that new constitutional arrangements will be necessary to preserve a Canadian community. Whatever arrangements are made, Ontario, as a political entity, is as certain to endure as is Québec.

Our new edition celebrates the province's 200th birthday. We have taken the opportunity to revise some material, correct errors and omissions, and to extend the contemporary section – Ontario since the Second World War – to incorporate the NDP election victory of 1990.

We have seen no reason, however, to alter dramatically our view of Ontario. The province remains a place where balance and moderation are considered to be both virtuous and desirable by native residents and newcomers alike. Viewed objectively, this posture has strengths and limitations, of course, but it is the direct product of the province's long and distinctive historical experience.

We are constant, as well, in our debts to the archivists, librarians, and curators in the province who have so generously given their time and advice to this project. We salute as well photographic artists who were the original creators of the images collected here. And finally our thanks to Toronto's Dundurn Press, a firm that has played no small role in shaping Ontario's understanding of itself.

RH and GD, Toronto, September, 1991

Introduction

Ontario sprawls across the Canadian map "the vital centre," "the heart of the country," "the golden hinge" of promotional tracts and travel brochures. But Ontario is undeniably real, certain, and solid, the firmest bulwark in the definition of English Canada. And Ontario speaks for and gives shape to much of what is English Canada. It is the largest and most populous of all the English-speaking provinces and, to the everlasting chagrin of Maritimers and Western Canadians alike, the industrial and commercial focus of the country. Ontario's pre-eminence is both its strength and its weakness. While virtually everyone agrees that Ontario is decidedly Canadian and that a major chunk of Canada is Ontario, few people know what Ontario is, or what it means to be an Ontarian.

Ontario, in true Canadian fashion, faces an identity crisis. Canada itself has always been a compromise. How could a nation so young, so diverse, and so vast be anything else? Besides, Canada is a country of distinctive and enormously varied regions, some as idiosyncratic geographically as others are culturally and socially. But is Ontario a distinctive region, except in a vague political sense? Few would deny that Newfoundlanders and Maritimers have a unique society and a corresponding historical tradition. Québec's special character is beyond any doubt, and westerners lay convincing claim to their particular identity. The drums and alarms don't sound the same way for Ontario.

Ontario's elusive identity is a tantalizing problem for historians. Only in legal terms is it easy to get a working definition. Ontario is, unquestionably, a province of Canada, and has been one since Confederation in 1867. Before that Ontario was called Canada West and before that Upper Canada,

the latter name being applied because the province stretched along the upper reaches of the St. Lawrence River system. It isn't difficult to project Ontario's modern borders into the past and trace Loyalist penetration into the region after the American revolution, or before that to chart the activities of early French traders. Anthropologists and archaeologists can uncover much about the Indian societies that existed here, and hypotheses abound, curving backwards into time, analysing the area's occupation by primitive man.

Sketching in the borders of a region and projecting them into the past isn't enough. Ontario requires social, cultural, and psychological definition as well. And this is where the difficulty lies. The idea of Ontario has become fused with that of Canada as a whole. The historian must grapple with the notion of Central Canada, separate out the elements that are "national," and analyse the residue to discover a regional definition for Ontario. The job is complicated by the fact that what was essentially English-speaking Canada for most of the nineteenth century became exclusively the province of Ontario.

Some historians have argued blatantly that Ontario no longer exists, that after Confederation it slowly turned into an abstraction, with its regional identity lost because of an intense identification with Canadian "national" affairs. They allege that Ontario's literary and artistic traditions are derivative, explaining that in Southern Ontario's rather featureless geography the inhabitants are indifferent to the natural setting. Additionally, they blame their fellow historians for being preoccupied with national problems, particularly national politics, at the expense of the region. Generally these scholars agree that in the nineteenth century Ontario existed as a distinctive entity with a firmly rooted culture and society; consequently they have turned their full professional attention to that period. It is tempting to join those who argue that Ontario no longer exists, but there is much evidence to suggest that the body is still warm; occasionally, indeed, there are flickers of life still.

So far as *Ontario: Two Hundred Years in Pictures* has a theme, it is that Ontario flourished from its eighteenth-century beginning until shortly after the Second World War. During that century and a half a singular society found its roots in the province and fashioned a correspondingly unique outlook on the world. After 1945 Ontario both fell and was pushed into the mainstream of North American society. The war had catapulted Canada onto the world's stage, and Ontario right along with it. In a scramble to find a place in the new order of the post-war world, Ontario stretched itself commercially and industrially both within and without Canada. The result has been the gradual abandoning of traditional ideas and beliefs in favour of a new international style. If a date were to be placed on the death of Old Ontario it would have to be 1961 with the demise of Leslie Frost's government. Thereafter, to paraphrase Professor Arthur Lower, there would no longer be Ontarians, only people who happened to live in Ontario.

"*Ut Incepit Fidelis Sic Permanet,*" claims the province's official motto, and not without reason. Loyal Ontario began and loyal she remains. But loyal to what?

Ontario, one might argue, at one time was loyal to France, although the scrappy band of fur traders and bored soldiers who occupied it couldn't have expressed much of an Ontarian opinion. Champlain had explored the area early in the seventeenth century and missionaries had established themselves among the Indians, notably the Hurons centred at Sainte-Marie near modern Midland – a settlement recently uncovered and restored with a large measure of success by the Ontario government. But in 1649 the Huron nation was largely destroyed by the Iroquois, and some of the Jesuit fathers who had built and operated Sainte-Marie joined the long list of martyrs to their faith. Permanent European settlement was not a feature of the French occupation, but commerce and war necessitated the posts and fortresses that gave what scant substance there was to the French claim to

the area. The nuclei of modern Toronto, Windsor, Niagara, and – most significant at the time – Kingston were all established in this way.

During the Seven Years' War (from 1756 to 1763) the French abandoned most of the region to their English foes without a serious struggle. The exceptions were Fort Frontenac (now Kingston), which was taken by an Anglo-American force in 1758, blown up, and then abandoned, and Fort Niagara, which succumbed a year later after a short siege. When Governor Vaudreuil surrendered Montreal to the British in September 1760, a year after the battle of the Plains of Abraham, he was effectively surrendering Ontario too; the French fact was not to become significant in Ontario again until the twentieth century. After the peace of 1763, loyalty meant fealty to George III, his heirs and successors. What would become Ontario was absorbed into His Majesty's not especially loyal province of Québec as its borders were stretched westward beyond Lake Ontario into the Ohio Valley.

Ontario's loyalty to Britain really dates from the American Revolution. In 1775 the permanent population of the province consisted of a handful of French-speaking settlers in the Detroit/Windsor region. The revolution changed everything. Neither the fourteenth colony, Nova Scotia, nor the newest, Québec, swung to the American cause. Montréal's few hundred English merchants were fearful of losing their commercial links with Britain if they threw in with the Americans, and were equally frightened of American competition for their formidable fur empire which arched through Ontario's lakes and rivers as it made its way west. Inevitably the definition of loyalty had a self-serving economic edge.

By 1783 – the end of the American revolt – what had been a trickle of wartime refugees became a stream. An estimated thirty thousand came to Nova Scotia (which some labelled in disgust "Nova Scarcity") and almost doubled the size of that colony. What was shortly to become Upper Canada saw an influx of five to six thousand. These refugees were the first sizable body of permanent settlers to occupy the area, and they were to set a tone and to fashion an ideology which became the crucible for Ontario's future.

Contemporary Ontario is often labelled as conservative, stable, wealthy, smug, and confident. In the eighteenth century Loyalist Ontario was conservative, unstable, poor, maybe a trifle smug, but with hardly any confidence. These traits came from the Loyalist migrations, or, at least, can be traced to what some scholars call "the Loyalist myth." It is worthwhile to distinguish the Loyalist reality from the mythology.

The Loyalists who made their way into the western parts of the old province of Québec were mostly American frontiersmen from Pennsylvania and New York. They were very different from the townspeople of the eastern seaboard who moved to Nova Scotia, the West Indies, or Britain itself. The frontiersmen were experienced woodsmen and well aware of the rough life that awaited them. A few had suffered terrorist treatment at the hands of their American neighbours; some had even been tarred, feathered, and run on rails. All were uprooted, or uprooted themselves, and became displaced persons or refugees. As such, in both Nova Scotia and Québec, they were not badly treated.

The Loyalist myth has it that these sturdy folk overcame great odds to establish themselves and a better world in the north. This was hardly the case. Few refugees anywhere have been treated as well. At first Québec governor Frederick Haldimand attempted to settle the Loyalists on the French seigneuries of the old regime. But this proved unsatisfactory; the seigneurial was a feudal system of land tenure complete with fiefs, duties, and binding obligations. It was a distastefully foreign concept to the refugees, and Haldimand, although he had some doubts because of possible Indian objections, finally determined to settle them in the western reaches of Québec province. The local Indian tribes, and the "forgotten" loyalists – those Indians, Mohawks and other Iroquois, who under their leader Joseph Brant had sided with Britain in the revolution eventually agreed either to sell their lands or to live beside the white men. It was a decision they would come to regret.

So Haldimand began his Loyalist initiative. At first he settled disbanded regiments in ranges of quickly surveyed townships stretched along the American frontier so that in the event of war these veterans would form a firm defensive barrier. Three main areas were selected: along the Upper St. Lawrence; around Kingston and the Bay of Quinte; and the Niagara Peninsula. A fourth area, near Detroit, was considered, but the surrender of that post to the United States postponed development.

Land, the only commodity the Imperial government had, was granted in lots from a hundred to a thousand acres. The allotments were based on status and rank: heads of families received a hundred acres; field officers up to, and eventually more than, a thousand acres. Additionally, clothing, tools, and provisions were supplied for three years to help prime the settlement pump. Although there were hard times, particularly the "hungry year" of 1789, these were very favoured displaced persons. And not a few disgruntled Americans – some would say land-hungry – moved north to join them. By 1790 Western Québec could boast a population of ten thousand in an area that a dozen years before had been a howling wilderness.

No matter where they came from the Loyalists soon showed that they had been in the forefront of political protest in the old Thirteen Colonies. Although they were not prepared to fight a war for colonial rights they would take every legal and constitutional means at their disposal to better their lives. Some were firmly committed to Imperial Britain, others had fought in the war for the King's cause, but most were simply small "c" conservatives who preferred familiar British institutions to American republicanism and democracy.

Britain was well aware of this. When constitutional demands were voiced in Québec the mother country responded cautiously, willing to grant her loyal subjects a certain amount of autonomy but very careful not to permit the "excess" of democracy which many British colonial officials and parliamentarians felt had contributed to the American revolt. Britain's measured response to the Loyalist and mercantile demand for a stronger say in government became the founding statute of Ontario – the Constitutional or Canada Act of 1791.

This new Imperial act superseded the old Québec Act of 1774. It split the colony into two separate provinces – Upper Canada to the west, and Lower Canada to the east along the St. Lawrence, where the inhabitants were mixed but predominantly *Canadien*. The act established in each province a lieutenant-governor, an executive council to advise him, a legislative council to act as an upper house, and a representative assembly. Policy was to be directed by the executive, which was responsible not to the assembly but to the Crown; it was British government but the model was a throwback to the Stuarts a century and a half before. No democratic spirit bubbled in the colonial assemblies: power filtered from the top; the lieutenant-governor and his chosen council reigned supreme; and the Anglican church was institutionalized in the provinces to tie the colonies more firmly to the mother country. (It was noted in Britain that the Anglican episcopate had never been formally established in the Thirteen Colonies.) A permanent appropriation of funds "for the Support and Maintenance of a Protestant Clergy" was guaranteed by devoting one-seventh of all lands in the province as reserves, with the proceeds from the sale or rental going to the church. Another seventh was set aside for Crown use, that is for Crown revenue, funds that the administration could raise from the colony without consulting the local assembly. These Crown and Clergy reserves were considered the firmest barrier against American influence.

But the land question that interested most settlers was not the reserves nor the many thousands of acres set aside for school or defence use. What pleased them in the Constitutional Act, and affected them most, was that the old feudal, seigneurial land-tenure system of the old régime was gone for good in the upper province. Land would be granted in the English manner – in "free and common soccage"; that is, freehold tenure.

The franchise, for the time, was fairly wide. A holding with an annual worth of two pounds entitled one to the vote in rural areas; in towns it went to those who owned a residence with a yearly value of five pounds or who rented one at ten pounds per annum. In Upper Canada membership in the Assembly numbered not less than sixteen (in more populous Lower Canada it was fifty) and the Legislative Council was made up of seven members (fifteen in Lower Canada).

The first leader of the government of this proud new province was Lieutenant-Colonel John Graves Simcoe, ex-commander of the American loyalist Queen's Rangers Regiment, MP for Bath in the British Parliament, inheritor of substantial wealth, and an eighteenth-century English gentleman of the first stripe. Simcoe was a man with a mission; he wanted to establish in Upper Canada a "superior, more happy, and more polished form of government" not only to attract further immigrants but, in the most naive fashion, to cause a "renewal of Empire" and so win Americans back into the British fold. In short, he set out to design and build a new society.

Simcoe has been called the "effervescent" governor and condemned for his unbridled enthusiasms. There is some truth to this. He was more soldier than politician and more tactician than strategist. Simcoe had troops build good primary roads in the province, principally Yonge and Dundas streets, the former leading north to Lake Simcoe (named after his father, or so he said). He planned to remove the government from Newark (Niagara) to a more defensible site in the interior which he named London, but Lord Dorchester, the governor-in-chief of British North America, chose instead a location at the Lake Ontario end of the Toronto Portage. Simcoe made the best of it, remarking that there was better salmon fishing there anyway. He was a strong churchman and supported the cause of the Clergy Reserves. He successfully set the primitive provincial and local government machinery in motion: land boards functioned, the judiciary began its rudimentary proceedings, in fact all the fledgling institutions were operating when he left in 1796. But he had always been a soldier, and that was his downfall. For him Ontario was to be a bristling military centre – Fortress Ontario. But Lord Dorchester saw little reason to defend an unsettled appendage or to antagonize restless Indian allies, or to excite further the ambitious Americans to the south. Imperial Britain agreed – after all the colony of Upper Canada was expendable, not least because it was expensive to run (twenty thousand pounds a year) and it returned nothing. Canada for the British still meant Québec, and Québec was to be defended by the omnipotent Royal Navy at the cost of any inland colony.

Simcoe was followed by lesser men, men without the same enthusiasm or imagination. First Peter Russell, faint-hearted and uncertain, then Peter Hunter, general and busy commander of all British forces in North America, and then Francis Gore, brimming with unfulfilled promise. Gore was lieutenant-governor from 1806 to 1817, but he was absent from the province from 1811 to 1814, the crucial years of war with the United States.

Gore was present in the province, however, for a taste of its tumultuous politics, "puddle politics" to some, "squabbling in the wilderness" to others, but politics not to be dismissed. The Constitutional

Act had created a party of favourites. Traditionally lieutenant-governors had chosen their executive and legislative councils from among men they could trust and understand, men who they felt shared the same solid, conservative values as themselves.

Upper Canada was a raw frontier community, and those who were literate and capable of running the machinery of government frequently were not the best choices – almost always they were either old or new Loyalists or British colonial appointments. Whichever, they were decidedly less than radical in their political opinions. These men quickly became entrenched in their favoured positions. They became a kind of Tory party permanently in power. Efforts to dislodge them, indeed to throw up opposition of any sort, were few and disorganized before the War of 1812. Those who did argue the side of the popular assembly did so over the control of money bills, the right of the assembly to have full charge of all the revenues raised in the province. Early advocates of an extension of the assembly's powers were Robert Thorpe and Joseph Willcocks. They have generally been viewed as demagogues and smoke-makers, but increasingly the opinion is that they were part of the Whig reform tradition, transplanted to Upper Canada from Ireland. However, reform was to be cut short by the War of 1812.

That war is a kind of Holy War in Ontario's history. It is the chief repository of all the Ontario myths and no small number of Canadian ones. The late C.P. Stacey, Canada's dean of military history, called it an event everyone can recall with satisfaction because everyone interprets it in his own way. For the Americans – it was a second revolution, a war where they defeated the vaunted British navy, particularly on the Great Lakes, and, of course, the army at the Battle of New Orleans (fought, alas, after the peace was signed). For Canadians, and especially Upper Canadians, it was "Invasion Repulsed," a heroic homeland defence in the face of a bitter foe. And for the English, fully occupied with Napoleon, the War of 1812, that is, the American phase, is scarcely remembered at all. They don't even know it happened.

The point is that it was Ontario's war. Ontario was invaded, violated, and in parts occupied. And Ontario had a large fifth column – the province's population was eighty per cent American in origin – which caused extensive war damage in both economic and human terms.

The war was the breeding-place of Canadian heroes. Among them are soldier-martyr General Sir Isaac Brock, plucky Laura Secord and her cow, and the strong, capable citizen militia that rallied to throw back the Yankees. Despite individual and collective heroics, capturing Upper Canada, twisting the Lion's tail, proved difficult for one reason only: the British army. The British army was not a cohesive force led by brilliant officers; rather, they made fewer blunders than the Americans. The Americans overestimated the importance of Upper Canada and wasted time and money in the wilderness when they could have cut off supplies by drawing a steel ring around the St. Lawrence.

When the war ended Ontario had established another tradition which would prove extremely durable: anti-Americanism, a keen refinement of the Loyalist stance. Besides, there was now a proved pantheon of heroes for the imagination to draw upon. Wartime service became a key to advancement and status in the province. To have served – even, like some, to have surrendered gallantly – was a mark of honour. One of the great ironies is that the American invasion probably kept Ontario British. If war had not come the Americans might have conquered the colony by peaceful immigration. But war did come, and with it the revival of Loyalism.

Upper Canada, like the rest of the British Empire, became a different place after the Napoleonic Wars. The great folk movement of millions of people shifting across the Atlantic to America began, and lasted a century. Upper Canada claimed its share of settlers. The province and its economy were still very primitive and very much under the mercantile control of the City of London, but increasingly the commercial emphasis was shifting from fur to grain. As well, local industries were developing. Yet the economy was still fundamentally agrarian, and the sale or lease of land was still the biggest business whether it was conducted through the government, through the ever-plentiful land sharks, through distinguished ventures like the massive British-based Canada Company, or through eccentrics like Colonel Thomas Talbot, whose vast personal domain stretched along the north shore of Lake Erie. The society was equally simple and, to visitors such as Anna Jameson, fundamentally rude. The principal towns (York and Kingston) were little more than wharves, warehouses, and a few pretentious public buildings. And the politics, always the politics, were as vicious as they were intense.

The War of 1812 made the Upper Canadian world safe for oligarchy. Those few in a position of power moved to consolidate that strength and to assure its smooth transfer into equally safe hands when they passed on. Political radicalism was dead in the years following the war and conservatism entrenched itself in a peculiar form called the Family Compact. Was it any wonder that the oligarchy thrown up by the Constitutional Act became entrenched by that war, and was it any wonder thereafter that they celebrated the British connection at all costs? After all, it was that link that had saved them. For these men and for their anointed leader, John Strachan (confidant and adviser to Lieutenant-Governor Sir Peregrine Maitland and eventually the first Anglican bishop of Toronto), the war was the sacred touchstone, the proof of one's acceptability.

The clique succeeded, however, as all cliques do, because it controlled patronage – it was more a persuasion than a party. The members had a Tory cast of mind more than anything else, and the names of a few prominent families – the Boultons, the Robinsons, the Jarvises, and so on – soon dominated everything. Many observers have labelled the Compact as corrupt, but this is not so. Recent evidence reveals that the group was rigorous and methodical in its administration, and thorough in its investigation of irregularities. The Compact had a strong sense of civic duty. For example, their support of the Welland Canal project, in the conviction that it would serve all Upper Canadian society, demonstrated their concern for the public good. But they were an oligarchy in a democratic age.

Opposition to the Compact was ill-organized and fragmented until the 1820s. Although it was not tinged with the racism evident in Lower Canada, the struggle between the Tory clique and reform in Upper Canada was fierce. Agitator Robert Gourlay, the celebrated "Banished Briton," was the Compact's first victim. He would be followed by others – the Bidwells, Mr. Justice John Willis, and, of course, William Lyon Mackenzie.

Mackenzie in a way is a typical Ontario figure.

Popularly considered a radical, he was in effect a camouflaged conservative. Like Stephen Leacock's knight who rode off in all directions, Mackenzie seems to have had no set policies except a vague commitment to the "common man." Frequently, he is thought to have been the chief advocate of responsible government, but he didn't really know the meaning of the phrase and generally favoured American republicanism. He apparently wanted for Upper Canada a kind of Jeffersonian dream, and envisaged a province composed of yeomen-farmers wedded to the soil, firmly patriotic, and ready to become political minutemen in the American colonial mould. He, like the Compact he so vigorously opposed, was a stranger to the forces and values that eventually dominated the nineteenth century: liberalism and industrialism. The rebellion that he plotted misfired when it broke out in 1837 because, like so many politicians after him, he failed to understand the basic conservative nature of Upper Canadians.

Perhaps if Mackenzie had realized that whiggery could be considered a form of conservatism and had appealed to the populace in those terms, his violent phase would have been unnecessary. As it was, that lesson had to be taught again a decade later, in the 1840s, by the solemn, short-lived dynasty of William and Robert Baldwin. But the impetus for real change could come from only one place. It might be accelerated by advocates in the province but fundamental change had to be initiated across the Atlantic in Imperial London.

It came in the form of a slightly foppish, egotistical young English aristocrat, John George Lambton, Earl of Durham. His acquaintance with Upper Canada was brief but conclusive. He spent most of his time in the colony gazing in wonder at thundering Niagara Falls, but his political recommendations for the place were sound, even though they were for a time ignored in London.

Durham's report set in motion a scheme that had long been considered – recombining Upper and Lower Canada into a single unit. The idea had been advanced, albeit as a merchants' plot, in 1822, and revived periodically. By Durham's time Upper Canada had a population of more than four hundred thousand, but it had no seaport, as the noble lord reminded the Imperial Parliament. Further, the unruly French needed to be swamped in a sea of English and, more importantly, the economic potential of both colonies would be enhanced if the Canadas were one. All this, Durham insisted, could easily be achieved under the grant of responsible government, the simple democratic expedient whereby the cabinet is responsible to the Assembly rather than to the Crown.

The Imperial mother nodded her approval of everything except the framework of responsible government, and in 1841 Upper Canada's short history came to an end. The province ceased to exist; for the next twenty-six years, it would be called Canada West.

From 1841 to Confederation, the affairs of Ontario were once more bound up at least officially with those of French Canada. Although there was considerable co-operation among political leaders during this period, the two provinces very much went their separate ways; the 1850s were strongly marked by a sense of regional identification called "sectionalism." Sectionalism grew out of grievances as much as distinctive interests. The Act of Union had created a single province in which the two halves enjoyed equal representation in the legislature. Presumably this had been done to avoid a French-Canadian dominance of the Assembly; if so, it was a serious error, for immigration would soon turn the balance of population in favour of Canada West and the English-speaking settlers. Another great limitation was the Imperial decision to withhold responsible government. A string of colonial governors from Lord Sydenham (Baron Sydenham of Kent and Toronto) through Sir Charles Bagot and Sir Charles Metcalfe (dubbed Charles the Simple by reformers) attempted half-measures, stalling tactics, and, in the case of Bagot, helpful compromise, but the road was tortuous. Robert Baldwin in the upper province and Louis Lafontaine in the lower persevered, however, and as one historian of the period has stated, showed the Imperial officials two important facts: that Canada could not be governed without the French; and Canada could be governed with the French.

In 1846 the Imperial Parliament scrapped the protective Corn Laws, the laws that controlled entry of foreign grain to the British market, and Britain and her Empire entered the era of free trade. Thus the chief mercantilistic argument in favour of not granting responsible government – the need for colonial dependence on the mother country – was removed. In that same year Lord Grey, Durham's brother-in-law, became colonial secretary. The following year Lord Elgin, his son-in-law, became governor general of British North America. The grant of responsible government followed, when after a successful election, in which their party won a clear majority in the Assembly, Baldwin and Lafontaine were called by Elgin to form a government.

The economy of the province was hard hit by the Imperial abandonment of the Corn Laws. Agriculture in Canada West was greatly dependent on Imperial markets, even more so when wheat became the primary cash crop. The lumber industry was the second strength of the economy, and this too was susceptible to fluctuations in British markets. American competition further threatened prosperity. The old Laurentian fur-trade route which now funnelled a commercial flow of manufactures and produce through Montréal seemed lost forever by the repeal of Imperial protection and in 1849 certain Montréal merchants in Canada East clamoured for annexation to the States.

Canada West was more secure, and instead of appealing for American annexation the Tories of Ontario began serious consideration of a British North American union. Even so, some replacement had to be found for the lost Imperial markets, and certainly in 1849 a union would not produce a sufficiently large common market. The answer lay with the United States – not annexation but reciprocity, a common lowering of trade barriers and cancelling of various tariffs and duties. Elgin fostered the idea and sold it on both sides of the border with a winning combination of tact and generous helpings of champagne. Reciprocity began in 1854 and ran for ten years.

The result was that Canada West boomed. Agriculture was no longer based on scrappy subsistence but on cash crops; wheat production leaped forward, as did dairying and, to a certain extent, mixed farming. Lumbering too grew to hitherto-unknown importance, and much trade shifted to a north-south axis rather than an east-west one. But British links remained; the outbreak of the Crimean War in 1854 reopened the British market to Canadian produce and the British, in turn, invested heavily in Canada West's future – primarily in railroads.

Railroads were the nineteenth century's magic elixir, the wonderful tonic that would cure all ills –

economic, social, political, cultural – and Ontario was soon laced with an expanding network designed to suck and syphon commerce from every corner, not to mention drawing the trade of the American west through Canada. But the costs of these railroads were enormous and frequently outweighed their advantages. Communities were knitted together, but often at the cost of bankruptcy. Railroads brought huge public debts, created higher tariffs in order to pay for them, and thrust government into a common corner with the railroad companies – a prime situation for corruption and graft.

Railroads and the commerce which was both their cause and effect helped to lay the basis for British American union. At the same time, it was obvious that the Union of 1841 was a dismal failure. Canada East retained its distinctive French laws, its Catholic religion, and its strong sense of nationalism, a patriotism which ironically had been rekindled by Durham's attempts to drown the French in a sea of English. Instead, the English-speakers had flocked westwards to the upper province. Government became a shaky compromise between English and French interests, and the development of a solid, colony-wide provincial party structure seemed not more than a remote possibility. Besides, Canada West was seething at the situation. They considered the old balance of parliamentary representation struck by the Act of Union absurd. "Representation according to population" became the rallying-cry in the more populous west and soon "rep by pop" became a universal slogan.

In the face of these pressures the old Baldwin-Lafontaine alliance of the 1840s fell away, and distinctive sectional political parties emerged. In Canada West the most significant move was the development of the Clear Grit party, so called because its adherents had to be tried-and-true reformers, "clear grit" all the way. Increasingly, they became the voice of the new Ontario, particularly of Toronto, although they retained much active support in the farming communities and small towns and cities of southwestern Ontario. Their leader was the forceful George Brown and their chief mouthpiece his newspaper, the Toronto *Globe*.

The opposition rallied around a bright capable young Eastern Ontario lawyer named John A. Macdonald. Early on in his career, Macdonald realized that some sort of basic alliance with the French would always be necessary for Canadian political success, and so he reached out to conservatives in Canada East and to non-radical liberals in Ontario. Thus was founded, in 1854, what would be Canada's first great political expression, the Liberal-Conservative party. In Upper Canada Tory roots dug much deeper than 1854, stretching back to the Loyalists and the Constitutional Act.

It is here that it becomes difficult to sort out Ontarian and Canadian politics – which is which? Does Ontario's Loyalist stream flow through Macdonald or Brown? The answer is, of course, that it moves through both. Here it is pertinent to focus on Brown, for he converted the "Grits" into a British North American equivalent of the British Liberal party – the party of free trade, industrialization, individualism, and the Empire. If Brown dominated the towns, cities, and countryside of Canada West, Québec increasingly fell under the sway of the Bleus, the Tories of that province. Political deadlock in the United Provinces parliament was the result of this marked sectionalism.

Ontario took the initiative for change. In 1859, the "Grit" convention endorsed the idea of federalism as a solution to Canada's problems. They resolved that local issues could be dealt with by provincial governments while matters of wider concern would be conducted by a central government. Behind the scenes, Ontario had its shrewd business eye on the old Hudson's Bay Company lands in the vast Canadian northwest and wanted their agricultural and commercial wealth to filter through Toronto. But it wasn't until 1864 that Brown suggested that the warring political groups establish a coalition to strike a general federation of all the provinces. Those negotiations and achievements do not require restatement here, except to note that Ontario's interest had helped to promote them and after 1867 would occasionally challenge but generally sustain them.

July 1, 1867. Canada's birthday, but also the birthday of the province of Ontario and of the three other founding provinces: Québec, Nova Scotia, and New Brunswick. Ontario in 1867 had a population of about one-and-a-half million, making it the most populous part of the country, and in economic terms, because of the fruits of reciprocity, it controlled the lion's share of the economy. More than a third of the nation's economic activity emanated from Ontario.

Ontario was not a completely homogeneous unit. Toronto and its hinterland might control the central area, but Brantford, Guelph, Hamilton, London, Belleville, and Berlin were all distinctive entities, and further afield the old river towns of Kingston and Cornwall and lake ports like Sarnia, or Goderich, or even old Niagara, were important local centres. A balance between provincial and local control had always been an Ontarian trait and it continued into the post-Confederation period. For example, powerful local school boards were an integral part of the network of state schools. Although Ontario was still fundamentally agricultural, the economy rested upon different bases in different locales. Increasingly after Confederation, and with the opening of the prairie West, Ontarian farmers turned to local and regional markets, and away from "King Wheat." So orchards grew up in the Niagara peninsula, dairying and cheese production developed in Eastern Ontario, especially in the area of Kingston and its off-shore islands and in Prince Edward County, and tobacco was cultivated in southwestern Ontario.

As the province became industrialized fewer workers grew their own vegetables, so that it became profitable to do truck farming for a local city or town market. Railroads opened distant markets and mechanized farm machinery increased productivity and helped accelerate the shift of population from the country to the towns. The post-Confederation era also saw the beginning of the breakdown of the old farm family as the traditional working unit. Ontario farming rested on the family structure, a structure, incidentally, in which pioneer women were the keystone. Women produced and raised the children who in turn became the primary labour force. Women also fed, clothed, and ministered to all the members of the working unit.

Small towns and cities characterized the Ontario of this period. They flourished because they provided the service needs of small hinterlands. Manufacturers sprang out of village stores, local breweries thrived, small carriage works and furniture factories were set up in every town. Some of these businesses, because of railroads and the protective tariffs of John A. Macdonald's National Policy, grew into substantial nation-wide concerns in the late nineteenth century and helped to make Ontario the kingpin of Western Canada's development. Ontario's industries boomed as the province

(and its banks) clamped a developer's hand on the prairies.

After an initial setback George Brown's "Clear Grits" came to dominate the political scene. Ontario's first premier was John Sandfield Macdonald, who is still frequently confused with his mentor, Sir John A. Macdonald. Sandfield was Sir John's designated hitter, his nominee, for control of Ontario. He was premier from 1867 until his death in 1871. For many years he was considered merely Macdonald's mouthpiece, but the view now is that he was more a traditional moderate than a Macdonald Tory, more the inheritor of Baldwin and Lafontaine than anything else, and not a bad caretaker in a difficult time of transition.

In 1871 the old "Clear Grits," now newly christened as Liberals, formed the provincial government. At first they were under the shaky control of the brilliant but erratic Edward Blake, who soon abandoned the province to turn his unsteady hand to national politics which, in turn, he abandoned in the 1890s for Irish-Imperial politics in Britain. The Liberal leadership and provincial premiership shifted to Oliver, later Sir Oliver, Mowat. He was political boss of Ontario for twenty-four years. A pious, serious man and a canny politician, he delightedly referred to himself as the "Christian Statesman." He was one of Canada's first truly modern leaders. His style would appeal to us now, since he was what is called a "brokerage politician"; that is, he steered a moderate course, playing to the electorate, served popular causes, and was not above inventing issues he knew would be popular. Ontario's Tories of our time copied his style with success.

Mowat also had many substantial achievements to his credit, particularly in the fields of "provincial rights" and provincial expansion. In these days of Québec nationalism, cultural sabre-rattling, and Alberta's oil-rich smugness, it is hard to remember that a century ago Ontario was the great champion for increased provincial powers. It is almost inconceivable that a contemporary Ontario crowd could be raised to an emotional frenzy over Ontario's rights, but Mowat had that power.

The provincial-rights movement was a natural outcome of the "Clear Grits" platform of "rep by pop," and it was extremely popular. Primarily at stake were the western provincial boundary and control of the region north and west of Lake Superior. Ontario wanted this vast land and all the mineral and lumbering advantages it promised. If the region went to Manitoba the federal Tories would be able to claim considerable revenues because the natural resources of the western provinces were under federal control (and remained so until the Depression). And like the duel between Brian Mulroney and Clyde Wells, the Mowat-Macdonald confrontation was a bitter personal rivalry – in fact Mowat had once worked in Macdonald's law office in Kingston.

Related federal-provincial questions were: who would control the lucrative liquor trade, who would control Ontario's waterways, who would license taverns or hotels? The final arbiter in all these matters was the Judicial Committee of the Privy Council in England, and that committee came down most firmly and frequently in favour of Ontario rather than Ottawa. Provincial rights owe much to Oliver Mowat, and Sir Oliver and his government were cheered time and time again at the polls.

Industrialism established its Canadian bridgehead in Ontario during the Mowat era, and threw up as many problems as it offered solutions. Industrialization changed the face of Ontario as surely as it did everywhere else it appeared; in Ontario it erased the self-sufficiency of country villages and towns. Most of the insulated communities would linger on until the First World War, but thereafter would be swamped by larger service centres and be reduced to mere dormitories. Migration to the prairies contributed to the depopulation of the Ontario countryside, as did the choice most immigrants made to try their unskilled luck in an urban environment rather than on farms. Industrialization also brought a pressing need to open the province's mineral-rich north, much ignored until the late nineteenth century because of its unsuitability for agriculture. Lumbering firms were soon operating extensively in the Canadian Shield, and pulpwood for paper production was becoming an important industry. Many great mineral discoveries resulted from the construction of the CPR – for instance the great nickel deposits at Sudbury. Discovery of gold at Porcupine in 1909 and three years later at Kirkland Lake focused much attention on the region, but more "practical" minerals such as copper were being uncovered as well. The Ontario government with its sponsorship of mining education in the universities fostered commercial exploitation of the North; this government interest was in sharp contrast to Québec, and helps to explain Ontario's lead in northern development.

Ontario had one serious limitation in the industrial stakes: it was without vast coal resources for energy. This handicap was soon overcome by the extensive and early development of hydro-electric power, which guaranteed industry a cheap source of renewable energy. Public power would be a later development. Industrial expansion meant growth in financial institutions too, and the period from Confederation to the First World War is a great heyday of Ontario finance. Banks, insurance companies, and trust companies all flourished in a frantic rush to fuel the development of Ontario's North and Canada's West. Montréal, of course, shared in this development, as did British portfolio investors and, to the later distress of Canadian nationalists, the American branch plants which were forced by Canada's high tariffs to establish themselves within the country. It should be noted that Ontario's towns and cities in the late nineteenth century fell over themselves in a desperate struggle to attract branch plants.

Sir Oliver Mowat's long reign came to an end in 1896. He was followed by two lacklustre Liberal premiers, A.S. Hardy and the rather more dynamic G.W. Ross, but the period of their premierships, 1896–1905, was largely dominated by the spectacular rise in Ottawa of Sir Wilfrid Laurier's Liberals, with their open advocacy of the twentieth as "Canada's Century." Indeed, Mowat had shifted to Ottawa himself to become a member of Laurier's cabinet.

Once more Ontario's development and history seemed enmeshed with that of the nation as a whole. The short burst of patriotic fervour which accompanied the chest thumping "Canada First" movement of the 1870s had promoted Canada, but it did so with the voice of British Protestant Ontario. Tory politician D'Alton McCarthy's anti-papist oratory and his bigoted Equal Rights Association with its attacks on Québec represented much of Ontario and English Canada. So had the general cry for Louis Riel's blood. By the turn of the century, a definition of Ontario would contain all these opinions and more; Ontario was diversifying, as was Canada.

Ontario remained, however, unquestionably the British heart of Canada, and that heart beat loyal still. On the federal scene Ontario had largely rejected the old Dominion Liberals' campaign for renewed reciprocity with the United States and favoured, at least until John A. Macdonald's death, the Tory alternative. But Laurier and prosperity coincided, and Ontario wanted its full share. That is not to say that the Liberals didn't have to tread warily in Ontario – Ontarians cheered Queen Victoria's Diamond Jubilee as throatily as any Briton, they embraced the idea of Imperial federation fervently, they supported Canada's contribution to the Boer War and in the years before the First World War, as Europe became two armed camps, Ontarians generally believed in Canada's responsibility to contribute to Imperial defence.

But the province was changing fundamentally, and it wasn't simply because of the influx of overseas immigrants. In the late nineteenth and early twentieth centuries French-speaking Québeckers helped to open Ontario's near north and new north, and to the west of the upper Ottawa River the population balance began to shift. This new French-speaking population demanded French schools – separate but equal. The trouble was that the Ontario government didn't consider them equal, at least not by the standards set for English schools in the province, and in 1912 issued Regulation 17 of the Department of Education, which severely cut back the teaching of French in schools. This anti-French policy would not be modified until 1927, and in 1917 would contribute, at the height of the First World War, to Canada's gravest clash between the language groups.

But in 1905 all that seemed a long way away. In that year a new government was elected and a new political force established itself in the province. It was the end of a long Liberal reign, the first expression of the lengthy single-party control which has become characteristic of Ontario politics. The Tory government of Sir James Pliny Whitney *was* different, different because it recognized the major shifts that had been going on in Ontario society. Whitney understood that electoral power had shifted, as surely as the population had, from a rural to an urban base. So his party platform was designed to appeal to the middle-class "liberal" – churchgoing, educated, urban – and it was given a new, truly Canadian title: "Progressive" Conservatism.

Some viewed it as mere middle-of-the-road government, but it was more than that. It was a de-

cided policy and in sharp contrast to the hapless provincial Liberals, who now seemed locked into forgotten rural concerns such as prohibition. The First World War would show that these rural interests still had considerable vitality, but in the meantime Ontario strode with full confidence into the twentieth century. Expansion, prosperity, growth were the commercial watchwords, but progressivism also meant political watchdogs, and there was a strong feeling of public political accountability clinging to Whitney's government. In a way, Whitney's Tories reached back to embrace some of the finer civic virtues of the old Tory Compact, but without the self-interested overtones: much as Upper Canada had been served by the Welland Canal, so twentieth-century Ontario would be served by Ontario Hydro power for the people.

Pre-war Ontario was the apogee of the development of the province's distinctive character: a healthy balance of small-town virtues (even if transplanted to growing cities), public concern for the growth and direction of society, prosperity and economic growth for all to share in, a smiling, educated professional and progressive citizenry, and overlaying it all a patina of muscular British Christianity. All of this confidently marched off to Flanders in 1914. Not all of it came back.

The First World War forms a massive barrier to a clear conception of our past; everything that went before seems forever locked away and everything that has happened since is "modern."

And, perhaps because of the horrors of the war, the pre-war past is remembered somehow as happy and prosperous. This conception holds true for Ontario as much as anywhere, and in many ways, in the Canadian context, Ontario was most affected by that war.

The war, however, did not mean the end of prosperity in Ontario; it had already come and gone. Ontario, during the hot summer of 1914, faced an economic recession. The province was also forced to look at the human costs of its rapid industrialization, overall expansion, and urban growth. What should be done about the plight of labour, slums, health care for the masses, unemployment, and urban poverty? These domestic concerns certainly didn't prevent Ontarians from answering the call to the colours with pride and enthusiasm. When Britain was at war, Canada was at war, and a wave of patriotism swept the cities and countryside. The enthusiasm was not lessened by the large number of British immigrants who had continued to swell the province's population. Plainly, Ontario's British links were strong. The spirit of Empire was celebrated regularly and formally in schools and churches and frequently and spontaneously in homes. Rare was the Ontario household that could not produce a portrait of the Royal Family. British capital still moved much of Ontario's economy. British manufactures were snapped up at the T. Eaton Company stores, and British culture was the highest ideal for Canadian achievers. Canadians, and especially Ontarians, relished their British connection and the "sense of power" that it brought to them.

The war had both direct and indirect effects upon Ontario. There was, of course, the question of recruitment, an activity that was aided physically and financially by the provincial government. Of course unemployment and poor prospects helped too. By June 1918, of Canada's 538,283 enlistments, 231,191 (forty-three per cent) were from Ontario, a province with 2.5 million, or thirty-one per cent, of Canada's eight million people. The war also made great demands on the province's labour force, and war-related industries contributed greatly to the continuing rural-urban shift. By the outbreak of war more Ontarians lived in the city than the country; the nation would not reach this stage until 1921.

Ontario's war industries were central to the Canadian effort. In 1914 Canada had no munitions plants; by the end of the war, all the implements of modern warfare from shells to ships to aircraft were being manufactured in Ontario. War also meant governmental controls for industry, and Ontario responded with the establishment of provincial regulatory bodies to complement the federal boards directing the war effort; particularly important in Ontario was the tight control maintained over power resources.

Agricultural production was also vital. Wars were won, Ontario farmers were reminded, by rations as well as regiments. So the war years saw an upsurge in farm production, but at the same time rural depopulation was on the increase. How was this? Production went up because of extensive use of machinery, and there were better yields per acre, though the rural farmer was not happy with the manpower situation. A sharp conflict was felt between recruiting in the city and the country; the

countryside was said to be dragging its feet. Hard-pressed farmers would remember this taunt.

Tory premier Sir James Whitney died when the war was scarcely two months old. His successor, Sir William Hearst, attempted to carry on the same government. But the demands of war meant massive cutbacks, especially in the penetration of the province's northland, or New Ontario as it was called. Besides, the war brought to a head two simmering social issues: prohibition and woman's suffrage. The latter movement had been championed by Dr. Emily Stowe as early as the 1880s, but wartime "manpower" needs forced a reluctant government to grant Ontario women the full rights of citizenship in 1917. Hearst, and the opposition leader, N.W. Rowell, were both anxious to promote prohibition and saw in the speedy demise of the "Demon Rum" a giant step towards winning the war. The churches applauded their initiative and in 1916 the restrictive Ontario Temperance Act became law.

A soldier returning to Ontario at the war's end in 1918 scarcely would have recognized the place. Cities and industry had expanded willy-nilly at the expense of the countryside, women now had the vote, the province was dry, religion was enjoying a resurgence. Imperial sentiment was on the wane, and big government was a prime mover of the economy. A year later the picture changed even more. In 1919 Hearst's Tory government was booted out of office and replaced not by the provincial Liberals who had split when their leader Rowell had answered his country's call and gone to the Union government in Ottawa but by a new rural force. Ontario was about to discover that despite "Progressive Conservatism" the countryside still had some kick, and could even win a few industrial labourers to its side. A rural protest movement, without a political leader, without much formal organization, without much money, and without much of a platform, and with the extraordinary name United Farmers of Ontario, was elected the provincial government. Farmers' grievances, which had never before had much concerted expression in Ontario, had been so sharpened by rural depopulation during the war that they were able to marshal enough sympathy to split the vote for the two traditional parties. No one was more surprised than the UFO itself, and no one as much as its head, E.C. Drury, who became Ontario's first post-war premier.

Ontario's bow towards farm politics was really as much a rejection of the status quo, and an expression of a general war-weariness and disillusionment as it was an embrace of any rural policy. The federal counterpart was the rise of the Progressive party which also found itself, to its amazement, a power broker in the post-war world. In the federal election of 1921 the Progressives won a remarkable twenty-four seats in Ontario.

The Drury government is generally remembered for its social welfare program, but recently it has been suggested that the changes made were quite in accordance with the slow progress march established by Whitney's and Hearst's Tory governments; in fact, mothers' allowances and other acts concerning women, including minimum wages, were a logical outgrowth of wartime exigencies. Drury's government, however, had its achievements – of a sort – and in spite of, or perhaps because of, the vast inexperience of the executive.

The great effort of the UFO, especially through the agency of its energetic attorney-general, W.E. Raney, was to cleanse the province with moral fire; the politics were those of moral "uplift." The enforcement of the Temperance Act became almost a crusade, with the formation of special liquor squads charged with searching out and clamping down on irregularities. Remarkably the chief distribution agency for booze was the medical prescription: until Raney's squads got to them, some doctors were squeezing out five hundred prescriptions a day. Raney also turned his cleansing fire on public morality by raising the taxes on racetracks and betting. For most Ontarians he went too far and was out of touch with the realities of the day. Uplift was desirable enough; bigotry and fanaticism in its pursuit were viewed as assaults on civil rights, sacred rights which, opposition members quickly pointed out, stretched back in an unbroken chain to the Magna Carta. Drury's government became an interlude, and in the election of 1923 the UFO was chased back into obscurity by Howard Ferguson and his Conservatives, who would rule the province until the Depression.

Ferguson was a shrewd and capable politician. He was the perfect Tory product: Old Ontario family, Anglo-Saxon, Imperial, Orange, rural roots, stable, but mindful of the need for "progress" in terms of commercial growth, and particularly the expansion of Ontario's northern mineral wealth. As a backbencher he was best remembered as chief advocate for the restrictive Regulation 17, which had limited the teaching of French in the schools.

He provided what the UFO had not – strong, forceful leadership for a modern, varied age, and he was one of the most astute premiers Ontario has ever had. Like Sir Oliver Mowat he understood the brokerage principle, and when he felt the sway of public opinion he offered what was wanted. By the mid-1920s he felt the need to water down Regulation 17 and the result was great personal popularity with both French and English, and an upsurge of Tory votes. He even sweet-talked the Orange Order into accepting the new situation – certainly the mark of a politician's politician. During a decade of provincial growth and expansion, marked incidentally by some degree of political scandal and intrigue, Ferguson emerged firmly in control with his integrity beyond question. When he shifted to the federal scene, and eventually went on to become high commissioner to Britain, George Henry took over the Ontario government and there seemed little reason to doubt that the Tories would go on forever.

But the Liberals had a challenger in the wings, Mitchell F. Hepburn, a prosperous St. Thomas farmer in his thirties, and federal MP for Elgin county. Hepburn liked the federal parliament and was a clear advocate for Ontario on the federal scene. He was personable, clever, and witty, and he spoke for the ordinary man. At least that was the way he liked to think of himself, and when he came to the provincial party he came on his own terms.

In the Ontario election of 1934 Hepburn came out swinging for the cause of the little man. His oratory, for such it was, swayed city and country alike. He branded the Tories as the very embodiment of corruption and big spending, and clearly at fault for the Depression, or at any rate, for the province's inability to pull out of it. Ontario liked what he had to say and he scampered to victory. His new government began with a thorough house cleaning and great publicity stunts (such as public sales of ministerial cars) to show that government economy would be a prime consideration. Judicial inquiries were launched to gauge the depth of Tory crimes, but in fact most of the enthusiasm was window-dressing. Neither Hepburn nor any other provincial parliamentary leader could do anything about the Depression.

And Hepburn in power seemed different. Hadn't he been the champion of the little guy? The image changed and the popular opinion grew that Hepburn was being dominated more and more by Toronto business interests. Neither did Hepburn get along well with Mackenzie King's federal Liberals any more. He felt that he should have a say in Dominion appointments and also considered himself the only logical successor to King as prime minister. Hepburn's "little man" appeal was completely spent in his vicious anti-labour policies. In 1937 there was a long, bitter strike of automobile workers at Oshawa. Hepburn considered them all dupes of foreign agitators (in this case, the American CIO) and a great danger to the Ontarian way of life. The Ontario Provincial Police were brought in as a small political army to smash the strike.

Hepburn's battles with Prime Minister King seemed unending. The premier claimed the right to make Hydro sales on his own authority to the United States, and then, more significantly, they scrapped over Canada's commitment to the Second World War. Hepburn moved a vote of censure in the Ontario House condemning the federal government's mediocre response to the war effort. A willing seconder was George Drew, the leader of the Ontario Tories. King successfully met this challenge in the federal election of 1940 when he swept Ontario, and the provincial Liberals began to conclude that Hepburn's one-man show might not be their salvation after all. They were right. Hepburn's chief legacy would be the destruction of the Liberal party organization. Finally, he resigned, and left in his stead a dull, earnest man, Gordon Conant, who lasted only a few months in the job, as did his successor, Harry Nixon. A date for a new election was fixed: August 1943, the height of the war.

George Drew, the Tory leader, in many ways was the culmination of the Ontario High Tory tradition. He had a fine, grand sense of aloofness which he converted into a kind of personal style. He was, and no one who dealt with him doubted it, Colonel Drew, and traced his Ontario lineage to the United Empire Loyalists. He surrounded himself with men of like persuasion: Protestants, small townsmen, British, war veterans, that is, men of tested loyalty.

Drew moved to victory in 1943 with his hastily contrived "22 points" program, a wide-ranging blueprint for social and economic development in the province drawn up with a firm eye on the post-war world. The platform promised health care, municipal tax reform, a revamping of education, old-age pension increases, the establishment of an Ontario Housing Corporation, plus extended redevelopment of minerals and agricultural production as the province's economic mainstays. The Tories won thirty-eight seats, the Liberals lost more than fifty, and were cut to sixteen, but the great surprise was that the socialist CCF took thirty-four seats. Drew was to conduct a minority government.

The situation did not last long, and Drew never actually directed his government as though it were a minority. He steamed ahead with the "22 points." In the meantime Hepburn had returned to lead the Liberals, and he and the CCF leader, Ted Jolliffe, were anxious to tear down Drew's government. When that government was defeated on a minor matter in the house, all sides cheered the opportunity for an election.

The Tories swept to victory, greatly aided by Ted Jolliffe, who stated on radio that the Drew government was actively maintaining a government spy-organization, or as he phrased it a "Gestapo," to ferret out information about the political opposition. The electorate didn't buy it, and the CCF was trimmed to a svelte eight seats. The Liberals lost one, reducing their strength to fourteen, two Communists lost their seats, and the Tories gained twenty-eight to add to their thirty-eight for a total of sixty-six in a House of ninety members. Drew won because of the "22 points" but also because the Tories had honed their election machine to a state of keen efficiency. "The Big Blue Machine" of the 1970s could trace its origins to 1945.

Drew set about to modernize Ontario. Popular measures such as extensive highway development and enlargement, or the switch of the electrical system from twenty-five to sixty cycles, or the introduction of great reforms in liquor laws (cocktail lounges, at last) were translated into Tory votes in the 1948 elections. But not all measures were so successful. The showy import of ten thousand British skilled workers by air was viewed by many as a threat to native Canadian working men and women.

Drew moved to federal politics in 1948 and for a while the Tory reins were held by Thomas Kennedy, his aging agriculture minister. In 1949, however, the nod went to Leslie Miscampbell Frost, called by one observer "the most successful politician in the province's history." On 4 May 1949, he became premier.

Frost, tall, kindly, exultant, eventually came to be called "Old Man Ontario." He also represented, and would be the last politician to do so, Old Ontario: the Ontario of small towns and the countryside. He liked to say that he viewed events from the perspective of the barber-shop in his home town of Lindsay. This was partly true and partly a clever disguise, but to many Ontarians Leslie Frost became Ontario, and a strong personal loyalty grew up towards him which the Tory party readily exploited.

Frost was the man who had been chosen to implement Drew's "22 points"; he did, and continued the middle-of-the-road program into his own premiership. He realized, however, that it would all have to be paid for, and the Frost era saw Ontario become economic handmaiden to the United States, which the premier felt eminently desirable as it provided for the new freeways, schools, and hospitals the province needed. In a way, the St. Lawrence Seaway epitomized his career, and is a monument to his pro-American commercial policies. Paradoxically, Frost's efforts to modernize were a direct contradiction to the Old Ontario he appeared to represent.

For our purposes Leslie Frost's government marks the end of this sketch of Ontario history; the termination or suspension of many of the distinctive and self-sufficient traits that we have noted as being representatively Ontarian.

Ontario by the 1950s was fully plugged into the North American marketplace; it was both consumer and consumed. The carefully tended rural-urban balance was no longer necessary, as improved communications (the traditional forms of road and rail and now radio and television) made the city as accessible to the country as the country became to the city. The country for most Ontarians increasingly meant a weekend at the cottage.

But there are many elements that survive. Ontario is still loyal, and not simply loyal to a middle-aged woman 3,500 miles away. Rather, Ontario is most frequently loyal to its collective past, to its own history and experience. Much of that loyalty was seen always in a sense of balance and moderation in political life, and some of that is still there. Ontario governments don't serve up distinctive ideologies because Ontarians aren't very ideological. Ontarians are the cautious centre, they are the elusive "Red Tories" of political science, they want big government, indeed are used to it, but not at the expense of surrendering free enterprise. Reforms, political or otherwise, are well and good as long as they are cautious reforms.

A delicate urban-rural balance most characterized Old Ontario, between city and country, or between a city and its hinterland. And that seems gone now forever. Perhaps the formal end came when, in the 1960s, the Ontario legislature stopped sitting according to the old spring planting schedule and the sessions stretched on to summer. Regionalism still plays a role in Ontario, but it is just one factor rather than the decisive factor. Leslie Frost understood small-town Ontario not because he was from there (which he was) but because he had to and wanted to. John Robarts, who followed him as premier, understood it because he had to. Neither William Davis nor David Peterson understood it, nor does Bob Rae – except symbolically. Government has become depersonalized as Ontario itself has become dehumanized. The word is not too strong. A government's survival today depends as much on the New York bond market as it does on the needs of the electorate. The soul of a distinctive province is hard to find in glistening, international Toronto. It is equally elusive in Hamilton, Ottawa, London, or Thunder Bay's sprawling suburbia. When we look for it we are drawn to the country, to the small towns, farms, and villages. Wedged in between automobile-service centres and fast-food outlets, Old Ontario is still there – and it is that Ontario that this book is chiefly about.

Upper Canada
1791-1841

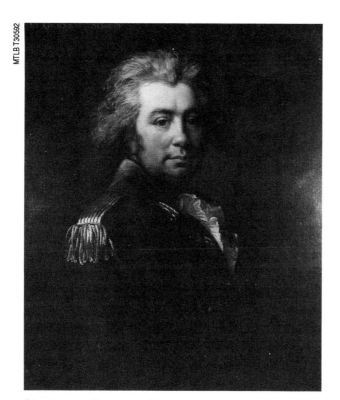

Lieutenant-Governor Simcoe

Upper Canada came into existence in 1791 when the Imperial Parliament passed the Constitutional Act which split old Quebec into two new provinces, Upper Canada to the west and Lower Canada to the east. John Graves Simcoe, first lieutenant-governor of Upper Canada (from 1791 to 1799, though he was actually in the colony only from 1792 to 1796), established the machinery of provincial government and attempted to set the tone for its nascent society.

At the first session of the provincial parliament held in the Freemasons' Hall, Newark (now Niagara), in September of 1792, he proclaimed:

> The natural advantages of the Province of Upper Canada are inferior to none on this side of the Atlantic. There can be no separate interest through its whole extent. The British form of government has prepared the way for its speedy colonization, and I trust that your fostering care will improve the favourable situation, and that a numerous and agricultural people will speedily take possession of a soil and climate which, under the British laws and the munificence with which His Majesty has granted the lands of the Crown, offer such manifest and peculiar encouragements.

Anglo-French Rivalry in North America – The Clash of Empires

What became British Upper Canada in 1791 had once been part of a vast French empire in America, which drew a loose ring around the British colonies hugging the Atlantic seaboard. Acadia and the Bay of Fundy were where French settlements had begun in the seventeenth century; they had then arched northward along the fertile, salubrious banks of the St. Lawrence River to embrace first Québec (which means "the place where the river narrows"), then Montréal by 1642, and beyond, into the *pays d'en haut,* the upper country, where commerce was the lure. In the eighteenth century a string of French forts marked the main waterways west through Ontario, and further west still into the prairies; another chain ran south through Louisiana and terminated at the mouth of the Mississippi.

In the Ontario region, trade-defence posts were erected at strategic points on the vital water routes: Fort Frontenac at the foot of Lake Ontario, Niagara with its important portage from Lake Ontario to Lake Erie, Detroit at the head of Lake Erie, and Michilimackinac where Michigan joins Huron. A small fort was also erected at "The Carrying Place," the Toronto portage. It was named Fort Rouillé after the minister of marine, who was responsible for the colonies.

The French in America were no strangers to war. The war with the Iroquois allies of the English colonies to the south raged intermittently for many decades. And the English fur interests to the north on Hudson Bay gave occasion for many sharp, vicious battles.

The eighteenth century saw the main event, however, a clash between the rival empires, a world war fought not only in Europe but in India and America. The climax was the Seven Years' War, 1756–63. In the beginning the French were most successful in the Ontario region, and maintained naval control of the lakes. But by 1758 British and American colonial forces turned the tide and France was forced into the narrow funnel of the St. Lawrence. British seapower was the determining force in the Atlantic war – first Louisbourg, the Cape Breton fortress without a fleet, collapsed, and then Québec where Montcalm and Wolfe ended their ambitions, and finally, a year later in 1760, the French capitulation at Montréal.

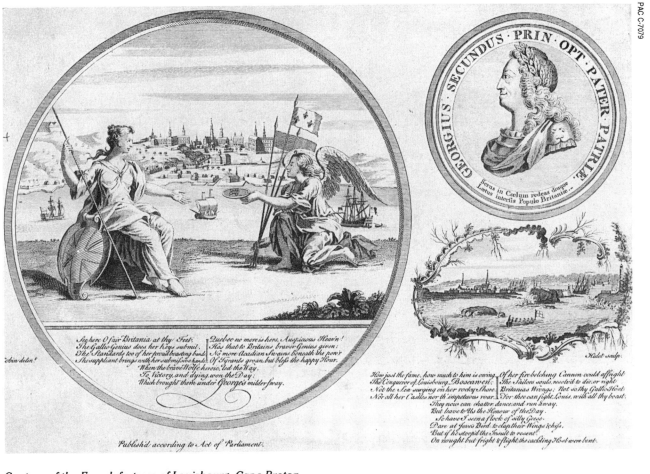

Capture of the French fortress of Louisbourg, Cape Breton, 1758 (right). Allegorical representation of the surrender of Québec, 1759 (left).

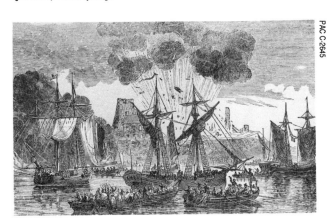

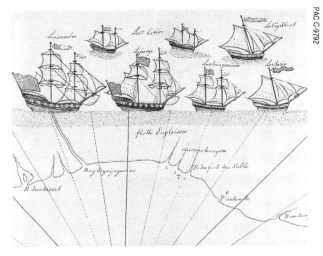

Capture of Fort Frontenac, 1758.

The English fleet, after a drawing on a map in the King's Library. British Museum, by Labroquerie, a French engineer at Fort Frontenac, 4 October 1757.

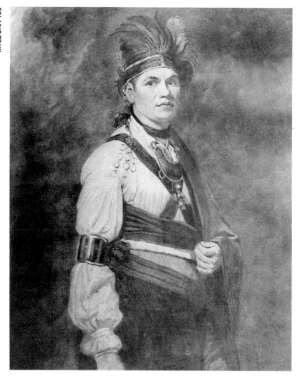

Joseph Brant, Six Nations leader. Mezzotint.

New France was British, but would it remain that way? In the peace of 1763 it might have gone either way, but the British wished to reduce the northern threat to their seaboard colonies and so Québec (and Ontario) became English. No one, of course, consulted the Indian inhabitants.

The Loyalists

The Loyalists were the first Europeans to settle permanently in large numbers in Ontario. They came in the aftermath of the American Revolutionary war which ended in 1783. Historians argue about the size of the influx, but most agree it was between five and six thousand. The Loyalists settled along the northern banks of the St. Lawrence and Lake Ontario, in the area of present-day Kingston and Prince Edward County, and also in Niagara. They should not be considered docile conservatives; many had led the opposition to British policy in the Thirteen Colonies before it entered its violent stage. Their hardships were real, but as refugees they were given many advantages by the British government and were comparatively well treated.

Frequently forgotten Loyalists are the Six Nations of the Iroquois Confederacy who had fought on the British side during the revolt; the fate of their lands, indeed their own fate, was not even discussed in the treaty. However, they were awarded a great tract in the Grand River valley "six miles deep from each side of [the river] beginning at Lake Erie and extending in that proportion to [its] head." This fine area eventually was chipped away by encroachments and hasty sales. Joseph Brant of the Mohawks, the Iroquois leader, was a most capable businessman and skilful negotiator who succeeded for a time in driving hard bargains for the Indian land. The Durham Report (1838) indicated that about one-third of the original Indian reserves in the entire colony was left to the native peoples. Originally, the British had purchased the Grand River valley from the Mississaugas before making the grant to the Six Nations.

Economic life still centred on the fur trade. Male fashions in Europe for many years featured a felt hat, made from beaver fur, and the trade was both long-lived and lucrative. It had its origins, of course, in the French régime, but the Hudson's Bay Company soon proved an able competitor. After the American Revolution, the French trade was assumed by American and Scots companies, the giant of which became the loose association called the North West Company. In the nineteenth century the fur rivalry between "the Bay" (HBC was said to mean Here Before Christ) and the Nor'westers almost bankrupted both concerns. In 1821 a union was arranged in which, effectively, the chartered might of the Bay swallowed the Nor'westers.

The Beginnings

The seat of government and the homes of the early provincial officials – William Jarvis called them "a roving tribe of Israelites" – were temporarily fixed at Niagara, the Loyalist settlement (named Newark by Simcoe). Yet by August 1793, the great defensible harbour of Toronto had pulled the capital of the new province away from the American frontier and a new government town, under Simcoe's name of York, began to rise on the west bank of the Don River, much to the distaste at first of army officers and officials who preferred the settled comforts of Niagara. Isaac Weld, an American visitor in 1796,

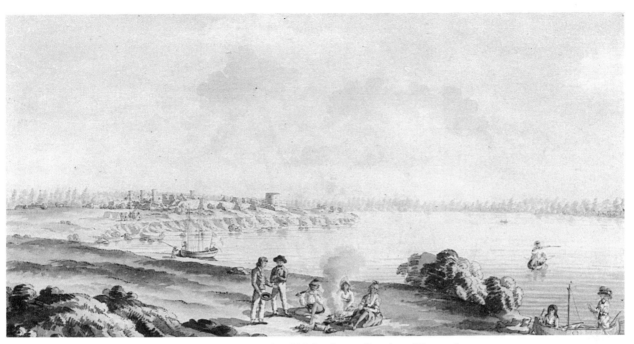

View of the Ruins of the Fort at Cataraqui (Kingston), 1783, by James Peachey. Watercolour.

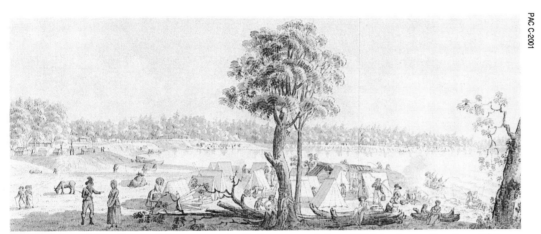

Encampment of Loyalists at Johnston, on the St. Lawrence, 6 June 1784, by James Peachey. Watercolour.

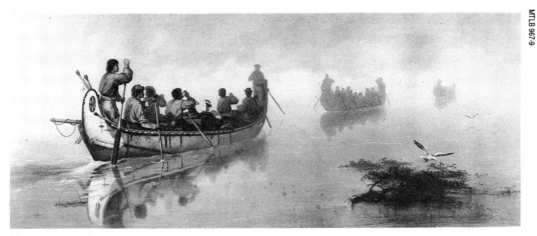

Fur canoes with passengers. Oil.

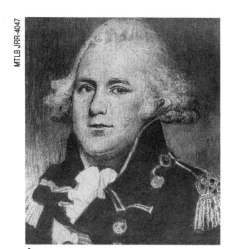

I

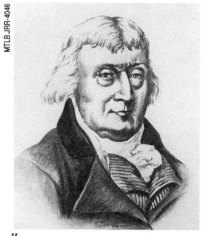

II

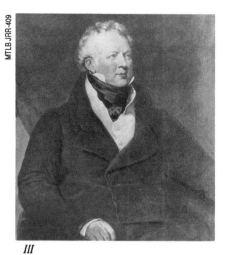

III

IV

I   William Jarvis, first provincial secretary of Upper Canada.

II   Peter Russell, receiver-general under Simcoe, administrator of the province 1796–99. By J.E. Laughlin.

III   Francis Gore, lieutenant-governor of Upper Canada from 1806 to 1817. Gore was absent from the province 1811–15, the crucial years which encompassed the War of 1812. Watercolour after Lawrence.

IV   Sketch map of Upper Canada, 1793, by Elizabeth Posthuma Simcoe, accompanying her husband's despatch (No. 19, 19 October 1793) to the secretary of state for the Home Department, Henry Dundas.

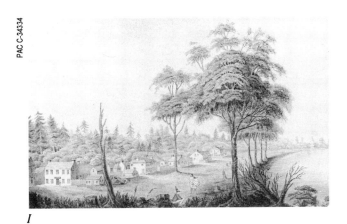

I

II

At a Meeting of the Inhabitants of the Township
of Grimsby this 5 day of march 1798 at the hous
of Mr Charles Anderson the following persons
were Elected into the offices annexed to their names

Andrew Pettit — — Clark
Solomon Hill }
John Smith toop } Assessors
John Green — — Collector
Isaac Merrit
Charles Meridith
William Laurance } overseer of Roads
James M'intire
Samuel Green

John Pettit Esqr } Town Wardens
Robert Nelles }
joseph Chambers — pound keeper

at the same time a vote passed that every
Inhabitant Shall pay one shilling for
every Wolf that is taken and killed in
this town and the sd one shilling is to be Collected by the
Collector and paid to John Pettit or Robbot Nelles Esqr
Town Wardens or either of them as they are apointed
to Inspect into the Wolf Scalps and they are to pay the
same to any persons that kills a Wolf in the Town

III

much regretted Simcoe's ardent anglicizing of local
Indian names and the loss of the name Toronto, not
to be regained until 1834. The new town rose from
zero population to just under 600 by 1810; much of
the original construction had been undertaken by
Simcoe's Queen's Rangers.

Elsewhere in the province local governments
were being firmly established and officers elected
to fill administrative positions. Titles and positions
were, of course, not nearly so grand as at York.
Grimsby's township minutes of March 1798 were
concerned, quite literally, with keeping the wolf
from the door.

Taking Up Land

Land, its purchase, cultivation, maintenance, and
sale, was the prime interest of Upper Canadians. It
was the only substantial source of wealth in the
colony. And it was, of course, for free land that
many colonists migrated. The following sequence
shows the procedures involved in an average grant
of land, in this case to a certain George Moot. A total of eight distinct steps were necessary before
clear title could be established.

*I View of part of the town of York, capital of Upper
Canada, 1804, by Elizabeth Francis Hale. Watercolour.*

*II View of the falls at Niagara. from the Canadian shore at
Birch's Mills, published 1807, by George Heriot. Hand-
coloured aquatint.*

*III Extract from minutes of Grimsby Township, Lincoln
County, 5 March 1798.*

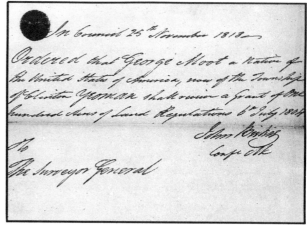

I

II

III

I Generally, to obtain a land grant, a settler submitted a PETITION to the lieutenant-governor-in-council. The petition might be accompanied by certificates of military service and oaths of allegiance.

II An ORDER-IN-COUNCIL authorizing the grant addressed to the surveyor-general was issued by the clerk of the executive council for presentation to the Surveyor-General's Office.

III In the Surveyor-General's Office the location was assigned and a TICKET of LOCATION, including the terms of settlement duties, was prepared and issued to the settler.

IV The settlement duties were performed within the time limit prescribed, and an AFFIDAVIT to this effect was prepared by the grantee.

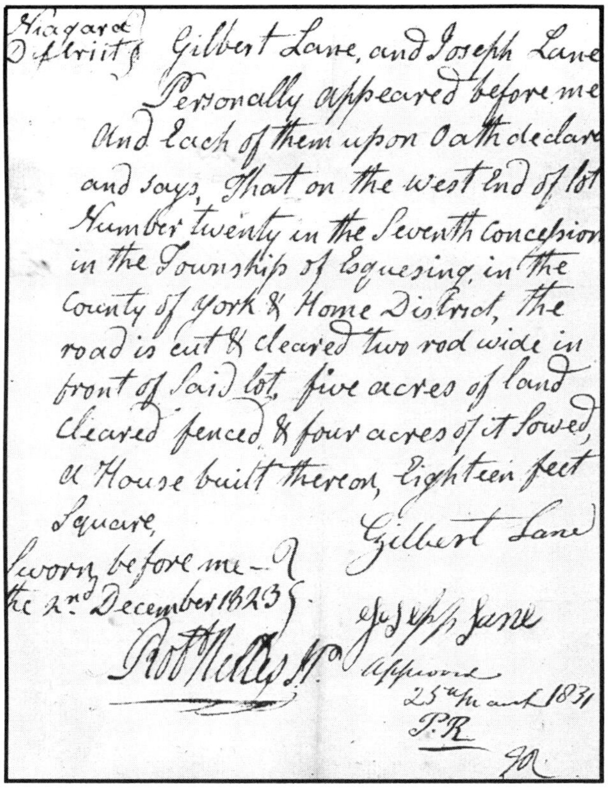

IV

V

VI

VII

V The grantee paid the prescribed fees eight years later, and submitted the receiver-general's RECEIPT to the Attorney-General's Office.

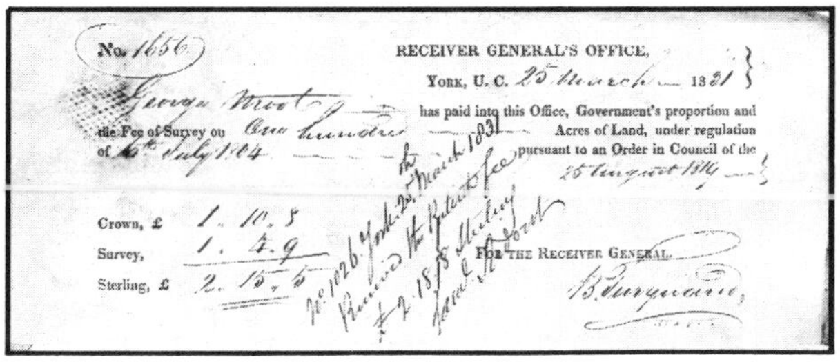

VI After receiving the receiver-general's receipt, the attorney-general issued his FIAT authorizing the preparation of a surveyor's description of the grant addressed to the surveyor-general.

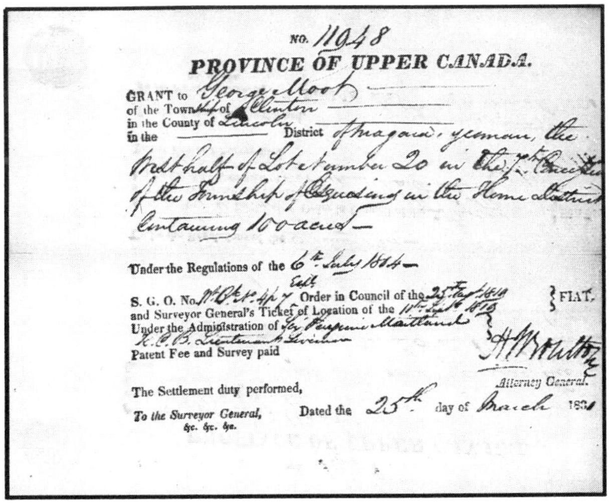

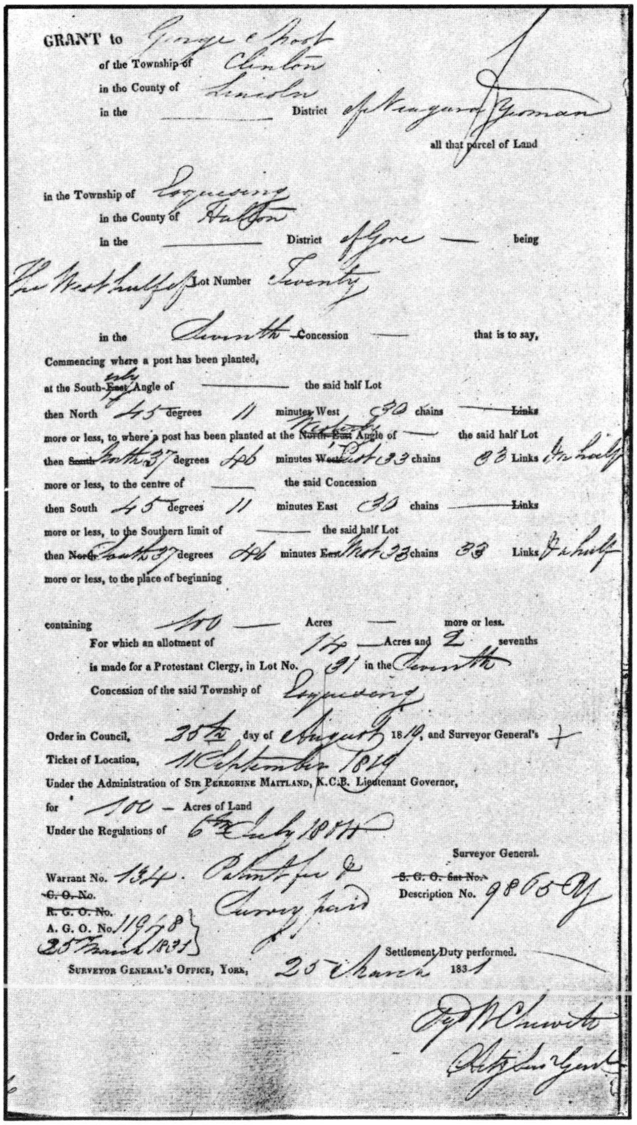

VII On the receipt of the attorney-general's fiat the surveyor-general prepared a detailed DESCRIPTION of the grant. This description was the provincial secretary's authority and guide for engrossing the patent.

VIII The PATENT (overleaf), engrossed by the Provincial Secretary's Office, signed by the lieutenant-governor, sealed with the Great Seal of the Province, and registered, was thereupon issued to the grantee who then had clear title to his land.

Hobbon

PROVINCE OF UPPER CANADA.

William

GEORGE *the Fourth* by the Grace of GOD of the United Kingdom of Great Britain and Ireland, King Defender of the Faith :—To all to whom these Presents shall come———Greeting :

KNOW YE, That We, of our special Grace, certain Knowledge, and mere Motion, have Given and GRANTED, and by these Presents, do Give and GRANT, unto *George Mott of the Township of Clinton in the County of Lincoln in the district of Niagara yeoman*

heirs and assigns for ever; ALL that parcel or tract of Land, situate *in the Township of Roguersing in the County of Hallow in the district of Ore* in our said Province, containing by admeasurement *one hundred acres* be the same more or less, being *The West half of Lot number twenty in the Seventh Concession of the said Township of Roguersing*

TOGETHER with all the Woods and Waters thereon lying and being, under the reservations, limitations and conditions, hereinafter expressed; which said *One hundred acres on* butted and bounded, or may be otherwise known as follows; that is to say:

Commencing where a Post has been planted at the Southerly angle of the said half Lot — then north forty five degrees eleven minutes West thirty Chains more or less to where a Post has been planted at the Westerly angle of the said half Lot then north thirty seven degrees but Six minutes East thirty four Chains thirty three links and one half more or less to the Center of the said Concession then South forty five degrees Eleven minutes East thirty Chains more or less to the Southern limit of his said half Lot then south thirty three degrees forty Six minutes West thirty three Chains thirty three links and a half more or less to the place of beginning

H. Throckton
attorney   *Amended 25 March 1831*

TO HAVE AND TO HOLD, the said parcel or tract of Land, hereby given and granted to *him* the said *George Mott* *his* heirs and assigns for ever; saving nevertheless, to Us, our Heirs and Successors, all Mines of Gold and Silver *that shall or may be* hereafter found on any part of the said parcel or tract of Land hereby given and granted as aforesaid : and saving and reserving to Us, our Heirs and Successors, all White Pine Trees, that shall or may now or hereafter grow, or be growing on any part of the said parcel or tract of Land hereby granted as aforesaid. **P**ROVIDED **ALWAYS**, that no part of the parcel or tract of Land hereby given and granted to the said *George Mott* and *his* heirs, be within any reservation heretofore made and marked for Us, our heirs and successors, by our Surveyor General of Woods, or his lawful Deputy, in which case, this our grant for such part of the Land hereby given and granted to the said *George Mott* shall, upon a survey thereof being made, be found within any such reservation, shall be null and void and of none effect, any thing herein contained to the contrary notwithstanding. **P**ROVIDED **ALSO**, that the said *George Mott* *his* heirs or assigns, shall and do within three years, erect and build or cause to be erected and built, in and upon some part of the said parcel or tract of Land, a good and sufficient dwelling house *to* the said *George Mott* or *his* assigns, not having built, or not being in *his* or their own right, lawfully possessed of a house in our said Province, and be therein, or cause some person to be therein resident, for and during the space of three years, then next ensuing the building of the same. **P**ROVIDED **ALSO**, that if at any time or times hereafter, the Land so hereby given and granted to the said *George Mott* and *his* heirs shall come into the possession and tenure of any person or persons whomsoever, either by virtue of any Deed of sale, conveyance, enfeoffment, or exchange; or by gift, inheritance, descent, devise, or marriage, such person or persons shall within twelve months next after his, her, or their entry into, and possession of the same, take the oaths prescribed by Law, before some one of the Magistrates of our said Province, and a certificate of such oath having been so taken shall cause to be recorded in the Secretary's office of the said Province. IN DEFAULT of all or any of which conditions, limitations, and restrictions, this said Grant and every thing herein contained, shall be and We hereby declare the same to be null and void, to all intents and purposes whatsoever; and the Land hereby granted and every part and parcel thereof, shall revert to, and become vested in Us, our Heirs and Successors, in like manner as if the same, had never been granted, any thing herein contained to the contrary thereof, in any wise notwithstanding.

AND WHEREAS, by an Act of the Parliament of Great Britain passed in the thirty-first year of the Reign of His late Majesty King George the Third, entitled, "An Act to repeal certain parts of an Act, passed in the fourteenth year of His Majesty's Reign, entitled, "An Act for making more effectual provision for the Government of the Province of Quebec, in North America, and to make further provision for the Government of the said Province." It is declared "that no grant of Lands hereafter made, shall be valid or effectual, unless the same shall contain a specification of the lands to be allotted and appropriated solely to the maintenance of a Protestant Clergy within the said Province in respect of the Lands to be thereby granted."——Now KNOW YE, that WE have caused an allotment or appropriation of *fourteen acres and two seventh to be made in lot number thirty one in the Seventh concession of the said Township of Roguersing*

Given under the Great Seal of our Province of Upper Canada: Witness our trusty and well-beloved *Sir John Colborne K. B. &c. &c. of our said Province & Major General Commanding our forces therein* this *twenty fifth* day of *March* in the year of our LORD one thousand eight hundred and *thirty one* and *first* of our Reign *in Council*

By Command *Wm Crawling*

25 augt 1819 — admitted by Six
Trenton Reg 6 May 1844. Barclay   *Sted Davis Entin worth to Auditor*
D F Span   25 March 1831   *J Throckton gr*

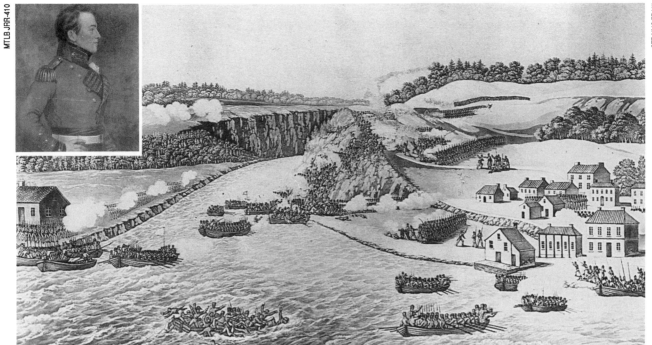

War of 1812

Inset above: *Major-General Sir Isaac Brock, administrator of Upper Canada (in Gore's absence), 1811–12. Brock's military genius and decisive actions combined to turn the edge of the American invasion in 1812 and keep the young province British. He lost his life in so doing at the Battle of Queenston Heights, 13 October 1812, and became Ontario's first hero and martyr. Watercolour from painting by G.T. Berthon.*

Above: *Battle of Queenston Heights. Engraving.*

Below: *The Battle of Put-In Bay on Lake Erie, where U.S. Captain Oliver Hazard Perry's squadron destroyed the entire flotilla of Captain R.H. Barclay, which had sailed out from Amherstburg, 10 September 1813. At a time when water routes were the principal means of transportation and communication, control of the lakes was all-important and hotly contested.*

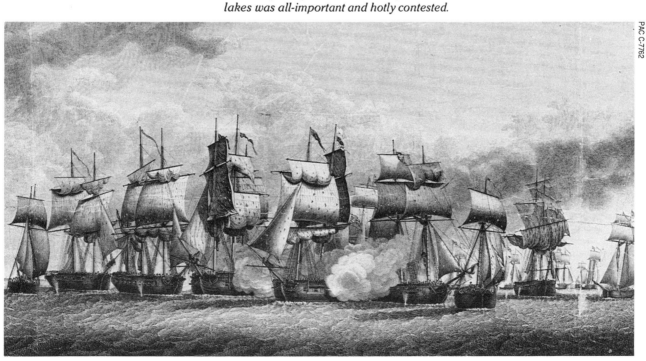

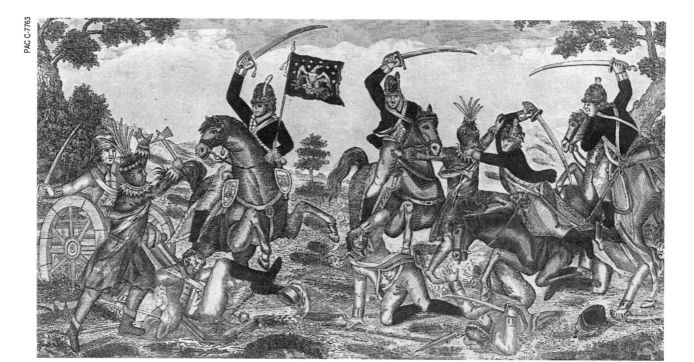

With Perry's victory on Lake Erie, the American forces recovered their balance and again invaded Upper Canada through Detroit. This time the retreating British and their Indian allies (including Tecumseth, the Shawnee chief) were caught at Moraviantown, on the Thames River, on 2 October 1813 (near present-day Thamesville). The invasion was not, however, followed up and corresponding American thrusts from Niagara met defeat at Stoney Creek. B. Rawdon's engraving shows an American cavalry unit charging a party of British gunners and Indians near Moraviantown. Engraving.

The Pioneer Province

In the history of Upper Canada it has long been customary to consider the Family Compact as the "villains of the piece." This is neither fair nor accurate. The Compact was simply the logical outcome of the Constitutional Act of 1791. It was a group of men of conservative leanings who were appointed to positions of authority in the province, and came to view the filling of those positions as their right. The War of 1812 was their testing time and in its aftermath they secured their hold over the executive government of the province.

The dominant figure became the Reverend Dr. John Strachan, a tough-minded Scots Presbyterian who had converted to the Church of England and eventually became first bishop of Toronto. Strachan had come to the province as a schoolmaster, a "merry dominie" as he liked to remember himself, and through a series of schools in Kingston, Cornwall, and York, instructed the future membership of the Compact on his own Tory principles. His star pupil was John (eventually Sir John) Beverley Robinson, who rose rapidly to become attorney-general and then chief justice of the colony.

Strachan's influence, and that of the Compact, was at its height during the lieutenant-governorship of Sir Peregrine Maitland, 1818–28. During this period Upper Canada acquired its first bank, the Bank of Upper Canada, in which Compact members played important roles.

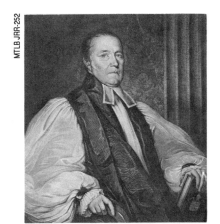

our townd'fosisors ware Putin By the Laster sesons for the year AD 1813 By keason of the wor that was decleards againet us By the States in the year : 1812 By the same keason our towndmetin war omited in the year AD 1814 and our Town officors war Put in the same manner

Upper Canada was saved by American faint-heartedness in both political and military terms, not to mention the presence of the British regulars. Violated perhaps, but not overcome, provincial life went on but was entirely disrupted as the minute book of the Township of Pickering reveals with ungrammatical simplicity.

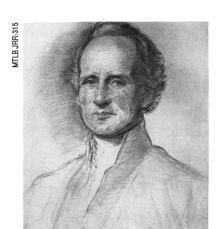

John Strachan, as bishop of Toronto.

John Beverley Robinson.

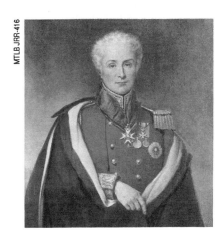

Sir Peregrine Maitland.

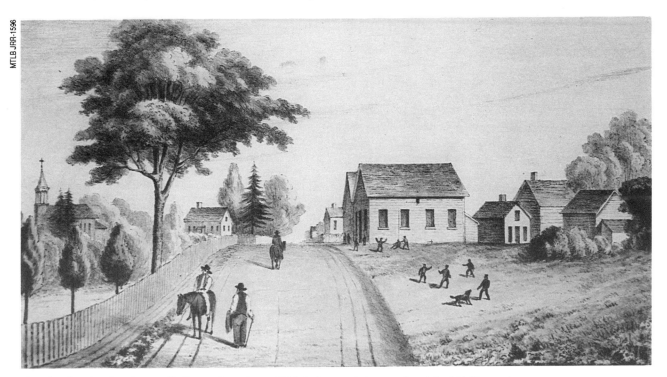

Strachan's school at Cornwall, Upper Canada, c. 1808. Lithograph from a sketch by J.G. Howard.

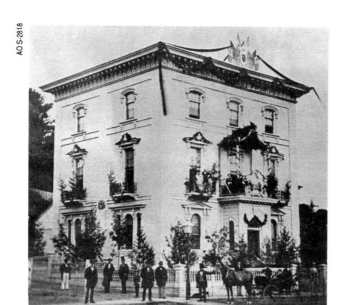

Bank of Upper Canada, Port Hope, 1860.

A growing demand in the 1820s for economic expansion and investment for major public works, like the Welland Canal, forced Upper Canada into banking. In the early years the province suffered from a bewildering array of private mercantile credit notes and coinage from Europe and America. Under pressure from Kingston merchants, who resented the intrusion of the Bank of Montreal into Upper Canada trading interests, London approved the first banking bill in 1819. With curious sleight of hand, however, Sir Peregrine Maitland set up the Bank of Upper Canada in York where government connections could be strong and condemned the Kingston initiative to ultimate bankruptcy.

The bank, a creature of the Family Compact, was largely funded and directed by the provincial government. Both its principles and its practices were fiercely criticized by William Lyon Mackenzie.

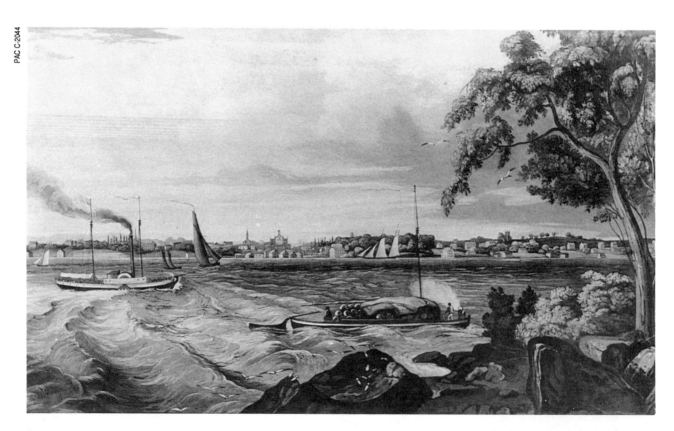

A substantial river town was Brockville on the north bank of the St. Lawrence between Kingston and Cornwall, founded by the earliest of Ontario's settlers, the United Empire Loyalists. Until it acquired its present name in honour of the hero of the War of 1812, Sir Isaac Brock, the town was known as Elizabethtown and was subordinate to Johnstown, which had boasted the seat of district govern-ment and judiciary since 1791. The substantial public buildings and riverside warehouses, sketched from one of the many islands across a busy waterway by John Gray about 1828, indicate its importance and commercial significance on the main route through Upper Canada.

A branch of the Bank of Upper Canada was still alive in Port Hope (September 1860), though close to bankruptcy, when E.E. Henry, a local photographer, captured its decorations in readiness for the visit of the Prince of Wales.

❖

Smooth transportation routes were seen as the key to successful development of the colony. Westward passage up the St. Lawrence River beyond Montréal was certainly more rapid than travel by land, but not without considerable obstacles at stages in the river where boiling rapids had to be ascended. With a canoe the obstacle became a customary portage to be climbed over and manhandled; navigating a flat-bottomed Durham boat or batteau – never mind a steamer (Lake Ontario saw its first in 1817) – was a different matter entirely. Prior to the sort of canalization begun at Lachine (1814), Welland (1824), and on the Rideau (1826), various ingenious mechanical schemes were suggested to move vessels from one level to another. One such plan as late as

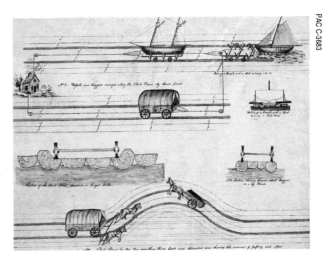

Railway scheme, St. Lawrence River, 1824.

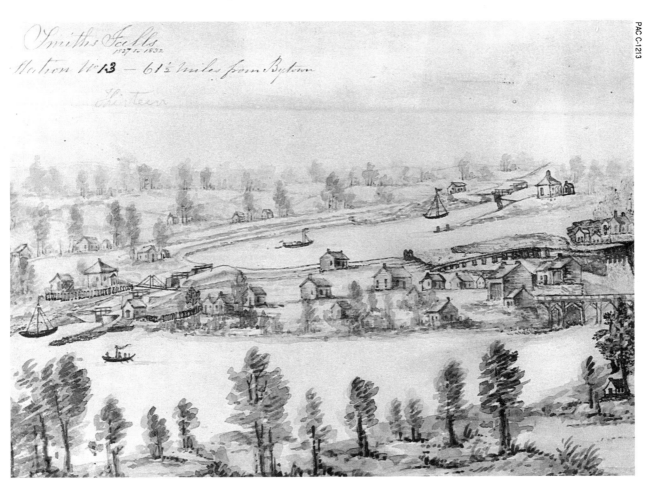

Smiths Falls, Station No. 13 – 61 ½ miles from Bytown. Wash drawing by William Clegg.

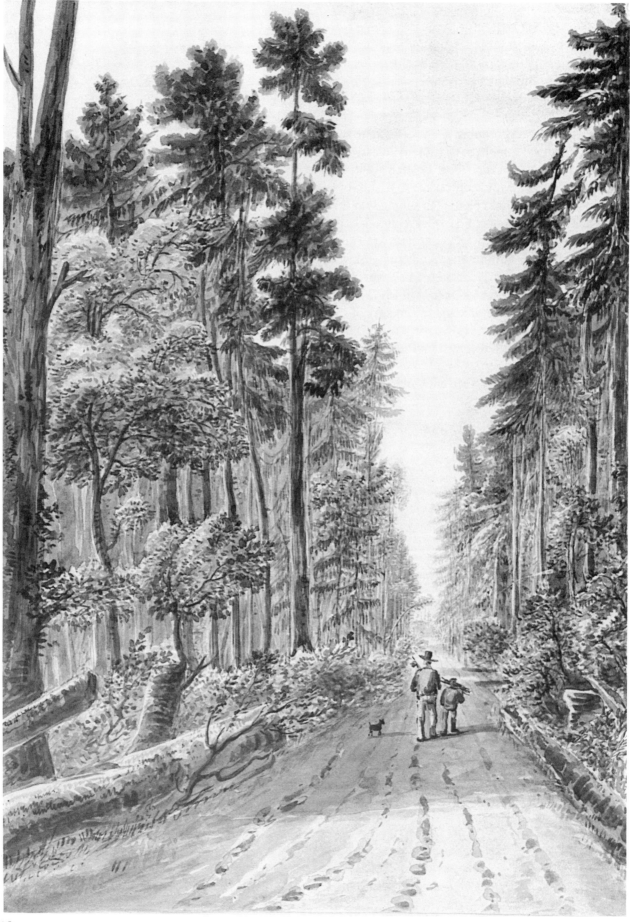

1824 envisaged a steam-driven railway for carting boats on wooden-wheeled cradles.

Facing the possibility of American seizure of the St. Lawrence River, British authorities after the War of 1812 searched for alternative routes to permit naval vessels to reach Lake Ontario unmolested from Montréal and the east. The most obvious path was through the series of shallow lakes between the Ottawa River and the mouth of the Cataraqui at Fort Henry, Kingston. Between 1828 and 1832, the enterprising military engineer Colonel John By (1781–1836) canalized the stretch from the Ottawa southwestwards through the Rideau Lakes, erecting a series of locks and block-houses to help and protect the passage of boats.

The waterway fast became a "white elephant" to the government of Upper Canada as well as the British military and was under-used even for commercial purposes until the pleasure-craft days of the middle of this century. The starting-point, the juncture of the Rideau and Ottawa, was called Bytown, a name retained until 1855, when it adopted the anglicized Algonkian name, Ottawa. Two years later, Queen Victoria chose it as the seat of government for Canada.

❖

Immigration and settlement became issues of prime importance in Upper Canada after the War of 1812. The door to Americans was shut by the Imperial government, and instead, cautious experiments were made with "systematic emigration" of Britons.

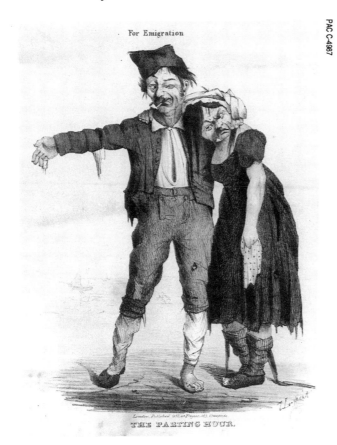

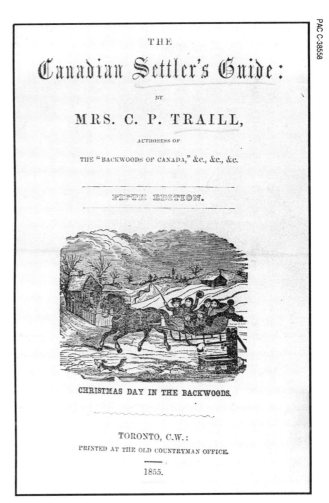

Opposite: *Some idea of the impenetrable forests and woods that pressed in upon the would-be traveller can be grasped from James Cockburn's watercolour of a stretch along the track between the towns of Kingston and York before the days of regular traffic (c. 1830). The best time to travel was winter, when the roads were frozen hard; the worst in the spring or fall when mud and ruts became axle-deep. George Head, in his* Forest Scenes and Incidents in the Wilds of North America *(1829), recorded a winter trip from Kingston to York as "Five days in the road, leaving ten miles for the last day's journey."*

Left: The Parting Hour, *by Tregear. Coloured print, published 1832.*

Right: Christmas Day in the Backwoods *on the title page of Catherine Parr Traill's famous* Canadian Settler's Guide, *already in its fifth edition by 1855 (and published in Toronto as well).*

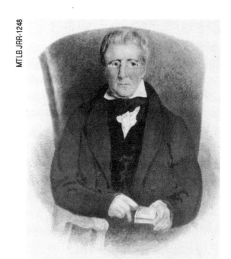

William Dickson. Watercolour from original by Hoppner Meyer.

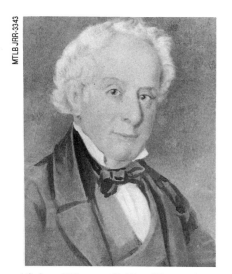

Colonel Thomas Talbot. Watercolour.

Right: Talbot Road, Back Road Junction, *by G.R. Dartnell.*

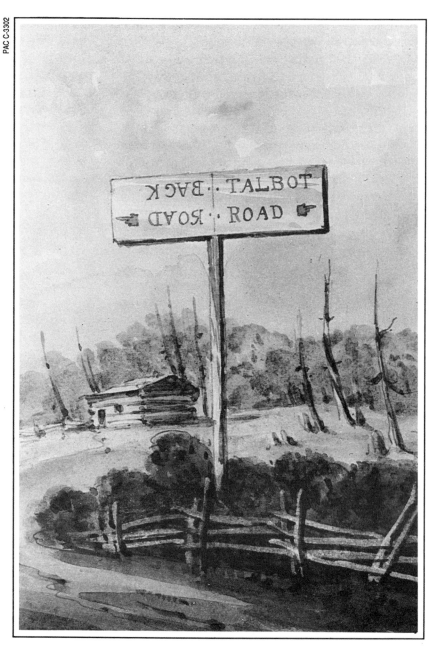

Efforts were made to sponsor pauper emigration as well, notably of Irish to Peterborough in 1823 and 1825, but they were soon abandoned because of the enormous costs. Generally emigration remained a private matter rather than one of government sponsorship.

In the 1830s emigration from Britain increased dramatically. Some 67,000 people arrived in Canada from British ports in 1833, adding to the almost 200,000 inhabitants of the upper province, though a good many newcomers moved on into the United States. Sir John Colborne, lieutenant-governor from 1828 to 1836, deliberately assisted emigration from the old country to combat a rising tide (now legal) from the United States. He posted agents along the route from Montreal to the west, appointed superintendents to settlement townships, assigned fifty-acre lots with a delayed payment for three years, undertook to build colonization roads and actively supported emigrant societies – unconsciously paving the way for the growth of violent Orange benefit societies and lodges in later decades.

Thousands of letters were sent home to Britain as advice and warning. In Britain itself, guides and travel accounts began to mushroom on publishers' lists, many of them highly coloured – and not all of them serious.

Land might be obtained from private individuals or land companies, as well as from the government. Almost everyone, blacksmith to bishop, speculated in land in Upper Canada.

William Dickson was a land dealer par excellence. A Scot who had moved to Upper Canada as early as 1792, he purchased a large section of land from the Six Nations Indians. He called it Dumfries after the town and county in Scotland, and advertised widely there for emigrants. The response was encouraging. Those who came were given some basic assistance in settling the land. Together with his superintendent, Absalom Shade, Dickson developed the area with enthusiasm and no small outlay of cash. Shade's Mills, the principal town, was renamed Galt in 1827 after Dickson's boyhood friend the Scottish novelist John Galt.

The Talbot settlement was different, and Colonel Thomas Talbot's scope stretched far beyond a single township. Talbot, who started his settlement activities in 1803, arranged a splendid deal for himself with the local government: for every settler he put on 50 acres of land, Talbot received a 200-acre grant from the government. Eventually he had a massive, unwieldy "principality" (as he called it), comprising 27 townships hugging the northern shore of Lake Erie, stretching far east and west of his base at Port Talbot. Anna Jameson visited him in 1837 and reported the population of his domain at about fifty thousand. "You see," he said to her, "I may boast, like the Irishman in the farce, of having peopled a whole country with my own hands." Towards the end of that year the colonel, an eccentric of the first order – high handed and a great lover of whisky – was forced to turn control of his huge estate over to the colonial government.

Another alternative to obtaining land from the government was to buy it from the massive Canada Company, a British-based land and colonization

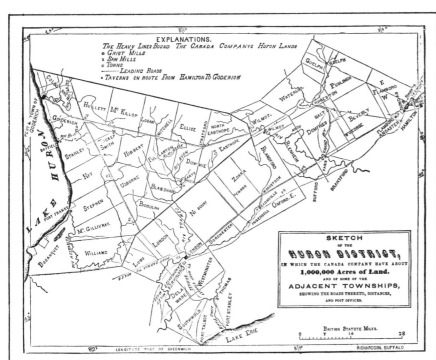

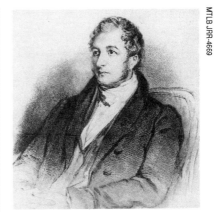

John Galt.

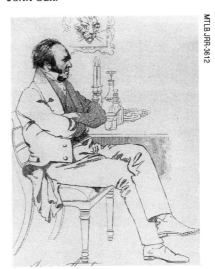

William "Tiger" Dunlop.

Left: *Canada Company poster.*

41

Lands for Sale
IN
Upper Canada.

The attention of Persons wishing to Purchase LAND is particularly called to that of the

CANADA COMPANY,

Situated in almost every Township in the Upper Province, and as it consists of scattered Lots, varying from ONE HUNDRED to TWO HUNDRED ACRES EACH—Blocks of from ONE THOUSAND to TWELVE THOUSAND ACRES, and a LARGE TRACT in the most fertile and promising portion of UPPER CANADA, containing upwards of ONE MILLION OF ACRES, the Company's Lands possess advantages, not even afforded by those at the disposal of the Government.

These *large Blocks* or *Tracts of Land*, are confined to the London and Western DISTRICTS.

In the former is the HURON TRACT, or COUNTY OF HURON, and on the completion of the DISTRICT BUILDINGS, now in progress at GODERICH, it will become a SEPARATE DISTRICT.

The Tract extends along the Shore of LAKE HURON about sixty miles, has an excellent Harbour at Goderich, and a Steamboat touching at it once a week, affords a water communication with Lake Erie and thence with Quebec;—superior Roads have been constructed—STAGES established, affording communication with the older Settlements,—MILLS erected when required—and neither pains nor expense has been spared by the Company to make their Settlement desirable situations for purchasers, or to promote their comfort and prosperity when established there.

The principal or District Town, situated at the confluence of the River Maitland with the Lake is called GODERICH, and contains Schools—places of Worship—and good Stores, with a population of about 600. From this point good Roads diverge to LONDON and GALT, or HAMILTON, and others are in progress.

The LANDS vary in Price according to situation—from 11s. 3d. to 15s. Some few from peculiar local advantages are charged from 16s. 3d. to 20s—but the average may be taken at 12s. 6d.

The usual terms of Payment are *one-fifth* of the Purchase Money in CASH—and the Balance by FIVE equal Annual Instalments, with Interest.

The superior advantages which UPPER CANADA holds out to the BRITISH EMIGRANT when fairly exhibited to him and properly considered will not fail to lead him onward, upon his arrival in the Lower Province. The climate is equally healthy, whilst at the same time, it is much milder as regards the degrees of heat in summer and of cold in winter, than that of Lower Canada; the soil is much more fertile, and the winter being shorter affords the great advantage to the Farmer of putting in his SEED WHEAT in the Autumn, whilst in Lower Canada his Farming operations for the season cannot commence before APRIL, and more generally MAY,—the population of UPPER CANADA and the LANGUAGE is of the same character as he has been accustomed to, an l instead of finding himself amongst strangers, both in feelings and language, as he would in Lower Canada—the probability is that the EMIGRANT, on his arrival in UPPER CANADA will meet with many who have formerly been his acquaintances or neighbours—and find the same religion administered as in the country of his birth.

The CANADA COMPANY'S COMMISSIONERS will be found at the Company's OFFICE in TORONTO and GODERICH, where persons desirous of purchasing LANDS will be afforded any information respecting those for sale by THE COMPANY.

The conveyances to the Upper Province are now comfortable. From Montreal, by Stages or Steam-Boats, either via the Rideau Canal or the St. Lawrence, to the various Ports on Lake Ontario, from whence Stages run daily to London, and thence one leaves twice a week for Goderich.

The distance from TORONTO to GODERICH, is about One Hundred and Fifty miles, or about One Hundred and Five miles from the Head of Lake Ontario.

The following are the ROUTES to the COMPANY'S PRINCIPAL SETTLEMENTS, and as they take in the Chief Places on the way, the TABLE will be found useful to the TRAVELLER, whether proceeding to the CANADA COMPANY'S LANDS or not.

ROUTE from QUEBEC to GUELPH and GODERICH in Upper Canada.

MONTREAL......................................By Steam-Boats.
PRESCOTT—at the Head of the River Navigation or KINGSTON, upon Lake Ontario, via the Rideau Canal.............................By Stages and Steam-Boats.
And from thence *Steam-Boats* ply regularly to TORONTO, HAMILTON, and the various Ports on LAKE ONTARIO.
From TORONTO and HAMILTON, Stages run regularly to LONDON and GUELPH—To the latter Place via GALT.—And from LONDON to GODERICH, twice each Week. — Between GALT and GODERICH, a Stage Waggon Weekly.

DISTANCES.

Via WILMOT	MILES.	Via LONDON.	MILES.
HAMILTON to DUNDAS......................	5	HAMILTON to BRANTFORD.............	25
GALT or PRESTON............	20	OXFORD...........................	20
HOBSONS to WILMOT.............	17	LONDON..........................	30
STRATFORD to EASTHOPE............	17	GODERICH.........................	50
MITCHELL to LOGAN.............	101		

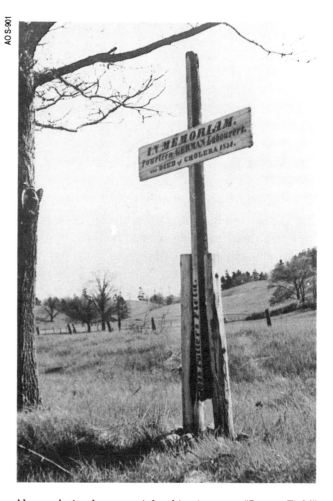

Above: *A simple memorial, taking its name "Potters Field" from Toronto, marked the burial mound of German labourers on the road between Cobourg and Peterborough as recently as 1948.*

Left: *Lands for sale.*

enterprise which operated in Upper Canada for over a century, beginning in 1824. The company was founded at the instigation of the Scottish novelist John Galt, who became superintendent of its Canadian operations in 1826. He brought with him to the province his close friend and fellow littérateur William "Tiger" Dunlop, who assumed the grand title "Warden of the Woods and Forests."

The company purchased the Crown Reserves, one-seventh of each township set aside at the time of the Constitutional Act, and was interested as well in acquiring the similar Clergy Reserves, when the Church of England intervened. The company instead bought the huge million-acre Huron Tract, a giant triangle of rich and fertile farm lands recently purchased from the Chippewa (Ojibway) Indians by the Imperial government.

At first the company was not a great success, and many years passed before its shareholders received a decent return on their investment. Eventually it proved to be a boon – although reformers thought the firm acted hand-in-glove with the Family Compact. Before John Galt was fired in 1829 and replaced by Thomas Mercer Jones, soon to be son-in-law to John Strachan, and William Allan, the firmest financial pillar of the Compact, the company had founded Guelph in what was called the Halton Block and Goderich on the shores of Lake Huron to the west.

The company shared in the benefits of the large emigration to Upper Canada of the early 1830s and augmented its sales program in the 1840s with a popular lease/purchase scheme. Many settlers found it more efficient and convenient to deal with the Canada Company than with the creaking, fee-ridden machinery of government. The company literature and posters reveal clearly its aims, purposes, and advantages.

Upper Canada was no more secure than Europe from the regular scourges of cholera that swept through the unsanitary buildings and polluted water supplies of most communities. Emigration, of course, increased the range and effectiveness of the disease, and by 1832 Canada had received a particularly bad dose. Medical science was ignorant of its treatment and largely of its causes too, and it was not unusual to explain its prevalence as caused by sin. The captain of the emigrant ship that brought Susanna Moodie to Montréal said it all: "That cursed cholera. Left it in Russia found it on my return to Leith – meets me again in Canada. No escape the third time." Again in 1847, with massive immigration into the country from Ireland (over a hundred thousand), typhus broke out; it was followed by cholera in 1849, first in Kingston and then Toronto. By 1854 cholera returned, though government health authorities in Québec and Toronto were by then better able to cope.

Nevertheless the *Canadian Freeman* could observe, even as late as April 1866, that "Toronto stands *facile princeps* as the dirtiest city in Upper Canada. Filth everywhere within the corporation limits stares one in the face. Go where you will,

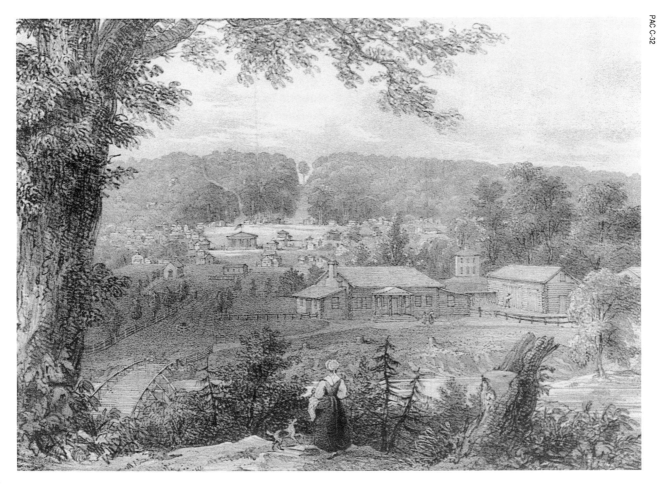

Guelph – Ontario's first company town, but with a difference. Exploitation of Ontario's mineral resources in this century has given rise to the one-dimensional phenomenon of the company town, dependent upon the exploiting company for its livelihood. Guelph would never qualify in this fashion but it was conceived, along with Goderich in particular, as the pride of the Canada Company's settlements. Founded by John Galt on St. George's Day, 1827, the town was designed as commercial and social centre for the company's eastern reserve. When criticized for the costs of erecting the place, Galt testily observed that the whole effort had cost less than a novel. The lithograph by G. Childs reflects the desirability of the settlement in its verdant rural setting during the first decade of its life.

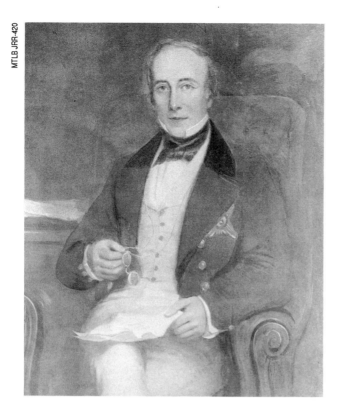

Sir George Arthur, last lieutenant-governor of Upper Canada, 1838–41. Watercolour from a painting by G.T. Berthon.

stagnant pools, pest heaps, lanes and alleys, reeking with the stench of decaying matter are to be dealt with."

Toronto, or more correctly the Town of York until 1834, eventually reached some approximation of the level of English civility so anxiously promoted by Simcoe. David Wilkie described the town with pleasurable recognition in his *Sketches of a Summer Trip to New York and the Canadas* (Edinburgh, 1837), recalling Sunday morning military parades and Toronto's citizenry walking in company to church. Wrote Henry Caswell in his *The Western World Revisited* (London, 1854): "Here the British flag, waving on some fortress, or the initials V.R., with the crown, or the likeness of a lion and a unicorn painted on a sign or exalted in a court-house, introduce at once a host of ideas, which pleasingly connect this vigorous young colony with the dear old fatherland 4000 miles away to the east." The lithograph (opposite page, upper) of the new courthouse, jail, and houses on King, east of Yonge, about 1830 confirms that impression in very flattering terms.

The site of Toronto (an Iroquoian word for "meeting place") was chosen because of its protected harbour. Wharves, piers, and warehouses soon developed at the foot of major streets and served a vigorous Lake Ontario trade. Cooper's Wharf, later called Maitland's Wharf, was at the foot of Church Street. Sir John Colborne in a despatch to the Colonial Secretary in 1833 advised that the area was filling up and much affected by "the effluvia of the marshes of the Don." He recommended that part of the military reserve on the waterfront be subdivided for civilian settlement, because the value of land near York had risen so steeply during the last few years.

An urban emigrant to Upper Canada frequently faced surprises. Not only would he and his family find themselves in the remote backwoods but what passed for civilization, and the concerns of government, frequently were very different from his British experience. Certainly, to a modern eye at any rate, a series of by-laws from the Township of Woodhouse in the southwestern portion of the province seems startling.

Religion and education proved a volatile mix in Upper Canada. Private schools had been the rule early on and it was only in 1807 that state-supported grammar schools made an appearance. Government elementary schools were founded after 1815 with much of the impetus being provided by the Reverend John Strachan. But the whole issue of schooling became sectarian in the 1820s. Strachan's fondest hope was to establish a university in the province to train and encourage a native-born elite.

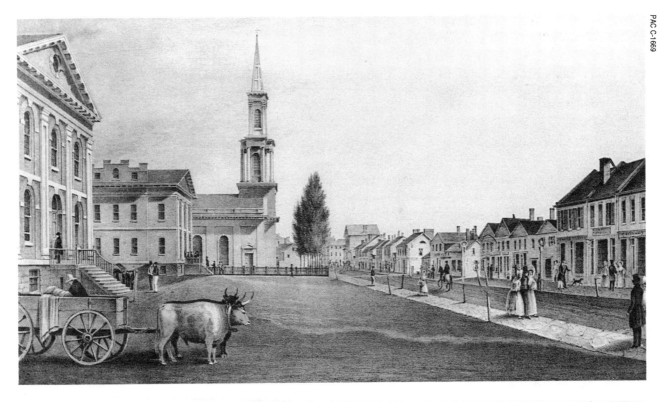

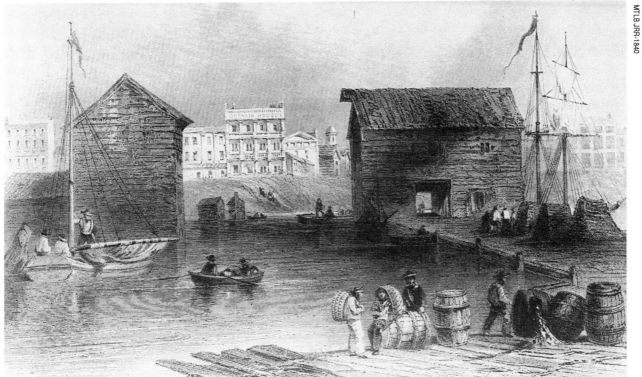

Maitland's Wharf, Toronto. Engraving after a drawing by W.H. Bartlett.

The result was, in 1827, the chartering of King's College in Toronto, endowed with some 225,944 acres of land throughout the province – the snag was that it had to be an Anglican institution. The religious proviso was strongly attacked throughout the province; the university, although it existed on paper, would not open its doors until 1842.

Sir John Colborne felt the province needed a good grammar school far more than a university, and under his prodding Upper Canada College came into being in 1829. It was endowed, at least in part, with the large amount of school lands set aside for provincial use.

The university and education question raged on through the 1830s with other religious groups founding their own institutions: for example, in 1836, the Methodists opened an academy at Cobourg, later to be called Victoria College, and still later to be shifted to and federated with the University of Toronto.

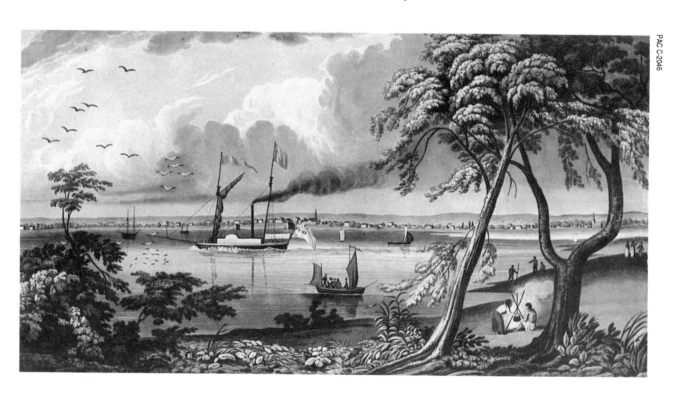

Two watercolours of Toronto Harbour a generation after Upper Canada had become a province. The region had been purchased from the Mississaugas in 1788. By the late 1830s it had developed an air of civic pride in its bustling activities. Soon it would lose its capital status to its competitor in urban "gravitas," Kingston, but at the height of the rebellions in 1837 there was no doubt that Toronto was the focal point for Lake Ontario navigation and commerce and could well confound Lord Dorchester's blasé observation on reaching Toronto Bay: "I know not what is meant by a Port in Upper Canada."

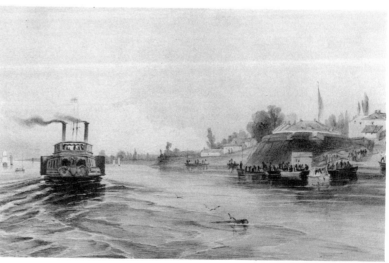

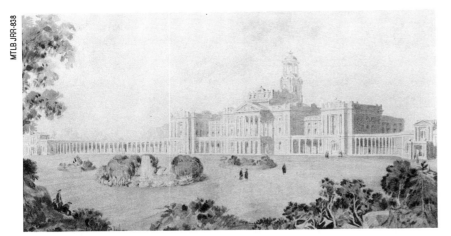

Left: *A proposal for King's College, 1835, prepared by J.G. Howard. Watercolour.*

Below: *Upper Canada College, Toronto, 1829. Lithograph, from a sketch by Thomas Young.*

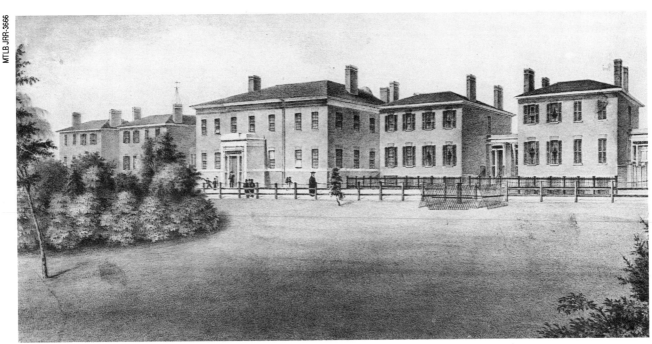

In many ways, the Upper Canada Rebellion of 1837–38 was a comic-opera affair, full of preposterous characters showing immense swagger and self-importance – William Lyon Mackenzie, the rebel leader, wrapped himself in layers and layers of clothing to deflect musket balls, and Sir Francis Bond Head, the lieutenant-governor, donned crisscrossed bandoliers and carried a brace of pistols. But there was death and tragedy as well. Lieutenant-Colonel Robert Moodie's death at Montgomery's Tavern on the evening of 4 December 1837 was both the beginning and in many ways the end for Mackenzie's Upper Canadian radicals. On 25 November, Mackenzie had proclaimed independent government and a date was fixed for a march on Toronto. The procession was badly coordinated from the start and commenced three days ahead of schedule on 4 December. Moodie, a veteran of the Peninsular War but also of the colonial military through the New Brunswick Fencibles, was a Yonge Street resident and fearful of rumoured rioting. Mackenzie, on that evening, was stopping all traffic on Yonge to prevent any information of rebel activities getting to Toronto, but at Montgomery's Tavern a group of rowdies met Moodie and his companions, who were riding south to see what was going on. Moodie discharged a pistol on being blocked and was in return shot from

47

A tableau of personalities in Upper Canada during the 1820s and 1830s. The series should, of course, be extended to include many others, and principally the members of the Family Compact.

I   William Lyon Mackenzie – editor, politician, rebel, gadfly. From a portrait by J.W.L. Forster.

II & III   The Baldwins, Dr. William and his son Robert – professionals, dynastics, moderates, chief advocates of responsible government. Lithographs.

IV   Sir John Colborne – veteran soldier, conciliator, High Churchman. Watercolour from painting by G.T. Berthon.

V   Sir Francis Bond Head – tragicomic swaggerer, galloper. Watercolour from painting by G.T. Berthon.

VI   Alexander Macdonell, Roman Catholic bishop at Kingston – soldier, priest, political underdog, infighter. Mezzotint.

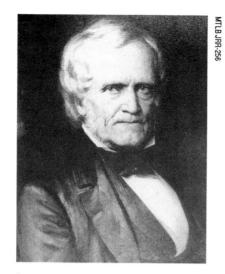

MTLB JRR-256

I

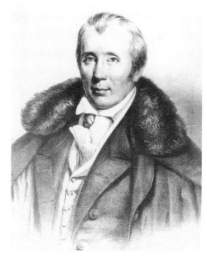

MTLB JRR-268

II

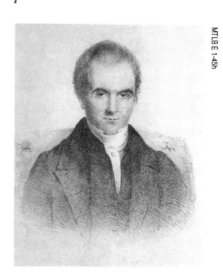

MTLB E 1-45h

III

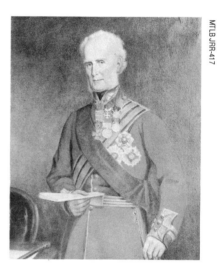

MTLB JRR-417

IV

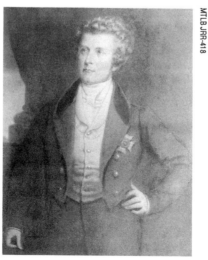

MTLB JRR-418

V

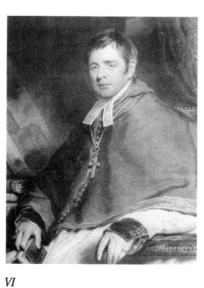

MTLB JRR-2506

VI

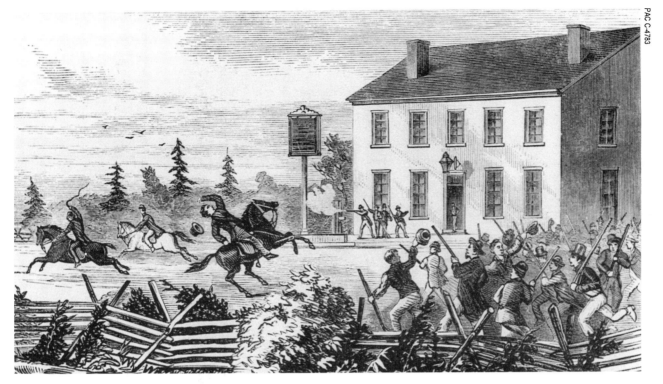

The shooting of Colonel Moodie. Sketch by Adrian Sharp.

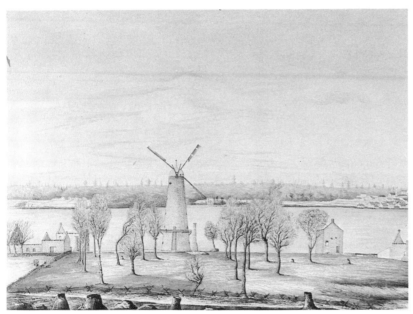

View of the windmill at Prescott as it appeared after the action. Sketch by H.F. Ainslie, April 1839. Watercolour.

his horse and taken to the tavern where he died three hours later. One of his companions slipped through rebel hands and reached Bond Head with the news before midnight. The town was warned and when the clash began in earnest the next day Mackenzie and his men were easily scattered. The fiery editor himself sped without much delay towards the United States.

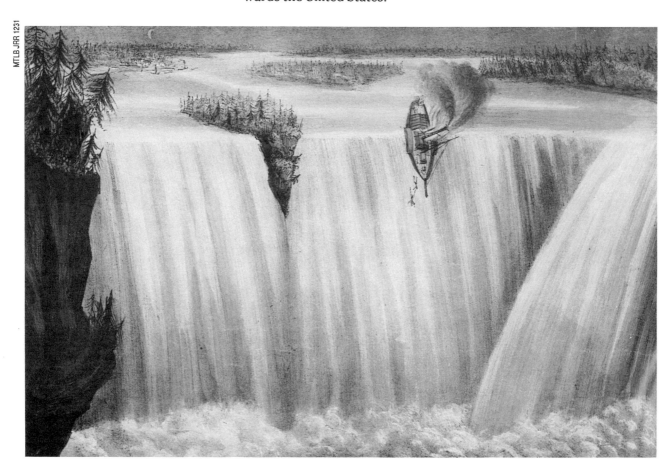

On 29 December 1837, the American steam packet Caroline, *which had been busily ferrying supplies to the rebellious camp of William Lyon Mackenzie on Navy Island in the Niagara River, after his melodramatic escape from the Yonge Street fracas, was taken by British naval authorities. It was set on fire and sent over the Falls. Ten days before, Mackenzie had appealed to the hearts of Upper Canadians by offering "three hundred acres of the most valuable lands in Canada" to any man who would join the "Patriot Forces" on Navy Island. In essence, the support for Mackenzie from settlers and farmers arose much more from resentment against York officialdom with its English overtones than from support for the mixed bag of "reforms" promoted by Mackenzie. The* Caroline *incident, a minor matter, remains a symbol of the British reassertion of power and authority, which took a sharper reality in the treason courts of Chief Justice John Beverley Robinson.*

Immediately before the outbreak of the rebellion, Sir George Arthur, a veteran colonial administrator with a dozen years' service in the British convict colony of Van Diemen's Land (now Tasmania), was appointed to Upper Canada with the clear purpose of maintaining law and order. Faced in 1838 with jails crammed with political prisoners, and constant harrying from American Patriot groups on both sides of the St. Lawrence, Arthur took a firm stand. Two unfortunate victims of the Mackenzie uprising, Samuel Lount and Peter Matthews, both popular farmers in York and supported by thousands of petitioners for clemency, were hanged as examples of no-nonsense authority. Secret Hunters' Lodges continued active infiltration from New York State across the St. Lawrence, however, and in November 1838 troops from Kingston repulsed rebels at the Battle of the Windmill and at Dickinson's Landing, near Prescott.

In August of 1838, at the height of the rebellions in Upper Canada, Philip John Bainbrigge painted this unusual scene of isolated figures aboard a St. Clair River ferry pulling across to the American side near Amherstburg. The juxtaposition of figures suggests a switch from conventional art depicting Upper Canada – frequently the draughts-

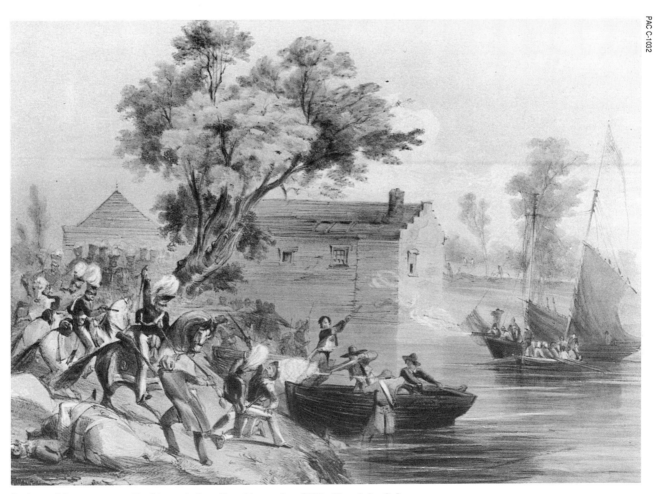

Defeat of Americans at Dickinson's Landing, November 1838. Sketch by Coke Smyth.

men's sketches of bored British army engineers stationed in the province. Bainbrigge, himself an army officer, is subtler, and in a way has captured the mood of the colony. The figures seem suspended in midstream; it is difficult at first to determine who is steering the ship and in which direction it is going.

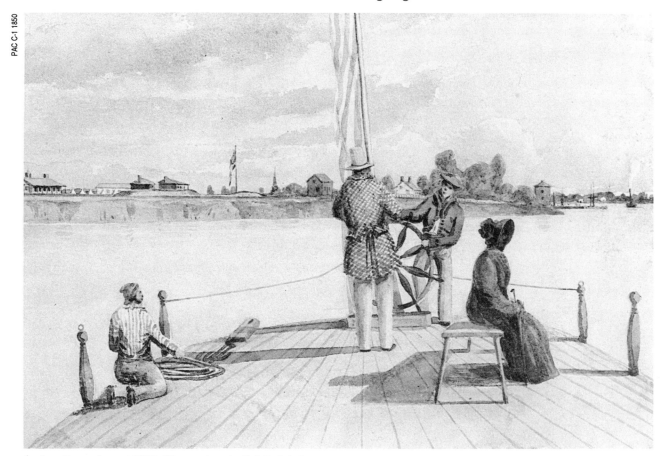

Amherstburg, August 1830. Watercolour by P.J. Bainbrigge.

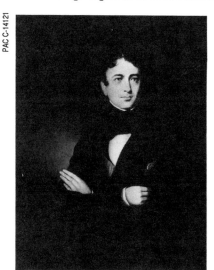

Lord Durham. Oil, by Sir Thomas Lawrence.

No document has had more probable effect on the growth and character of Ontario than the report that the Earl of Durham made to Lord Melbourne's cabinet in 1839 after a brief, tumultuous visit to the Canadas as governor-general. Most of his time was spent in Lower. Canada where, he believed, lay the key for resolving political problems. He found that far from a struggle between the people and the Crown executive there were "two nations warring in the bosom of a single state: I found a struggle, not of principles, but of races." His solution was, predictably, the English view of his time – both narrow and confident: "I entertain no doubts as to the national character which must be given to Lower Canada; it must be that of the British Empire; that of the majority of the population of British America; that of the great race which must in the lapse of no long period of time, be predominant over the North American Continent." This was no question of revenue disputes, as in 1822 when a Bill of Union was mooted, nor was it to go as far as a federal union with the Maritimes, as in 1867. Instead, Durham recommended a legislative union of Upper and Lower Canada to begin as quickly as possible, and to follow the principles of responsible government.

Canada West
1841-1867

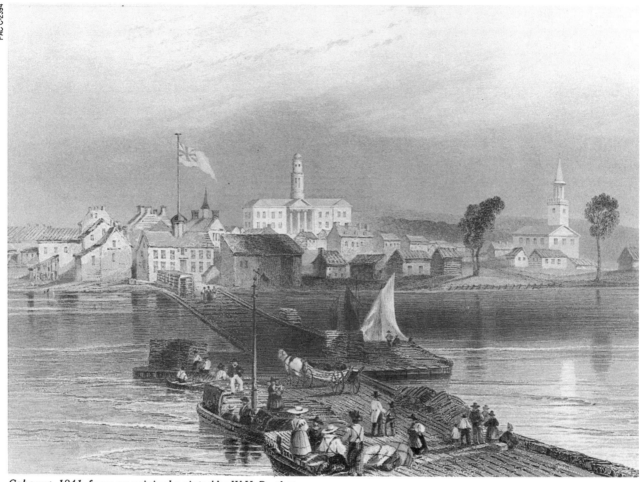

Cobourg, 1841, from an original painted by W.H. Bartlett.

The Union Bill passed the Imperial Parliament in 1840 and Kingston became capital city of the United Provinces in 1841. For more than two years the small limestone garrison-town at the confluence of the Rideau Canal and the St. Lawrence River had thundered for such glory against the "frontier" towns of Montréal and Toronto. Ironically, Bytown on the Ottawa River was dismissed, as not being on "the great line of communication to the upper country." The *Kingston Chronicle and Gazette* was ebullient at securing the seat of government and could not resist heaping misery on melancholy Toronto, its traditional enemy in the province, by gleefully observing that "the Public Records will now be placed in a situation equally secure from foreign invasion on the one hand and from internal insurrection on the other."

Cobourg, Canada West, was carved out of almost impenetrable cedar swamps by United Empire Loyalists in the first few years of the nineteenth century. Known, not lovingly, as "Hardscrabble" in its pioneer days, the town passed through the names of Buckville (after the first innkeeper, Elijah Buck), Amherst, and then Hamilton, before being rechristened in 1819 to honour Princess Charlotte who married Leopold of Saxe-Coburg. Following an influx of immigrants in the 1830s and completion of the harbour and pier in 1832, the lakeside town fast became a stopping-place for Durham boats and Lake Ontario steamer traffic.

The town was home to some notable provincial figures, including the great stagecoach boss, William Weller (who broke the record by driving Governor General C.P. Thomson, later Lord Sydenham, from Toronto to Montréal in less than thirty-eight hours in February 1840), and Egerton Ryerson who in 1841 became first principal of Victoria College – originally founded in 1835 as the Methodist Upper Canada Academy. Ryerson played a direct role in the development of public schooling in Canada West in succeeding years. Victoria College handsomely dominated the townscape.

The Earl of Elgin proved to be one of the best appointments made to Canadian government. He was well-connected politically – his wife was Lord Durham's daughter and the niece of Earl Grey, the colonial secretary. But it was more than politics that attracted Elgin to Canada: he needed the money. Elgin arrived in the province at the height of the terrible sufferings of Irish emigration, during the worst commercial slump in years, and in the face of alarming provincial deficits caused by rampant "canalization" in Canada West. It was Elgin's triumph to be able to secure the reality of responsible government. No longer would Westminster try to preserve its idea of an insulated harmony between executive and legislature as governors general Sydenham and Metcalfe had laboured mightily to do. Government was to be accountable to whichever political party dominated the legislature, or as Grey had shrewdly admitted to the lieutenant-governor of Nova Scotia, Sir John Harvey, in 1846: "it is neither possible nor desirable to carry out the government of any of the British provinces in North America in opposition to the opinion of its inhabitants." And indeed, as if to test the political waters

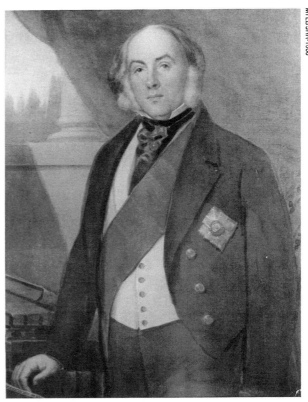

James Bruce, Eighth Earl of Elgin and Kincardine. Watercolour from a painting by Berthon.

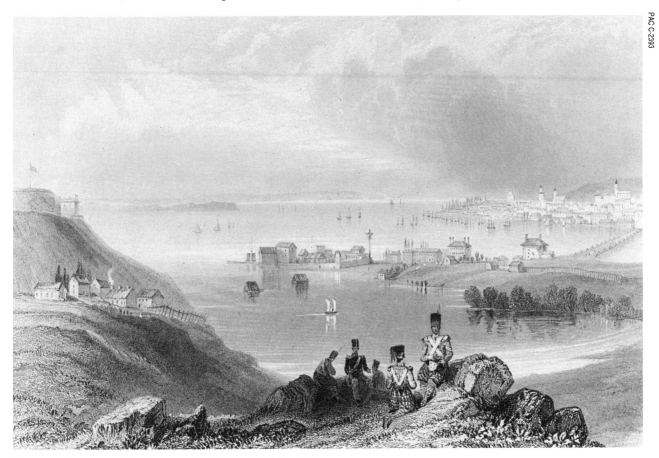

Kingston, from an original painted in 1842 by W.H. Bartlett.

in Toronto and Québec, but really to escape the violent Montréal of 1849 (to which government had removed from Kingston in 1843), the capital of the Canadas was to alternate until Queen Victoria chose Ottawa in 1857.

Army life in Canada had its moments of excitement after the War of 1812, notably the Mackenzie skirmishes and the Battle of the Windmill. But if you were not an officer and could not take advantage of the social privileges of your rank, the posting was dull and the life uncomfortable. Ordinary soldiers and their families, for example, found themselves crushed eight to a bed in most barracks. There would be little change until the horrors of the Crimean War became public knowledge.

Between the rebellions and the Fenian disturbances just before Confederation, the British forces in Canada had little occasion to practise their profession. In fact Earl Grey, the colonial secretary, reduced the military establishment in Canada and the Maritimes by twenty percent in 1852, assuming that the amateur soldiers of the sedentary militia were formidable enough. On paper the volunteer units which had flocked together in Upper Canada by 1839 (the Militia Registrar had nine artillery companies on his books for Toronto, Kingston, Gananoque, Brockville, Cornwall, and Niagara) looked impressive, but outside Toronto and Kingston militia activities didn't amount to much.

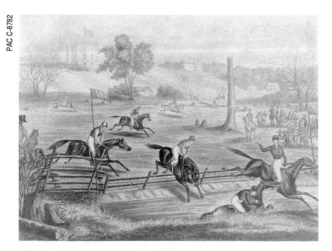

"A Grand Military Steeplechase." Engraved from a drawing by Lady Alexander in London, Canada West, on 9 May 1843.

Education might be dragging its feet a bit in the sketch opposite but the basic common-school education in Canada West is clearly shown. Grammar-school education was always available for the well heeled, but parliamentary grants were scarce for all schools. Lord Durham's Report led to the Union's Education Act (1841); nevertheless Canada West was so dissatisfied with the attempt to forge a unity between French and English cultures that it pushed through an act in 1843 which effectively made education a matter of local support, made religious institutions a matter of conscience, and assured all children the right to education. Under the advocacy of Egerton Ryerson, chief superintendent of education for Canada West from 1850, non-sectarian education flourished and separate schools were allowed to exist to ensure religious freedom for Roman Catholics. As well, Ryerson set up a provincial Normal School for the training of teachers and made the government responsible for grants, texts, and general supervision of teaching.

John Strachan's cherished University of King's College finally opened its doors in 1843 but attacks upon the essentially Anglican nature of the place continued, centring upon its exclusive control over lands set aside as university endowment. Robert Baldwin in 1849 finally secularized the college and brought it under government control. Strachan was enraged and fought the move, but without success, and on the first day of January, 1850, the "godless" University of Toronto, modelled after the University of London, came into being.

Bishop Strachan, then in his seventy-second year, determined that he would start again and create a church university. Gifts and donations poured in, and Strachan himself journeyed to England lobbying for both funds and a charter. He was immensely successful, and the cornerstone of the large building shown here was laid in April of 1851 on a site on Queen Street West in Toronto. Eventually, Trinity became federated with the godless University and in the 1920s moved to the central St. George campus where a similar building to the original Queen Street structure was erected.

Opposite above: *Trinity College, Queen St. West, Toronto.*

Opposite below: *"March of Intellect." Sketch by William Elliott of a rude schoolhouse in Adelaide village near Strathroy, Canada West, 1845.*

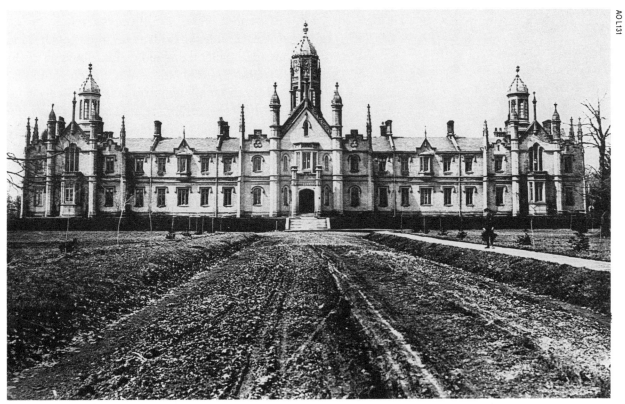

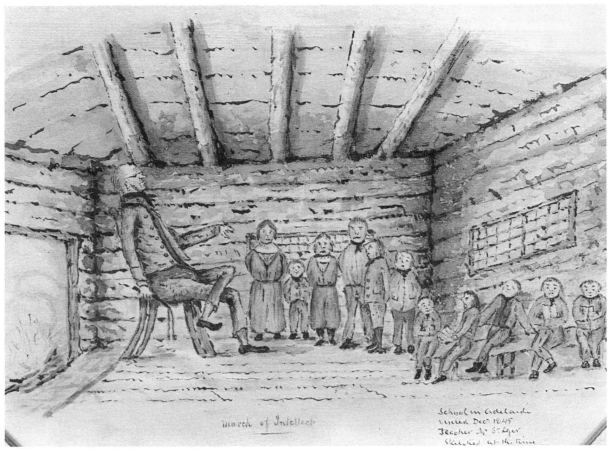

march of Intellect

School in Adelaide
visited Decr 1845
Teacher Mr St Leger
Sketched at the time

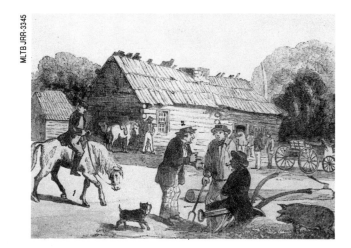

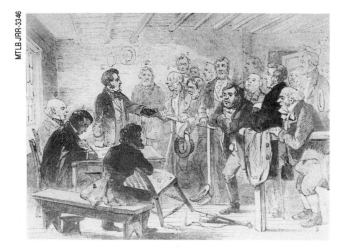

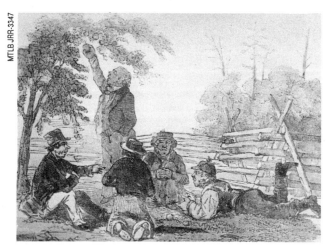

Backwoods justice.

Presented here are three sketches by Lucius O'Brien, first president of the Royal Canadian Academy, depicting judicial business at the Eighth Division Court at Mono Mills, Simcoe County, 1855. All three recall the informality involved in meting out backwoods justice, and some of the principal characters have been identified. The first sketch is the exterior of the courthouse, an ancient log house which for twenty-five years had been the home of George McManus, clerk of the Mono Mills Court, and subsequently the clerk of the Eighth Division Court. When he moved (to a fine brick house) the old home became the new courthouse. Number 1 is James McLaughlin, local farmer and resident. Robert Keenan, number 2, was a merchant of Keenansville, some nine miles away, and is here seen discussing the upcoming case.

The second sketch depicts the interior of the court. The first figure is the judge, James (later Sir James) Gowan. Number 2 is O'Brien, the artist. Three is McManus, the clerk. Four is John Haffey, bailiff, seen here tendering the oath to a witness. The Reverend John Fletcher, Anglican clergyman at Mono Mills, is number seven, and eight is an old settler, James Darragh, hanging over the bar. Court sessions even today cannot be photographed, and artists' sketches must be used. The final sketch shows the jury deliberating upon the case. The problem at the courthouse was that there was no other room in which the jury of five could consider their verdict. Consequently they were charged by Judge Gowan to go outside, and on their honour not to speak to anyone until they returned. The jury went to a nearby orchard, and after some serious reflection as pictured here rendered a verdict.

The Reverend Josiah Henson, 1789–1883, is thought by many to be the Uncle Tom of Harriet Beecher Stowe's classic abolitionist novel, *Uncle Tom's Cabin*. In fact, Henson was not Uncle Tom, nor had the story of his life as a fugitive slave contributed anything to the novel, although he once claimed that it had. But the myth continues, and is fused with legends of the Underground Railroad, the northern escape route to Ontario and freedom used by so many black American fugitives after the passage of the restrictive Fugitive Slave Act in 1850. There is no doubt that Ontario was a happier place for the blacks, but it is wrong to suggest that prejudice didn't exist here. After the American Civil War ended in 1865, large numbers of American blacks returned – emancipated – to the United States, lessening the potential for racial friction in Canada and permitting Canadians in general and Ontarians in particular to be self-congratulatory about their role in black history.

❖

Railroads were seen in the mid-nineteenth century as the ultimate expression of progress, and Canada West's Thomas Keefer, civil engineer, always provided the last word – usually with eloquent and fervent evangelism. In 1850 he published *Philosophy of Railroads* in which he extolled their construction and use in the most Victorian of moral tones, and urged their speedy acceptance in the province. "The civilizing tendency of the locomotive," he wrote, "is one of the modern anomalies, which, however inexplicable it may appear to some is yet so fortunately patent to all that it is admitted as readily as the action of steam, though no substance be visible and its secret ways unknown to man."

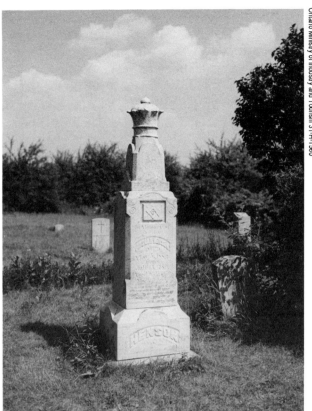

Josiah Henson's grave, Dresden, Ontario.

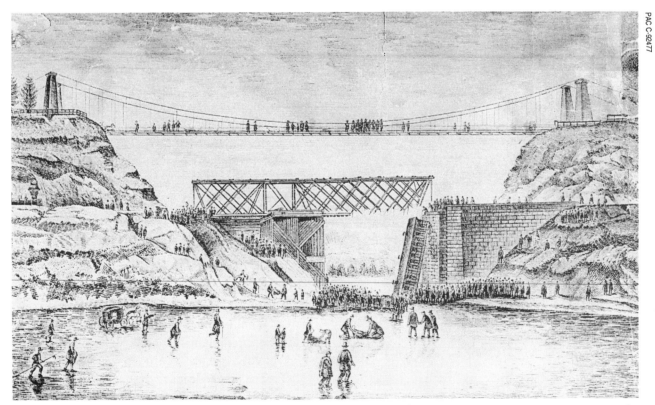

View of the railway disaster, Hamilton, Canada West, Thursday, 12 March 1857. Lithograph taken from a Daguerreotype by D.N. Preston.

If the 1820s through the 1840s were Upper Canada's canal era, the 1850s saw Canada West launch strenuously into railroad construction and connect, via feeder lines, to the busy American network across from Niagara and Windsor. Municipal credit for rail projects advanced by the provincial government brought untold speculation, however, and in 1857 when the inflating bubble burst, Canada West paid the price of boom. Even the great Grand Trunk line, completed from Montréal to Sarnia by 1859, barely kept above water (as a matter of fact in some places the rails actually were flooded over), and never did compete with the established American systems.

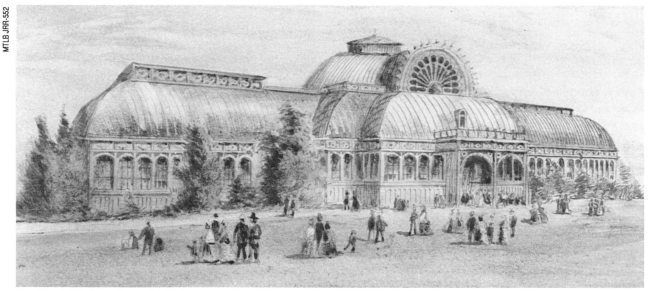

The Crystal Palace, Toronto. Watercolour.

TO THE RIGHT HONORABLE THE MAYOR, ALDERMEN & COMMON COUNCIL,
— OF THE CITY OF TORONTO —
THIS ELEVATION OF AN OBELISK SUGGESTED TO BE ERECTED AT THE JUNCTION OF KING & YONGE STREETS.
IS MOST RESPECTFULLY INSCRIBED, BY THEIR OBEDIENT HUMBLE SERVANT
THOMAS GLEGG,
ARCHITECT
JULY 1840.

It is proposed that this Obelisk be lighted with oil until it is decided to introduce Gas into the City.
The requisite number of Lamps similar to the above to be made and the lamp posts to be cast of a Pattern as near as possible to agree in Design with the Obelisk.

Gas lamps. Photograph from original in Board of Works Office – Toronto City Hall.

Another hymn to progress was demonstrated by Toronto's very own "Crystal Palace": an imitation of the celebrated structure which dramatized the spirit of progress of the Great Exhibition in Imperial London in 1851. Designed by Sir Sandford Fleming (inventor of Standard Time and the first Canadian stamp, the "threepenny beaver," and a noted railway engineer), the Toronto palace, erected in 1858, covered fifty thousand square feet and sat on ground adjacent to the Provincial Lunatic Asylum on Queen Street West.

Gas was naturally seen in Canada West as a sublime indicator of progress, and was applied to all manner of inventions – such as the lamp obelisk proposed for the juncture of King and Yonge streets in Toronto. In a lecture delivered to one of the numerous Mechanics' Institutes in the province, at Hamilton in 1848, R.B. Sullivan captured the romantic spirit of the machine age:

> I have a great regard for the town of Dundas, because more than any other place in Upper Canada, it appears to depend upon its factories; its situation in the midst of a fertile and beautiful country; its ever work-

ing stream, turning wheel after wheel, and keeping in movement factory after factory; the neat cottages of the artisans, and the snug comfortable and unpretending appearance of the place, are highly interesting to the stranger.

Nobody considered using oil for energy in Canada before Confederation. Nonetheless it was a valuable commodity as a lubricant and a source of light. Kerosene or coal-oil with its smoky, smelly illumination had been in use for many years, but a supply of natural oil burned cleaner and required less purification. The railway expansion of the 1850s made oil for lubricating machinery an essential product as well.

Oil Springs, in Enniskillen Township in the southwestern part of the province, was the location in 1858 (and probably as early as 1857) of North America's first successful oil well. Others followed, and by 1860 the region saw nearly a hundred producing wells. A refinery was established in the following year. Two years later there were ten refiner-

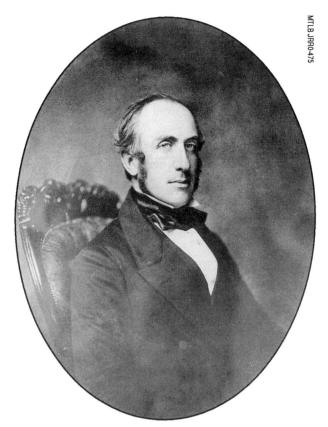

George Brown.

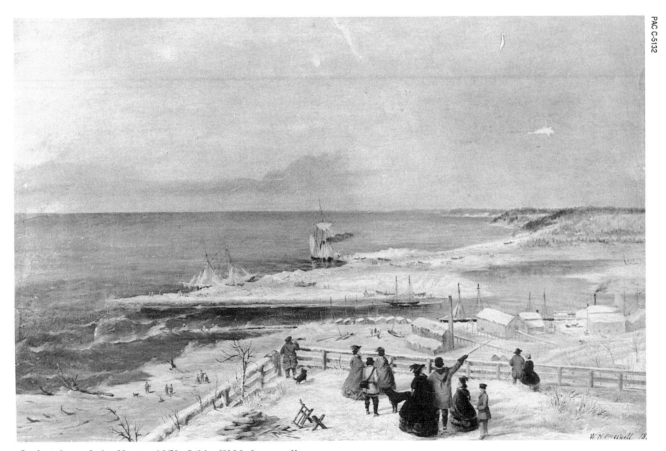

Goderich, on Lake Huron, 1858. Oil by W.M. Cresswell.

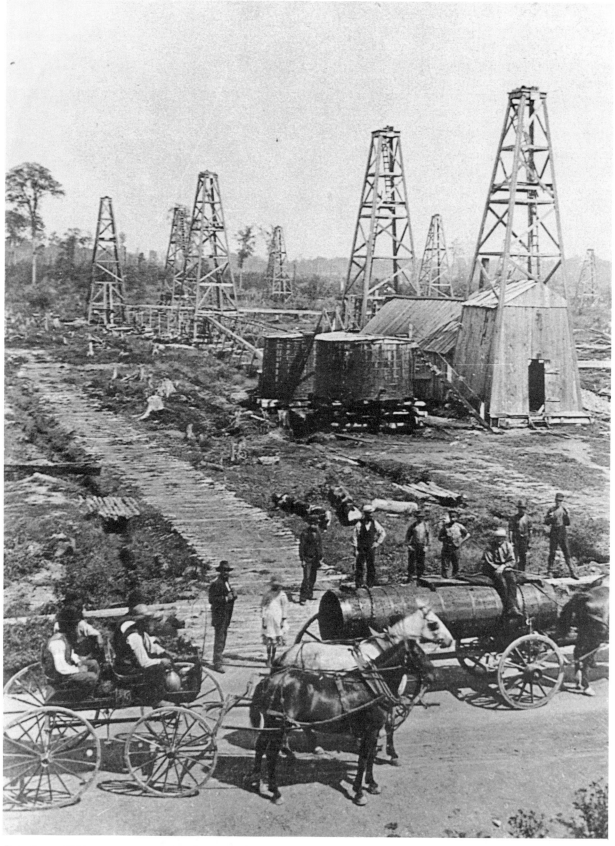

Petrolia, c. 1870.

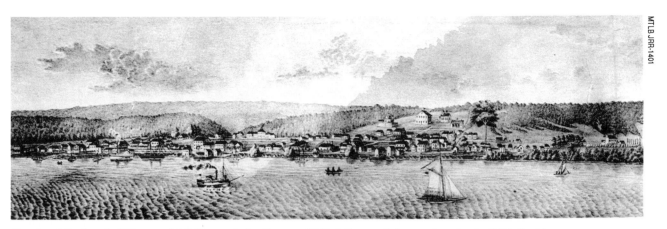

Barrie, at the head of Kempenfeldt Bay on Lake Simcoe, 1853. Lithograph from a drawing by W.H. Grubbe.

ies at Oil Springs and more at Petrolia, Bothwell, and Wyoming. Early producers banded themselves into a kind of consortium, the Canada Oil Association (a local OPEC), which fixed the price of crude at 50¢ per barrel.

The Bothwell field's heyday stretched from 1863 to 1866. George Brown, the Clear Grit leader and editor and publisher of the Toronto *Globe*, owned a large estate nearby – he was called "Laird of Bothwell" – and supplied wood for the Great Western Railway. His own fortunes, like those of the province, were tied up with the success of the rail

boom. A portion of his woodshed was used as an oil exchange; eventually he became extensively involved in the oil business himself.

The development of nearby Petrolia came later and was much better controlled than at Oil Springs or Bothwell. In 1866 crude oil was selling for $3 per barrel, and Petrolia was directly linked to the world by rail, assuring a flourishing export trade. The Petrolia field, in fact, was productive for forty years, well into the modern era when oil would be used as a source of power as well as lubrication and light.

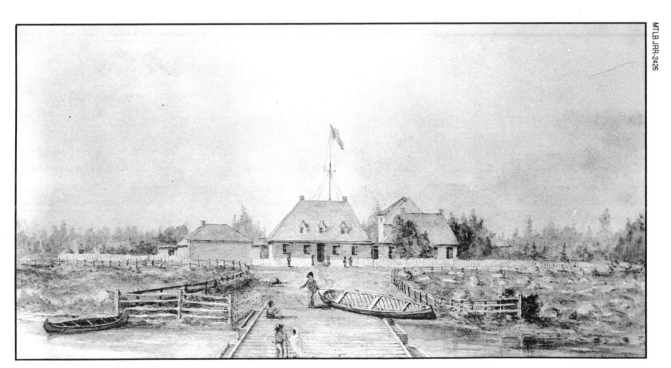

Hudson's Bay Company trading post, Sault Ste. Marie, 1853. Watercolour by William Armstrong.

By the mid-1850s shortage of good land was driving settlers into contact with the lumbering and fur-trading interests of the north. The Hudson's Bay Company, which since 1670 had ruled the enormous western tract called Rupert's Land, expressed a willingness to sell settlement lands to the government. "If land could be settled, it should be," was a recurring cry of the last decade before Confederation, and Canada West fixed an eye on Red River, the prairies, and, further west still, the Pacific coast. The visit in 1860 of the Prince of Wales, together with the Duke of Newcastle, colonial secretary, confirmed the need to support British-Canadian bulwarks against American influence and the threat of invasion. For some emigrants to the upper province, the west would seem a good deal more attractive than the mean living to be eked out in the rock-bound soil of the Haliburton Highlands.

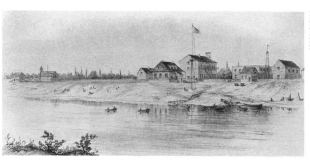

Top right: *Elgin Mills, Queen's Birthday Games, c. 1855.*

Right: *Ontario's first English settlement and oldest fur-trading post – Moose Factory, built in 1673 by the Hudson's Bay Company. Drawn as it appeared in 1854 by W. Trask. Lithograph.*

Below: *A. Currie's house, Haliburton, c. 1887. Photograph taken 26 February 1922.*

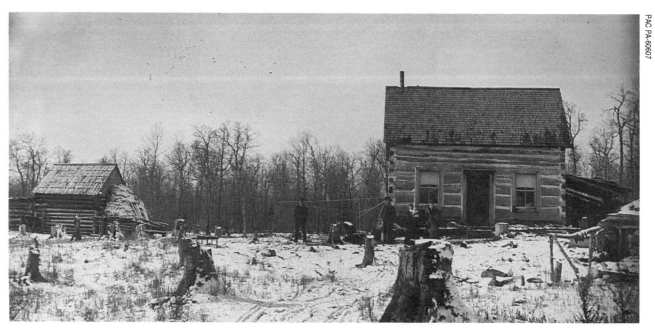

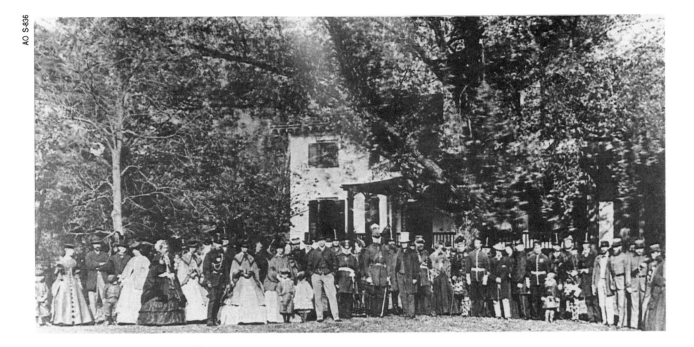

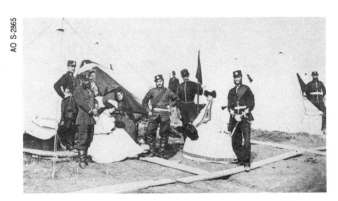

Above: *Rosedale, the elegant home of the York County Sheriff W.B. Jarvis, whose property stretched for 120 acres from Yonge Street eastwards, hosted a remarkable garden party on 23 October 1861. Survivors of the War of 1812, fought almost half-a-century before, and not easily forgotten in the colony, mixed with the prizewinners of the Fifth Military District Rifle Association.*

Officers of the 16th Regiment of Militia, Thorold, 1866.

British forces were swiftly reduced in the Canadas as an economy measure during the early 1850s, and commitments such as the Crimean War, 1854–56, persuaded Britain to make even more drastic cuts. Yet by the next decade the growth of Fenianism and the outbreak of the United States Civil War called for increases once more in military and naval activities in British America. The Irish Fenian brotherhood, hell-bent on separating Ireland from the British crown, seized upon Canada as a vulnerable British underbelly. Grandiose plans were laid to rendezvous along the Canadian border and to attack Hamilton, London, and Kingston (via Wolfe Island), taking over the Grand Trunk railroad lines and paving the way for a capture of Toronto. Secret agents employed by the Canadian government secured advance information on Fenian activities,

however, and John A. Macdonald, attorney-general of Canada West, was able to call out 14,000 of the volunteer militia within twenty-four hours for deployment along the frontier.

On 1 June 1866, a Civil War veteran, Captain John O'Neil, led a force of Fenians over the Niagara River. During that day and the following, they skirmished with groups of militiamen from Toronto and Hamilton at Ridgeway, midway between the mouth of the Welland Canal (Port Colborne) and Fort Erie, then in the hands of the Fenians. When that indecisive encounter was over, the brave volunteer gunners of the Welland Canal Field Battery, most of them with only bayonets and carbines, found themselves swamped by the disillusioned Fenians, now moving back towards the border to regroup.

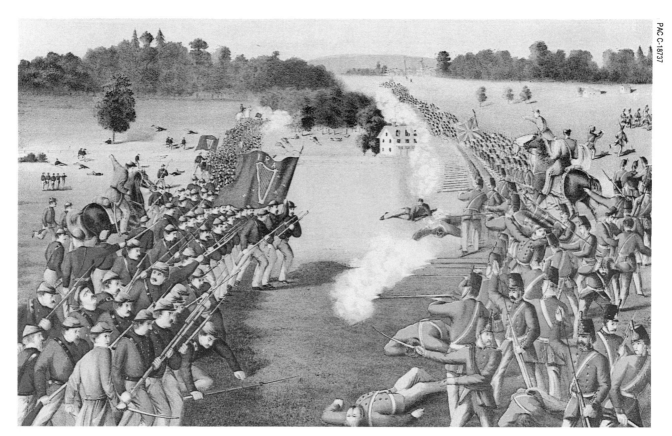

Battle of Ridgeway. Lithograph.

The events of June 1866 revealed the inadequacy of defence plans and the lack of proper field arrangements and military training. Defence expenditure increased markedly, and under Colonel Garnet Wolseley a "Volunteer Camp of Exercise" was set up in August 1866 at Thorold to provide a week's training for regular and volunteer units serving together. By March 1869, however, the press was reporting sale of cavalry and artillery horses as the British Army, Canada's garrison since the Conquest, began to pull out. The country's permanent force was now to be paid out of domestic pockets.

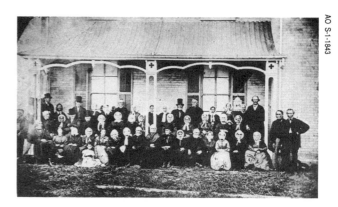

Pioneers at Peter Wood residence, 1867.

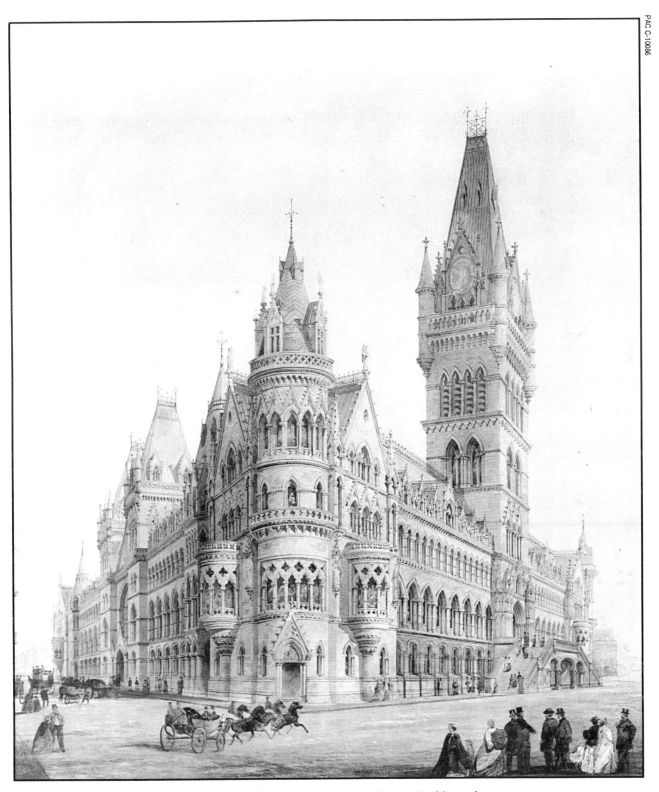

An architectural drawing submitted for design of the new Canadian parliament buildings. Anonymous.

Ontario at the time of Confederation: Three contemporary studies reveal first the ambition of the country as expressed in a proposed palatial Gothic parliament for Ottawa (previous page), then the ideal as portrayed in this flattering watercolour of Picton as a virtuous and elegant country town, and finally, the rougher reality, not without its charm, in the photograph of Bond Head, a village some twenty-five miles north of Toronto, west of Yonge Street.

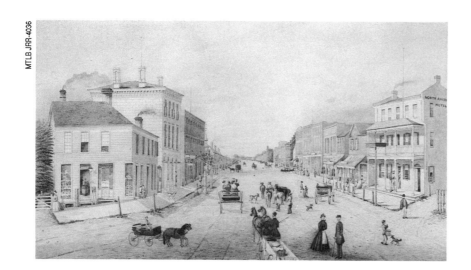

Left: *Picton, Prince Edward County, at Confederation. Watercolour by George Ackermann.*

Below: *Bond Head, York County, 1868.*

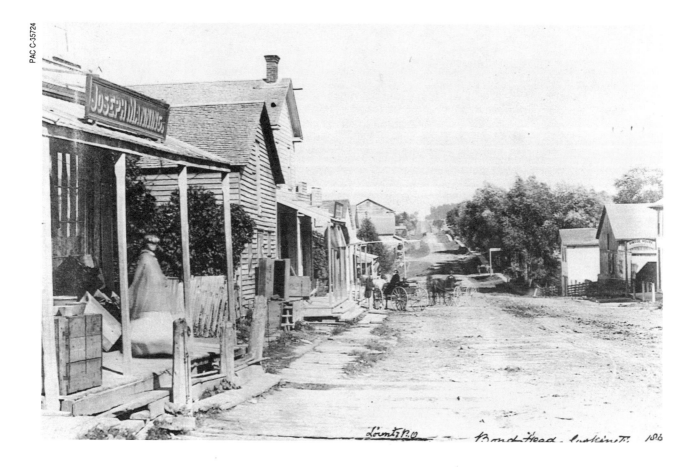

Ontario
1867-1991

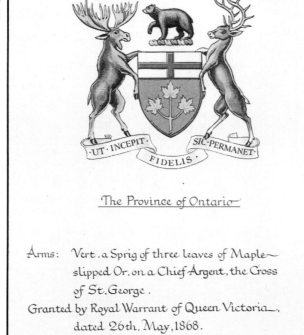

The Province of Ontario

Arms: Vert, a Sprig of three leaves of Maple slipped Or, on a Chief Argent, the Cross of St. George.
Granted by Royal Warrant of Queen Victoria, dated 26th. May, 1868.
Crest: On a wreath of the Colours, a Bear passant Sable.
Supporters: Dexter, a Moose; Sinister, a Canadian Deer, both proper. Also the Motto.
Granted by Royal Warrant of King Edward VII, dated 27th. February, 1909.

Arms of the Province of Ontario, 27 February 1909.
Watercolour and tempera.

Ontario at Confederation

Ontario in 1867 might have been considered "new" by the definition for a federated Dominion of Canada, but it was in fact very much the product of its past, and resembled still the solid, loyal, and British province of the first half of the century. The population was getting on for one-and-a-half million, with an annual rate of increase of over four per cent. Well over half were native-born, and most of those who were not came from the British Isles, particularly Ireland. The largest city was Toronto, whose population in 1861 stood at 44,821, more than double its nearest competitor, Hamilton (19,096), and far outdistancing its old rival Kingston at 13,743.

In any case most Ontarians lived in the countryside, and by Confederation there were still considerable areas of arable land to be taken up. But Ontario was beginning to be industrialized, and the province's trade pattern had shifted significantly with American reciprocity. In 1866, at the treaty's conclusion, the greater number of imports were still from the United Kingdom, but, significantly, most exports were to the United States. Wood and wheat remained the backbone of the export trade, and generally Canadian imports were of woollen and cotton manufactures, although there was a pronounced increase in industrial machinery and equipment produced both in the U.S. and in Britain.

Despite railroads and the centralization of the provincial government, regionalism continued to play an important role in Ontario life. The society was by no means homogeneous notwithstanding British backgrounds, and the old divisions of race, religion, and education also guaranteed variety if not conflict.

Ontario's first legislative buildings, of course, were in Newark (Niagara), but the first structure in York designed specifically for the purpose stood (in 1796) at the foot of present-day Berkeley Street, not far from Parliament Street. These slight, wooden buildings were destroyed in the War of 1812, and a series of temporary shelters used until 1820 when the provincial parliament moved to a new building on the site of the old. Four years later, however, it too burned down, and it was not until 1829 that work began on a large, attractive building on Front Street between John and Peter.

The Union of the Provinces in 1841 caused the government to shift from one city to another and for a number of years the Toronto building was

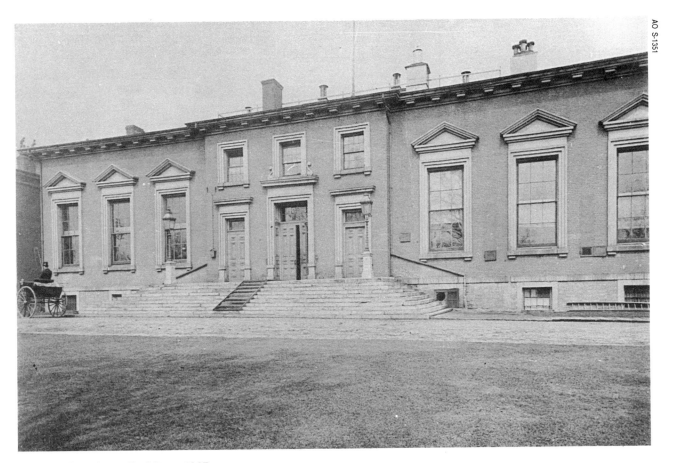

Ontario's Legislative Buildings, 1867.

used for university purposes and even as a mental asylum. Finally, with Confederation in 1867, the building returned to its original purpose. The legislature met here from 1867 to 1892, when it moved to more commodious quarters at Queen's Park. The old building was then demolished.

When Ontario became a province in 1867, the government was neither Liberal nor Conservative. It was carefully structured to be moderate, and not to revert to the old, rabid partisanship of the Union period. John Sandfield Macdonald, an associate but no flunky of Sir John A. Macdonald (notably, he had opposed Confederation), became the first provincial premier. Macdonald oversaw a cabinet of six – three Tories and three "Coalition Liberals" – and in a house of eighty-two members could count on fifty supporters. An opposition bloc, however, soon clustered around Archibald McKellar and Edward Blake. They reiterated the interests of the old Clear Grits and soon conducted themselves as a party; in 1871, as the provincial Liberals, they captured Sandfield Macdonald's government.

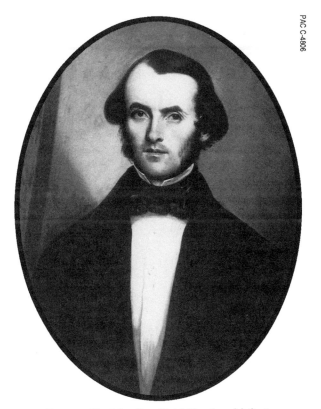

The Honourable John Sandfield Macdonald, first premier of Ontario. Oil by Théophile Hamel.

71

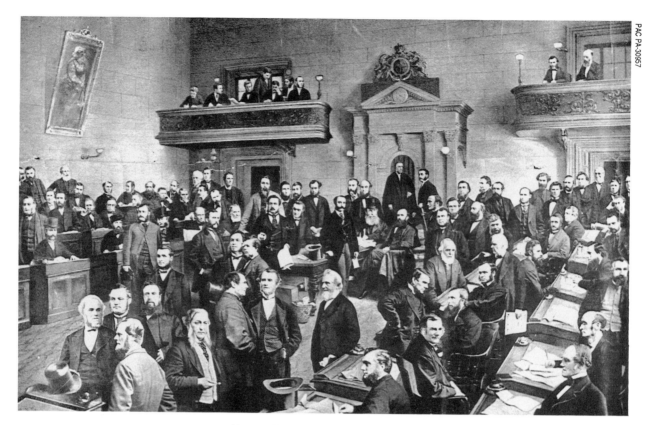

Above: *Ontario's first legislature, 1867–71.*

Below: *The library of the Ontario legislature, c. 1890. The Reverend William Inglis, librarian, standing.*

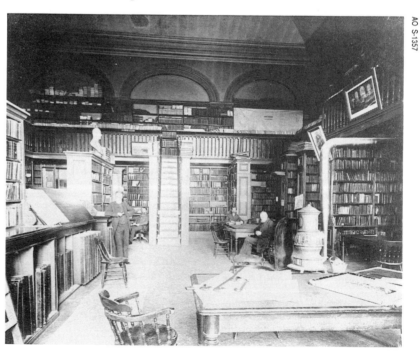

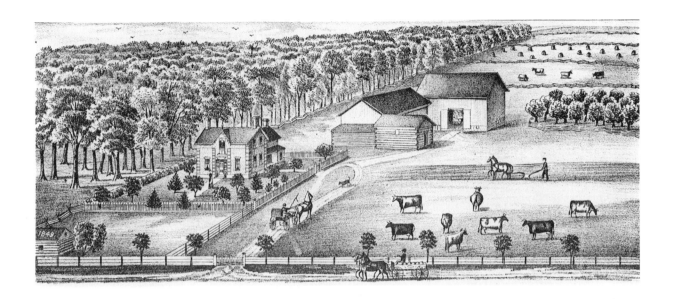

Above: "Elmdale," the prosperous farm of Septimus Hogarth, Concession 2, Lot 13, Stephen Township, Huron County, as portrayed in H. Belden's Illustrated Historical Atlas of the County of Huron, Toronto, 1879.

Below: Toronto, Yonge Street looking north from Front Street, c. 1872.

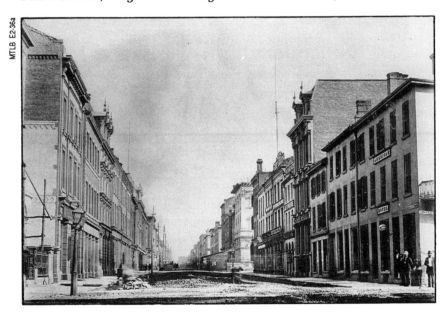

It is interesting to note that in 1867 parliamentarians could hold seats in both Ottawa and Toronto. Most of the tried talent from the old parliament went to Ottawa anyway. Only thirteen members in the new House in Toronto had any parliamentary experience.

Ontario's wealth had always been based on agriculture, and farming still provided the nucleus in 1867. Ready markets – augmented by American reciprocity, the U.S. Civil War, and the Crimean War – gave tremendous advantages to Canadian farmers, and their new-found prosperity took substance in the form of prosperous new farmhouses with spacious vistas. Traces of former wealth and power were still in evidence everywhere, but the old power élite was in decline. A new commercial class took social and economic precedence, and Ontarians joined the ranks of mid-Victorian Liberals with a vengeance.

Toronto was considered by some to be a Canadian Manchester and its citizens were proud to have the comparison made. After all, they fancied themselves as everything that a Samuel Smiles or a Horatio Alger promoted – individualistic, enterprising, ambitious, Christian, thrifty, virtuous, free, open, and "liberal." They had nothing to fear.

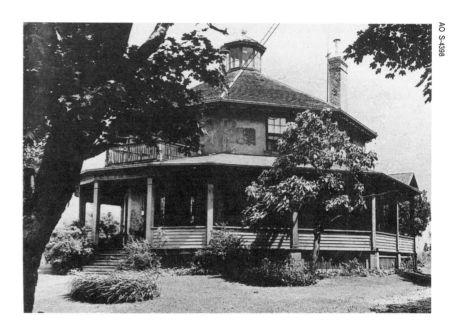

Octagonal House, Ameliasburgh, Prince Edward County.

Ameliasburgh, a hamlet in Prince Edward County, was once called Roblin's Mills, after Owen Roblin, a miller who in 1842 began a business here that eventually produced a hundred barrels a day and exported to Britain and the United States. Roblin as well ran an apple evaporator and a sawmill. In the late nineteenth century the village boasted a cooperage, a shingle mill, and a carriage works that employed upwards of a hundred and fifty people. The name Ameliasburgh, which is also the name of the surrounding township, comes from Princess Amelia, the youngest child of George III who was on the throne when the original township survey was made in 1785. Ameliasburgh, in its nineteenth-century heyday, was a typically Ontarian wedding of country village and farming hinterland, each serving the other.

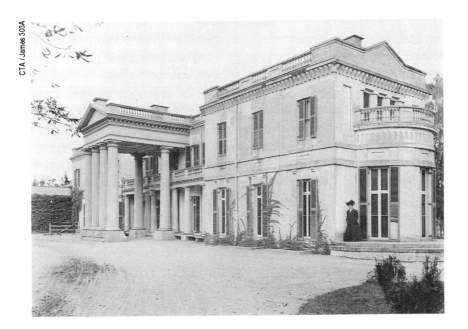

Dundurn Castle., Hamilton, c. 1900.

Sir Allan MacNab's splendid mansion, Dundurn Castle, contributed substantially to the wreck of his fortune. MacNab, a Rebellion of 1837 hero, led the government of the United Canadas from 1854 to 1856, and was an inveterate railroad speculator. After his death in 1868, his house served as the home of the Upper Canada Institute for the Deaf and Dumb, and then for many years as a civic museum before it was restored as a Centennial project in 1967. Bishop Strachan's massive house, near Front and University streets in Toronto, did not fare so well. The house was probably the grandest residence in Upper Canada when it was built in 1819. Strachan's Aberdonian brother, upon first seeing it, exclaimed, "I hope it's a' come by honestly, John?" Notably it had no outside doorknob on the front door – why would it? Strachan's butler would always be there to answer the bell. Bishop Strachan died in 1867, and the house, formerly known as The Palace, became the lowly Palace Boarding House until it was torn down in 1896.

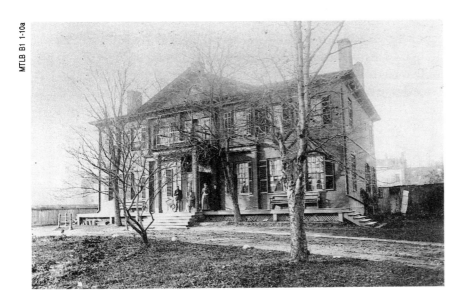

John Strachan's residence, Toronto, c. 1890.

75

The Canada Company was moving into its stride at Confederation. Founded in 1824, it would continue to sell land in Ontario until 1951 when it went out of business for the best possible reason – it ran out of land to sell. Shortly after the company was established in Upper Canada, it moved into the former residence of a wealthy York merchant, Quetton St. George, at King and Frederick streets. This Georgian house was the first private residence in York to be made of brick. The well-known Toronto architect, John G. Howard (who on his death gave High Park to the city), early in his career occupied an office on the main floor.

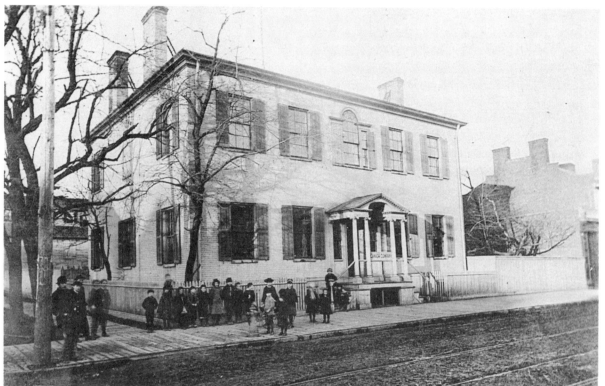

Canada Company building.

Toronto, capital of the new province of Ontario, was more and more commercial in its core, and the core had shifted by 1867, away from the axis of the old town of York, to the west and north. Residential districts were becoming the vogue, a movement soon to be facilitated by extensive street-railway networks. Commercial growth in the city was slowed by the depression of the 1870s and Toronto felt the bite of unemployment during that decade. As well, labour disputes were becoming more common. In 1872 the Typographical Union struck for a nine-hour day. The restoration of the economy and the growth of industry in the 1880s brought an expansion of unions, and investigations into working conditions, child labour, and hours of work. Toronto in the 1870s was not yet Toronto the Good. City Hall was the nexus of graft, bribery, and boodle. Violent crime was a considerable problem, and it is evident that much white-collar crime infected the commerce of the city as well. Intemperance and prostitution were considered the chief social evils of the time.

The Mohawk Chapel at Brantford was the first Protestant church built in what became Ontario, in 1785, with a grant from George III. In 1869 it was visited by Prince Arthur, third son of Queen Victoria, who was greeted by Simcoe Kerr, the grandson of Joseph Brant. Originally the photo caption read "Two Princes of the Blood." The Brantford *Expositor* was delighted with the visit, labelling it a "right royal" affair and describing it in detail:

> The procession then went on to the Mohawk Church where several thousands of persons were in waiting, including nearly all the Indians and squaws upon the Reserve. Loud cheers rent the air as the party reached the Church grounds and alighted from the carriages. At the door of the building a number of painted Indians with clubs, spears and knives stood guard and kept back the crowd. His Royal Highness before going into the Church stood upon the steps and was photographed with the painted Indians ranged on either side of him.

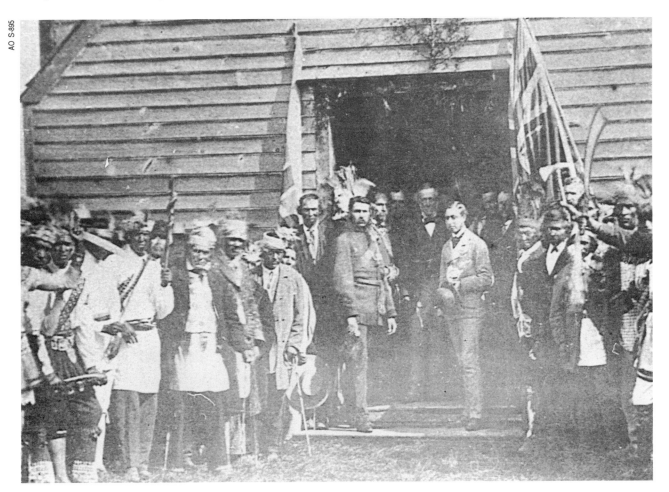

Reception of Prince Arthur, the Duke of Connaught, at H.M. Chapel of the Mohawks. Brantford, 1 October 1869.

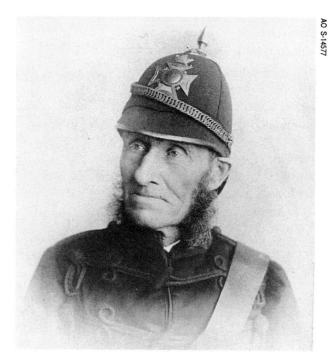

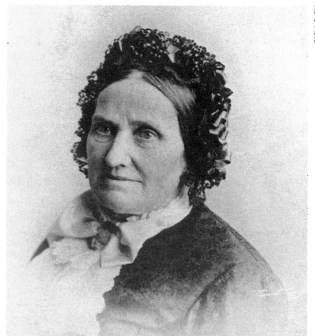

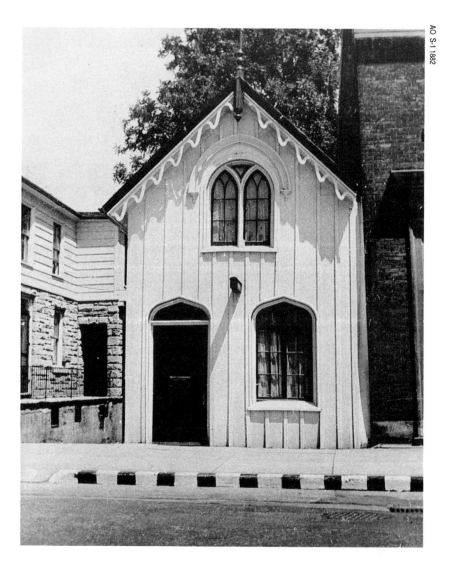

Above: *Lieutenant-Colonel J. Armstrong (shown wearing the cap and badge of the Wellington Rifles) and his wife, Mrs. Mary Armstrong, Ontarians.*

Right: *Surgery of James Ross, B.A., M.D., Dundas, Ontario.*

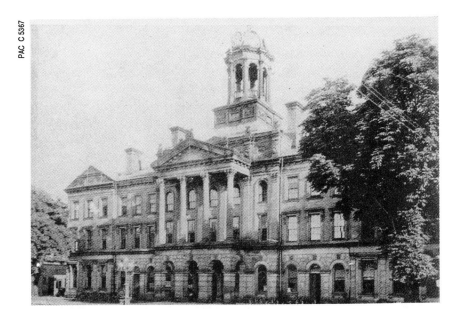

Victoria Hall, Cobourg. The confidence and commercial optimism of the mid-Victorian era are clearly captured in Victoria Hall. The huge Palladian building is, in fact, Cobourg's town hall, and houses the municipal offices and courts. Designed by Kivas Tully of Toronto, the building was opened by the Prince of Wales in 1860. The cost ($110,000) threw the town into debt for many years.

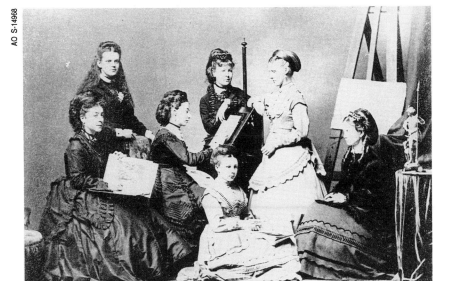

Mr. Gilbert's painting class, Toronto, c. 1870.

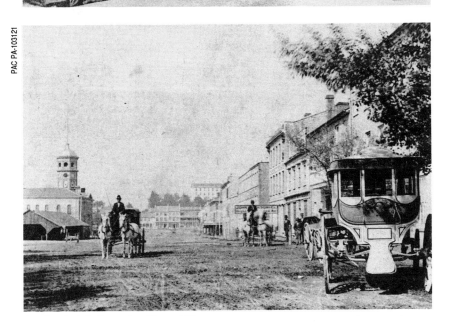

Guelph, c. 1870. The old Canada Company town was now almost half-a-century old. It was settled, permanent, and prosperous, and in 1879 became a city. The presence of the Royal Mail Coach to the right and the broad vista beyond give the impression of a town in West Country England.

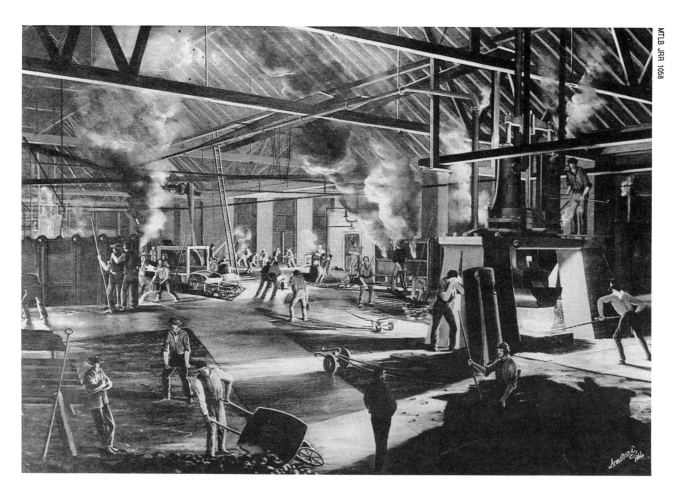

MTLB JRR 1058

Railroads meant the creation of heavy industry. The Toronto Rolling Mills, decidedly "dark and satanic," were built and managed by C.S. (later Sir Casimir) Gzowski. They were not only the largest manufacturing industry in Toronto but also the largest iron mills in the whole Dominion. The firm's best customer was the Grand Trunk Railway, but when it was shown that steel rails were superior to iron, and the costs of re-tooling the mill calculated, the Grand Trunk business went elsewhere and the place was dismantled.

Above: *Toronto Rolling Mills, 1863–69. Sketch by William Armstrong, 1864.*

Below: *Toll sign of the Hamilton & Saltfleet Road Company.*

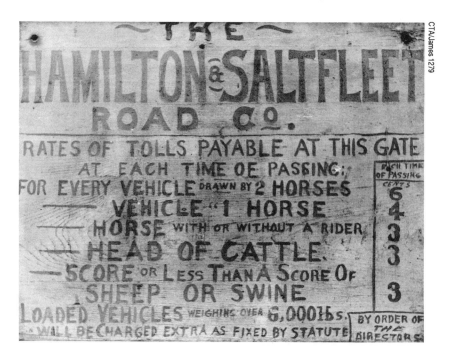

CTA/James 1279

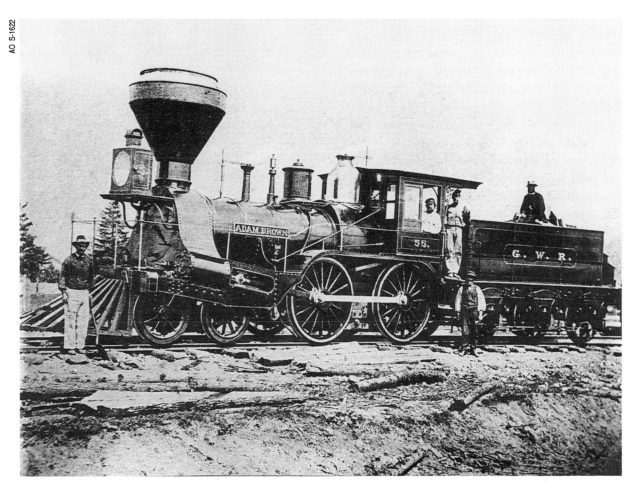

The "Adam Brown" of the Great Western Railway, the first train out of Elora, Dominion Day, 1870.

Adam Brown's long life ably represents the business spirit of the era. Brown, merchant, railroader, and politician, lived to be a few months short of 100 (1826-1926). Born in Scotland, he immigrated to Montréal with his parents in 1833 and was established in business there at the tender age of fourteen. Ten years later, in 1850, he moved to Hamilton, Canada West, and became a partner of a large wholesale grocery business. He went on to serve as one of the "fathers" of John A. Macdonald's protectionist National Policy, and was a pioneer Ontario railwayman – the first president of the Wellington, Grey and Bruce Railway and of the Northern Pacific Junction Railway; in fact both lines owed their existence to his persistent efforts and organizational skills. He represented Hamilton in the federal House of Commons from 1887 to 1891 when he was appointed postmaster of Hamilton, a position he held until his death.

Oliver Mowat's Ontario

The election of the Liberals to provincial power in 1871 marked the beginning of a trend in Ontario's political history: long single-party reigns. But the first overseer of Liberal fortunes stayed only a few months. Edward Blake, premier from 1871 to 1872, is one of the great enigmas of Canadian and Ontarian politics. Blake, touted by most to become federal prime minister, never did; in fact, he seemed always to back away from opportunities when they appeared. In 1872 he abandoned the provincial premiership and shifted to the federal scene; he remained there, continuing to promise much more, as a cabinet minister and leader of the Opposition, than he ever delivered. Eventually he became an Irish M.P. at Westminster and a constant supporter of "home rule."

If Blake's tenure in the province was short, his successor made up for it and more – for he remained in office, as premier and attorney general, for upwards of twenty-three years, the longest premiership in Ontario's history. Oliver Mowat (after 1891, Sir Oliver) was the perfect man for the times, and the place; he wore Ontario like a glove.

Mowat was Liberal by choice, not by inheritance nor by pressure nor by opportunity. Two phrases stuck to him, and he approved of both: "Christian statesman" and "practical politician." Mowat is frequently recalled as the champion of provincial rights, the man who, at the Judicial Committee of the Imperial Privy Council, most successfully slew the federal dragon. This is accurate enough; under Mowat's prodding, Ontario's boundary was pushed far westward and Ontario gained great advantages in terms of minerals, pulpwood, and power-sites. The opportunities won would eventually permit Ontario to become the most developed of the Canadian provinces, and the most advanced in terms of economic diversification. But Mowat provided more. He was a moderate and cautious reformer at a time when Ontarians wanted common-sense politics. He took a middle course in all things. For example, religion: the Ontario Liberals moved from being bigoted Clear Grits to being a party that embraced all creeds (and both language groups). Besides, Mowat had a sixth sense about appealing legislation. He knew when Ontario wanted "progress," the sacred calling of the nineteenth century, and he gave it with a flourish. He reduced the property qualification and ex-

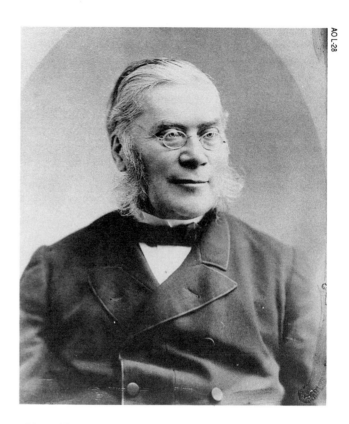

Oliver Mowat, premier of Ontario, 1872–96.

tended the franchise to give municipal votes to women. He was skilful too in manipulating the growing clamour for prohibition, and took refuge in plebiscites and court decisions rather than party platforms. It was a skill those who followed him in Liberal leadership did not possess.

Internally, he looked to party organization and was careful to mend political fences or construct new ones. Most important, Mowat understood the central significance of agriculture to Ontario's growth and stability. He made farming profitable and Ontario's produce competitive, and achieved a healthy balance between agriculture, business, and industry; in a similar way, he united town and country. Both flourished during his premiership; moreover, the Ontario countryside took on that distinctive look of established prosperity that it still possesses.

That is not to say that Mowat never made mistakes. He was, for example, too eager to encourage immigration to the Canadian Shield, clearly unsuitable for agriculture. Neither did he understand that timber had to be treated as a renewable resource, and during his premiership exploitation of the forests was extensive. Nor did his vaunted educational system, which proudly ranged from kindergarten to university, deserve the praise that his ministers bestowed on it – frequently the teachers were of inferior calibre. And Mowat was attacked by many critics for using patronage and pork-barrel politics a little too freely; certainly his placemen were everywhere.

But when all is considered, the advantages of Mowat's liberalism outweigh the negative elements. The basis for a multi-faceted modern province was laid during his régime: the Agricultural College at Guelph was begun; labour laws focusing on minimum wage and maximum hours (plus government standards for the worksite) were established; a Bureau of Industries aided industry and business; a

government Mines Department, a Board of Health, a Children's Aid Society, public libraries, and provincial parks all had their start during his time in office. And all of this was paid for – Mowat left the treasury in 1896 a million dollars richer than it was when he had taken over more than two decades before.

The lieutenant-governor's large residence was situated on a suitably grand plot of land at King and Simcoe streets, in Toronto, and is shown decorated in anticipation of a visit by Lord Dufferin, governor general from 1872 to 1878. "Welcome Lord Dufferin" can be seen over the main entrance.

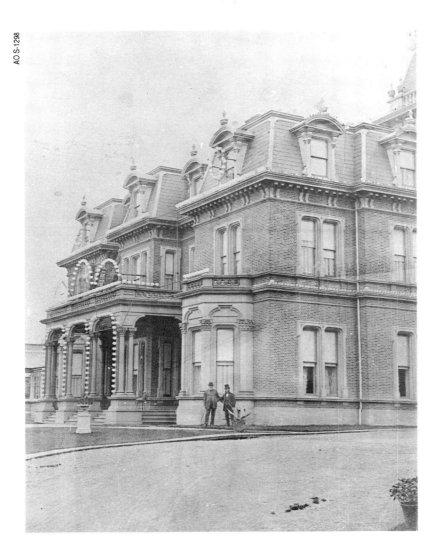

AO S-1298

Edward Blake, premier of Ontario, 1871–72, "The Light that Failed." Cartoon published in Vanity Fair, *1894.*

AO S-1801

Government House, Toronto, 1870s.

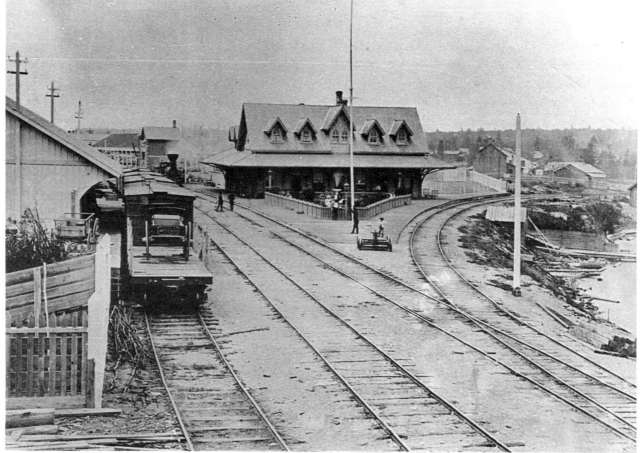

Above: *Allandale Station was a significant junction on the Northern Railroad from Toronto, at the point where the lines of the old Ontario, Simcoe and Huron Railroad Company (known affectionately as the "Oats, Straw and Hay") through line to Collingwood parted from the Muskoka Lakes tourist route. It sprang up outside the town of Barrie owing to a mixture of local political and engineering problems and it is said that the OSHRC engineer vowed "to make grass grow in Barrie's streets and pave Allandale streets with gold." That never happened despite the summer traffic moving through the junction.*

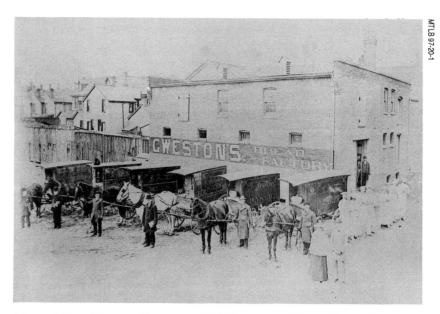

Weston's Bread Factory, Toronto, c. 1885. George and Emma Maude Weston stand in front of the Weston Bakery, with their bakery and delivery staff ranged behind them. George Weston died in 1924. His son, W. Garfield Weston, took over the business, and within ten years the firm had expanded to the United States and Britain.

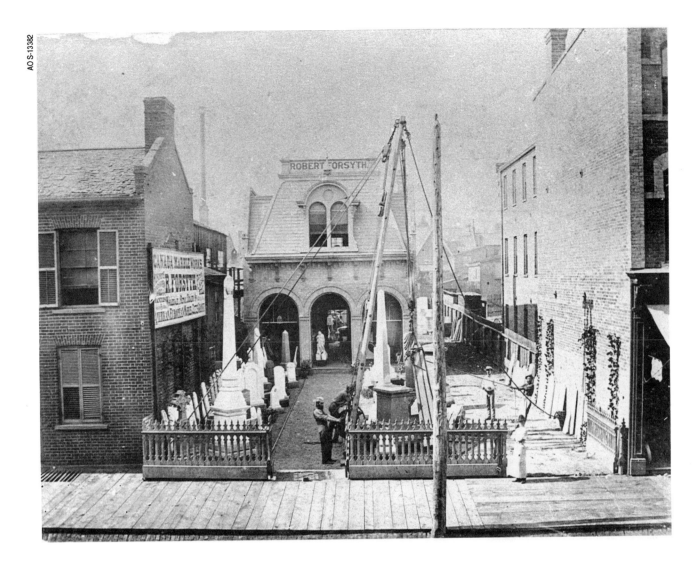

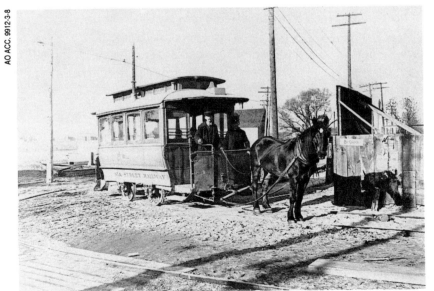

Above: *Canada Marble Works, Toronto, 1870s.*

Left: *Sarnia Street Railway, 1875. Sarnia, named by Lieutenant-Governor Sir John Colborne in 1836, was considered an excellent position for a fort to counter the American encampment across the St. Clair River. Forty years later it had become a flourishing lakes port with an active waterfront and railroads. The Sarnia Street Railway provided regular cross-town transport between Grand Trunk and Great Western depots.*

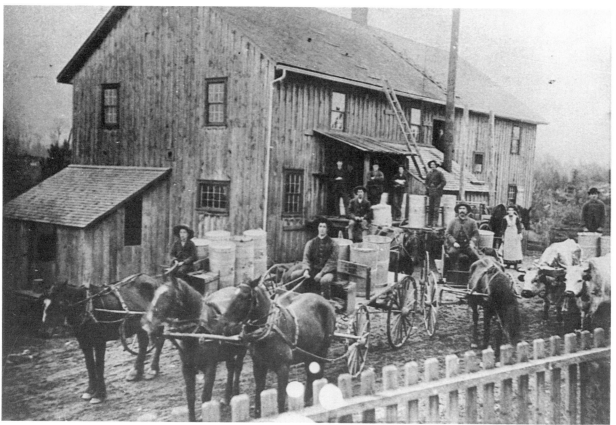

Cheese Factory, Warsaw, 1880s.

Dairying and cheese manufacturing were on the rise in Ontario during the post-Confederation period. Perhaps the most significant area was Ingersoll, near London. There resided, as well, one of Canada's worst poets, James McIntyre, remembered, when he is remembered at all, as the "Cheese Poet." When the good cheese makers of Ingersoll decided in 1866 to mould the biggest cheese ever (a monster that weighed over seven thousand pounds), McIntyre recorded the moment in verse:

Ode on the Mammoth Cheese

We have seen thee, queen of cheese
Lying quietly at your ease,
Gently fanned by evening breeze,
Thy fair form no flies dare seize.

All gaily dressed soon you'll go
To the great Provincial show,
To be admired by many a beau
In the city of Toronto.

Cows numerous as a swarm of bees,
Or as the leaves upon the trees,
It did require to make thee please,
And stand unrivalled, queen of cheese.

May you not receive a scar as
We have heard that Mr. Harris
Intends to send you off as far as
The great world's show at Paris.

Of the youth beware of these,
For some of them might rudely squeeze
And bite your cheek, then songs or glees
We could not sing, oh! queen of cheese.

We'rt thou suspended from balloon,
You'd cast a shade even at noon,
Folks would think it was the moon
About to fall and crush them soon.

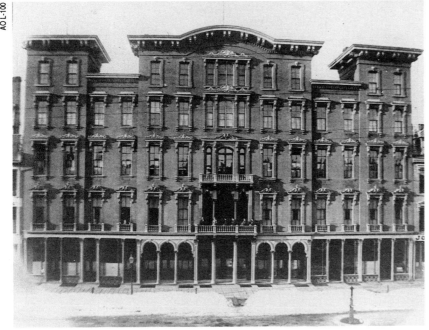

Wesleyan Ladies' College, Hamilton, c. 1870. Despite its name the college was nonsectarian, and attracted students from the United States as well as all parts of Canada. The building itself was a former hotel, the Anglo-American with 150 rooms. For many years a genteel education was overseen by the principal, the celebrated educationist Mary Electa Adams. The site, in Gore Park, is today occupied by yet another hotel, the Connaught.

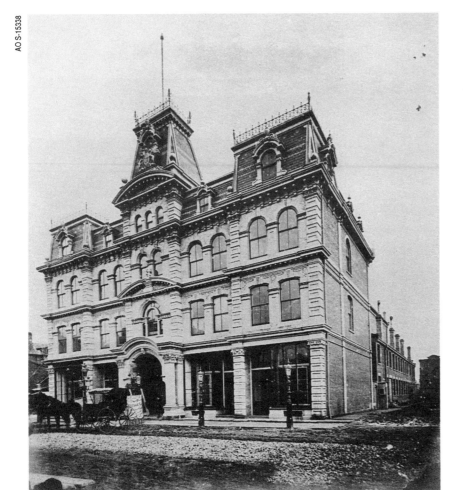

The Grand Opera House, Toronto (c. 1875), stood on the south side of Adelaide Street between Bay and Yonge. It was put up in 1874 by a joint-stock company, and managed by Mrs. Morrison, an accomplished actress. Finance was not her forte, however, and in 1876 the theatre was sold at auction. Three years later, on 29 November 1879, it burned to the ground, but was re-built in the remarkable time of fifty-one days. A contemporary account described it in 1882:

> *As a building the Grand Opera House ranks with some of the best in Toronto. It is of four stories, situated on the south side of Adelaide Street near Yonge Street. It is a handsome rendering of florid Parisian renaissance, the ground floor of which is rented for stores and a beautiful saloon, kept by D. Small. The apartments not connected with the theatre are utilized as offices. The interior of the theatre is large and so arranged as to prevent unhealthy crowding. There are ample means of exit.*

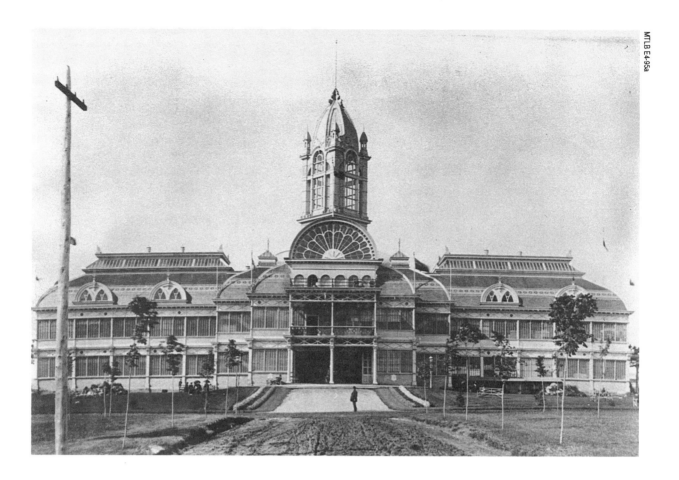

Above: *Toronto's Second Crystal Palace (c. 1884) was actually a reconstruction of the first. The old structure of 1858 was disassembled in 1879 and carted to Exhibition Park, where a ground floor and an ungainly cupola plus other "busy" features were added. The total effect was the destruction of a strong, simple design and its replacement by a clumsy monstrosity.*

Right: *Short, stocky Edward (Ned) Hanlan became a professional oarsman in 1876 after a celebrated career (throughout Ontario) as an amateur. That same year he became Canadian champion: two years later in 1878, American champion, and then, in 1880, at a meet held on the Thames in London, champion of the world. Hanlan retained the title for four years before losing it to William Beach, an Australian. He did not win the world title again, but continued to race, to the delight of Ontarians and Canadians, for many years. Altogether he won 150 professional races, and his efforts greatly popularized the sport in Ontario.*

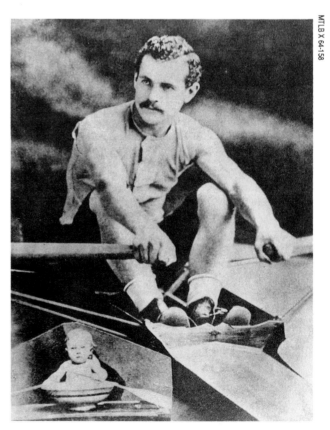

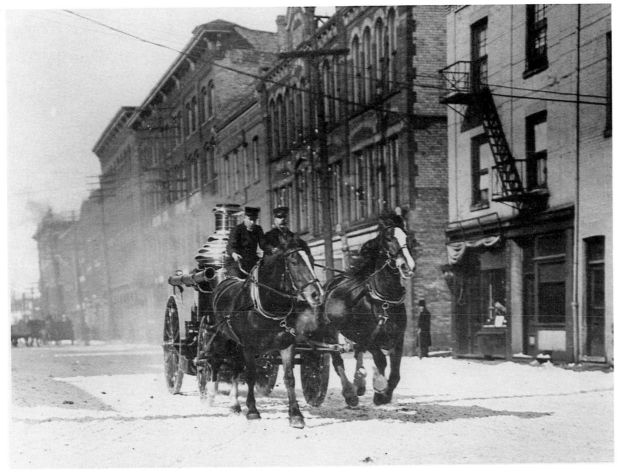

Fire engine in full flight, London, c. 1890.

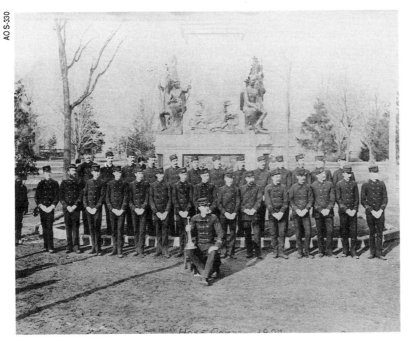

Volunteers were the backbone of fire-fighting in the nineteenth century, and in most communities it was thought both an honour and a symbol of civic pride to serve. The Brant Hose Company, twenty-nine strong, posed in front of the recently completed Joseph Brant Memorial, on Good Friday, 1887.

Fires were the great fear of nineteenth-century town dwellers. Toronto's core was devastated twice – once in 1849 ($500,000 in damages) and then again more seriously in 1904 ($10 million). The list of other towns hit is almost endless: Petrolia in 1867, Ottawa in 1900, and in the new northern towns (built usually entirely of wood and in a ramshackle fashion), hardly a season went by without a conflagration. Bucket brigades soon gave way to more sophisticated (and costly) equipment, much of which had to be imported. Needless to say Ontario's insurance business was brisk.

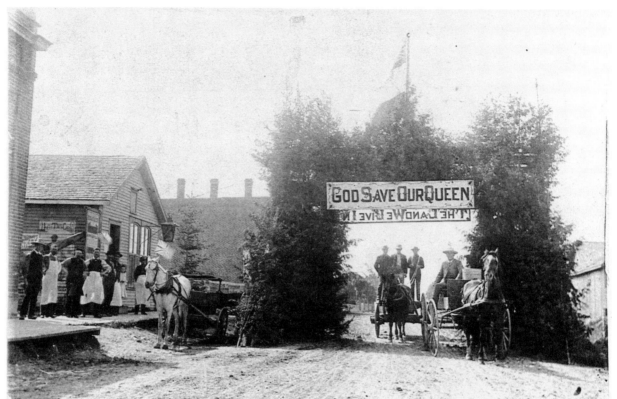

Port Perry, on Lake Scugog, 1889.

The decorated archway and flags declared solidarity with the Empire, but an advertisement on the walls of the restaurant to the left announced a performance of *Uncle Tom's Cabin*. American travelling theatrical troupes were a feature of Ontarian social life. *Uncle Tom's Cabin* always turned out the populace; it continued to do so in Canada long after its popularity had waned in the United States.

Sir John A. Macdonald was the commonest target for J.W. Bengough's cartoons in his satirical weekly *Grip*. But Oliver Mowat's Ontario was fair game too. Bengough had once worked for George Brown's *Globe* and was well aware of the inner workings of the Liberal party; he took great pains to expose both them and the general puffery of politics of the day. Bengough was no casual observer of the scene; he was a trenchant and witty editorialist, and his biting humour has not been lost with the passage of time. The cartoons reprinted here include his original explanatory comments. Oliver Mowat is shown, by turn, as a wielder of great patronage and influence, a friend to Roman Catholic votes, and the stern defender of provincial rights against Dominion encroachments.

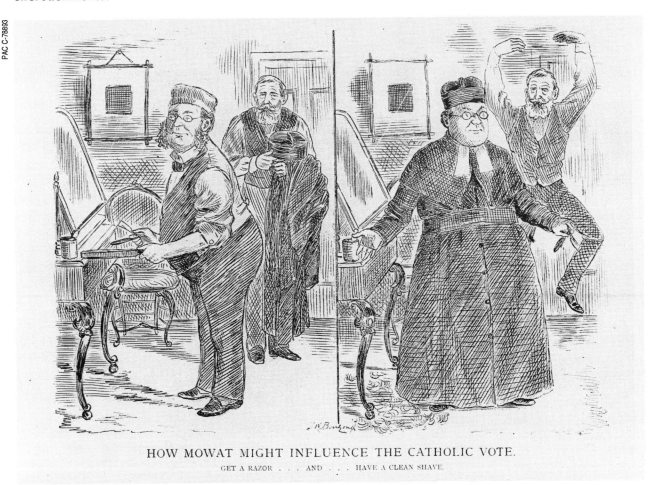

HOW MOWAT MIGHT INFLUENCE THE CATHOLIC VOTE.

GET A RAZOR . . . AND . . . HAVE A CLEAN SHAVE.

How Mowat Might Influence the Catholic Vote. *The Catholic voters of Ontario were believed to be amenable in the exercise of their franchise to the wishes of Archbishop Lynch, the provincial prelate, and it was an open secret that Mr. Mowat and the archbishop were upon terms of warm friendship. The joke of the cartoon is based upon the facial resemblance which, by a queer coincidence, exists between the two prominent dignitaries.* Grip, *14 October 1882.*

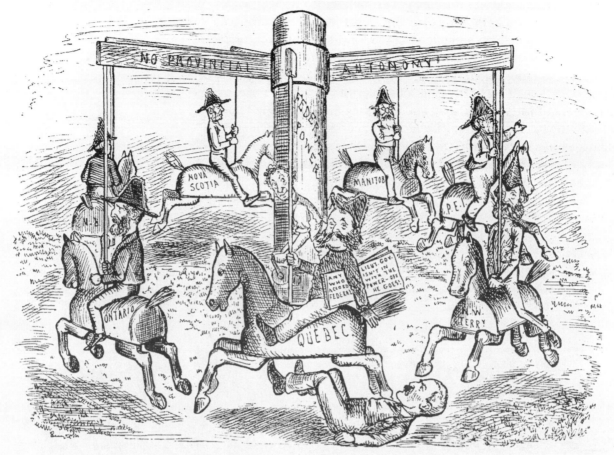

THE NEW IDEA OF CONFEDERATION.

Above: New Idea of Confederation. *The doctrine acted upon by the Government in the dismissal of Lt.-Governor Letellier was that provincial officers of that class are representatives not of the Crown, as had hitherto been supposed, but of the Federal authorities. This theory, which at once degrades them into mere automata, met with earnest opposition outside of Government circles, and it may be doubted if it was put forth seriously by its authors.* Grip, *2 August 1879.*

Right: Mrs. Ontario in Danger. *The* Mail *(at this time edited by Mr. Martin J. Griffin) was endeavoring to distract public attention in Ontario from the manifest design of the Dominion Government to overturn the Mowat Government,* Grip, *21 October 1882.*

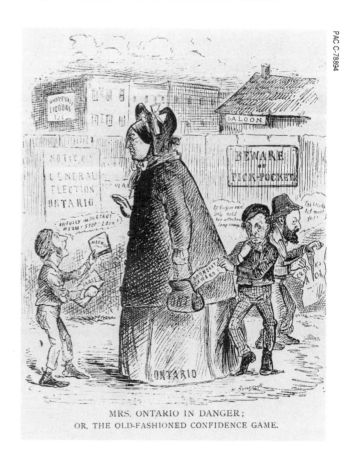

MRS. ONTARIO IN DANGER;
OR, THE OLD-FASHIONED CONFIDENCE GAME.

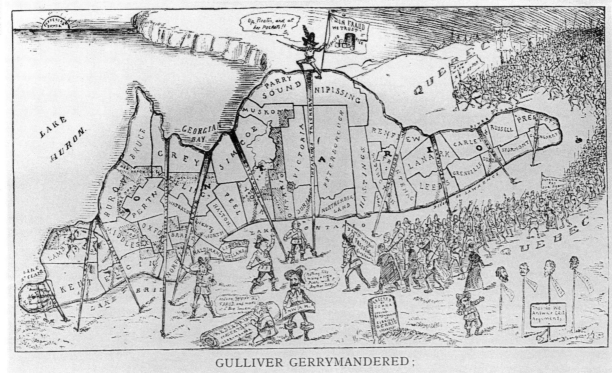

GULLIVER GERRYMANDERED;
OR, ONTARIO IN THE POWER OF MITEY SMALL STATESMEN.

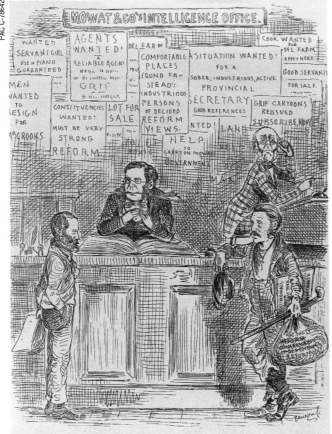

THE POLITICAL INTELLIGENCE OFFICE; OR, SITUATIONS WANTED.

Above: Gulliver Gerrymandered. *Under the pretence of "equalizing the population," the Government introduced a bill for a redistribution of seats throughout the Dominion. In Ontario the changes made were almost invariably in the interest of the Conservative party, and the measure has ever since been known as the "Gerrymander Bill."* Grip, *6 May 1882.*

Left: The Political Intelligence Office. *Hon. Adam Crooks, Minister of Education in the Mowat Cabinet, having been defeated in East Toronto, remained for some months without a seat in the House. Hon. William Macdougall, who had been politically "everything by turns and nothing long," and who had failed to get a lieutenant-governorship in Manitoba, or a seat in East York, was at this time showing a disposition to throw in his lot with the Reform Party, but met with small encouragement.* Grip, *30 January 1875.*

The Interpretation. *Certain public utterances of Archbishop Lynch had given rise to the belief that a claim was about to be put forward on behalf of the Roman Catholic Church for Separate Schools of a higher grade to supplement the Common Schools already granted. The "Adam" of the cartoon is Hon. Adam Crooks, Q.C., then Minister of Education for Ontario.* Grip, 4 November 1882.

The New Cromwell. *The long-continued Boundary "Dispute" was peremptorily ended by the Ontario Government taking possession of the awarded territory and appointing special constables, etc., to protect the settlers in the enjoyment of their rights.* Grip, 21 July 1883.

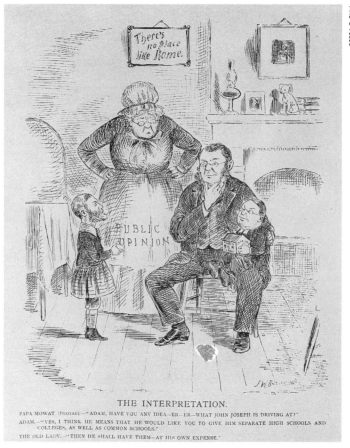

THE INTERPRETATION.

PAPA MOWAT (Puzzled).—"ADAM, HAVE YOU ANY IDEA—ER—ER—WHAT JOHN JOSEPH IS DRIVING AT?"
ADAM.—"YES, I THINK HE MEANS THAT HE WOULD LIKE YOU TO GIVE HIM SEPARATE HIGH SCHOOLS AND COLLEGES, AS WELL AS COMMON SCHOOLS."
THE OLD LADY.—"THEN HE SHALL HAVE THEM—AT HIS OWN EXPENSE."

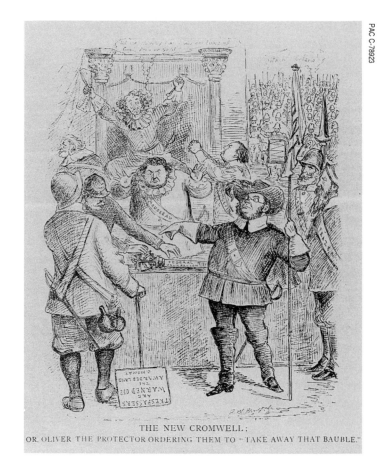

THE NEW CROMWELL;
OR, OLIVER THE PROTECTOR ORDERING THEM TO "TAKE AWAY THAT BAUBLE."

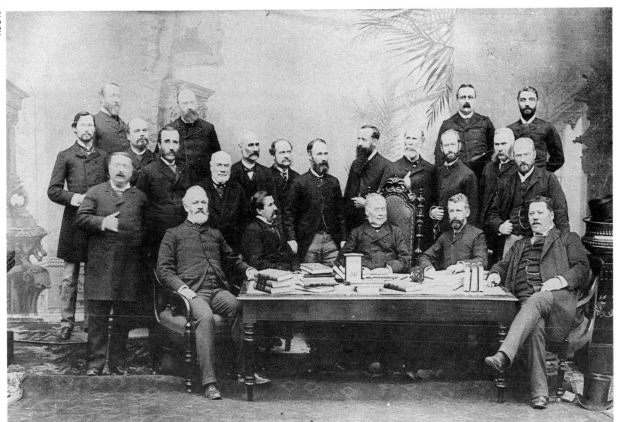

Québec Interprovincial Confer-ence, 26 October 1887.

In 1887, twenty years after confederation, an interprovincial Confer-ence was held at Québec "for the purpose of considering questions which have arisen or may arise as to the autonomy of the provinces, their financial arrangements, and other matters of provincial interest." Macdonald's federal government declined to send a representative, the federal Liberals kept their hands off as well, and the governments of Prince Edward Island and British Columbia also demurred. So the original provinces that comprised Canada, Ontario, Québec, Nova Scotia, and New Brunswick, plus Manitoba, came together for eight days at Québec under the chairmanship of Oliver Mowat. Ontario's interest was natural enough, and a logical extension of Mowat's suc-cessful provincial rights campaign. It seems certain that Ontario under Mowat viewed the Canadian confederation as a compact among the provinces, and one whose nature could be changed only by their will-ingness to act in harmony; in other words the restrictions of the fed-eral government might be sidestepped if the provinces acted in uni-son, or perhaps appealed directly to the Imperial mother for changes.

Although no distinct action came from the conference, it did re-veal the dissatisfaction felt with the federal bargain not just by Ontario but by the other provinces as well. Some of the resolutions passed sound familiar today: provincial selection of senators, clearer defini-tions of the legal machinery for sorting out provincial and federal ju-risdiction, and a simpler formula for fixing and restructuring provin-cial subsidies. Mowat had a keen interest in constitutional matters, and he also wanted to make sure Ontario would retain her favourable position if there were to be changes in the financial structure. As it turned out, the federal Liberals never picked up on the Québec resolutions and they were never debated in Ottawa.

For much of the time that Mowat's Liberals reigned supreme in Toronto, the Conservatives, under Sir John A. Macdonald, ran the Dominion government. The federal Liberals lacked decisive leadership, and they appeared unable to devise an acceptable, popular platform. Macdonald swung to victory in 1878 under the banner of his National Policy, a three-pronged interlocking combination of a protective tariff, a transcontinental railroad, and massive immigration to people the west and provide a home market. The Liberal counterproposal called for "Unrestricted Reciprocity" with the United States, an idea which was too frequently extended to include "commercial union," that is the removal of customs duties between the two countries. Canadian manufacturers and industrialists railed against the Liberal policy and warned that political absorption would follow any economic association.

Ontario's federal voters were by no means fickle, but they did change their support occasionally after Confederation. Macdonald, with some cautious chicanery, had done well enough in 1867. But the Pacific Scandal had turned voters against him in the early 1870s. Fortunately for him, however, the Liberal ascendancy corresponded with a global depression, and in the election of 1878, Macdonald promised a new economic deal. Protectionism was the tune of his election trumpet, and Macdonald eagerly took to the stump in Ontario. He sensed the urgency of taking the province: "If we fail in Ontario," he said, "I, for one, shall give up the fight in despair." Despair, however, was not the order of the day. The Liberals lost forty seats in Ontario alone, and the Conservatives marched to Ottawa with a clear majority of seventy-eight. The National Policy was the prime issue again in 1882, but provincial concerns swept into the federal arena as well. Macdonald, the Liberals argued, was simply the unwitting servant of Québec, or as one ditty put it:

> The tricky Tory Bleus
> Who Sir John as catspaw use
> Cannot rule the roost in Old Ontario

But they did, and would again, for Sir John A., parading himself as "the old Chieftain," easily vanquished Edward Blake's best efforts, notwithstanding Oliver Mowat's aid. Ontarians exhibited early on an ability to vote one way federally and another provincially. The twain met infrequently. In the 1880s the National Policy, or so people thought, showed positive results; Blake's long-winded criticisms were merely hot air.

The corpse of the Métis leader Louis Riel, hanged in Regina in 1885 after his abortive rebellion (in what was then called the Northwest Territories), also showed how federal matters could intrude into provincial concerns, and vice versa. Riel's death caused a spluttering outrage in Québec, but it was stoutly defended in Ontario, by both Grit and Tory alike, in a resurgence of the old anti-French, anti-Catholic feelings that had characterized the parties (especially the old Grits) of Canada West. Macdonald, in the federal election of 1886, took fifty-five of Ontario's ninety-two seats.

But in many ways it was the tumultuous federal election of 1891 that was most typical of Ontario's federal voting pattern. That election was the last for Sir John, and he faced a new opponent. Static Edward Blake had stepped down, and had been replaced by ecstatic, dynamic Wilfrid Laurier. Most were certain he would sweep Québec, and maybe Ontario as well.

Laurier, who had won many points for advancing provincial rights in the federal parliament, came out solidly for Unrestricted Reciprocity with the United States. Macdonald, in fear, pulled out all the stops, wrapped himself in a Union Jack, and went shopping for votes in Loyal Ontario. But he had to be careful, as the party he represented was now made up of a volatile mass. Riel and the reaction to Riel had eroded the old tolerant Ontario conservatism that had reached out to Québec's bleus. Ex-Tory D'Alton McCarthy's new Equal Rights Association in fact did not want equality but the supremacy of all things English (and Protestant), and Orange. British, Protestant Ontario nearly moved under his sway. Ontario farmers weighed loyalty carefully against the undoubted advantages of reciprocity with America. In the event it was a near thing but Macdonald took Ontario forty-eight seats to forty-four. It couldn't have been done without him, however, and, as the federal Conservatives were soon to discover to their regret, it wouldn't.

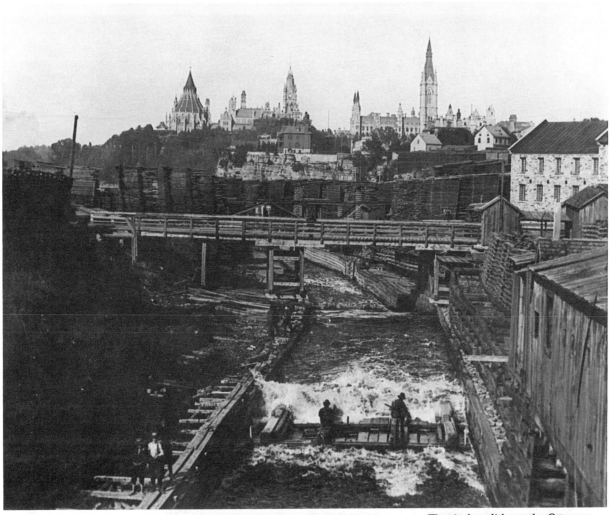

The timber slide on the Ottawa below parliament, c. 1880s.

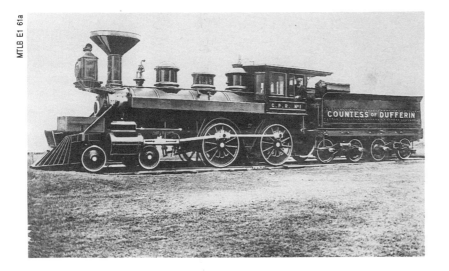

Left: *"Countess of Dufferin," the "first lady of the CPR." Engine No. 1 was a symbol of Ontario's role in the National Policy (even though the locomotive was actually built in Philadelphia, and had served American lines for five years in the 1870s). From an early period critics argued that the Canadian Pacific Railway and the National Policy were actually a form of Ontario imperialism, and that the chief beneficiaries of the legislation were the influential industrialists of the central province.*

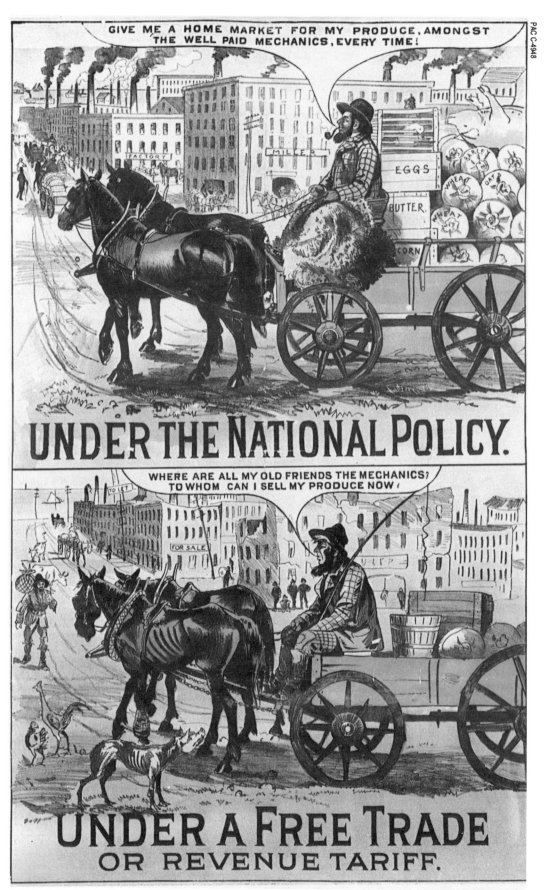

The dangers of free trade, as they were felt by proponents of the National Policy, were clearly shown in this poster published by the Industrial League.

Ontario in the 1890s

Queen's Park is the popular name for the Ontario legislature, but, of course, the term actually refers to the adjoining park to the rear of the present buildings. Not surprisingly the park itself is named after Queen Victoria, and was opened by her son, Edward, Prince of Wales, in 1860. It is surprising, however, that the ungainly, squat legislative building, erected 1886-92 (on the site of the first University of Toronto building), was the result of an international competition held in 1880. R.A. White, an English architect living in Buffalo, was one of the judges, and eventually, after a lapse of many years and much manoeuvring, succeeded in nominating himself as "the only architect" for the job. Under his direction the building was completed at almost twice the projected costs – $1.2 millions in all. (The twin turrets whose bases are completed in this picture were eliminated for this reason; hence the rather squat appearance of the finished building.) The land, incidentally, still belongs to the university, and an annual rent is charged – a peppercorn, or its cash equivalent.

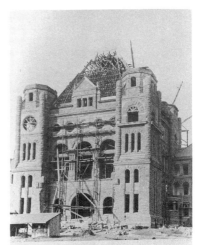

Queen's Park, Toronto.

The British North America Act assigned responsibility for education to the provinces, and for Ontario that meant not only primary and secondary education but also control of the provincial university, the University of Toronto. For many years the fortunes of the place rocked with the sway of provincial politics. But the institution made many advances in the decades following Confederation, notably with the admission of women students and the adoption of a distinguished honours curriculum. Money, however, was a constant source of difficulty, and not just for the "U of T," but also other colleges such as Queen's and Victoria.

A partial solution to increasing expenditures came with the federation movement of the 1880s which largely established the college system in the university and saw the move of Victoria College from Cobourg, and later Trinity from Queen Street to the central St. George campus. But the university still had to rely on its own financial resources; new buildings and new professorships had to be funded out of the dwindling university endowment, from fees, or from private benefactors.

Disaster of a different nature struck on the evening of St. Valentine's Day, 1890, when most of University College was burned out. Two college servants had been carrying a tray of lighted kerosene lamps. When one man slipped, the tray fell and fire tore through the dry, wooden interior of the building. The greatest loss was its library – thirty-three thousand valuable volumes, not covered by the meagre insurance policy.

Certain advantages came from the fire, however. The legislature granted $160,000 for rebuilding, and private citizens donated $60,000 specifically for the construction of a separate library building. A global appeal for books followed and met with a remarkable, willing response. Within three years fifty thousand volumes had been assembled, the nucleus of the library's present four million items. The fire also brought the university into the news, and official and unofficial notice was taken regarding both its finance and its direction.

University College, 15 February 1890.

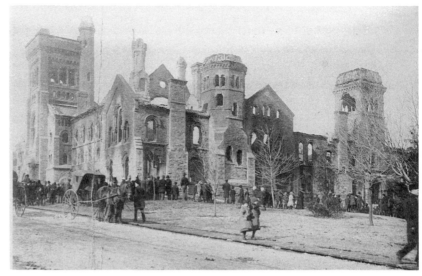

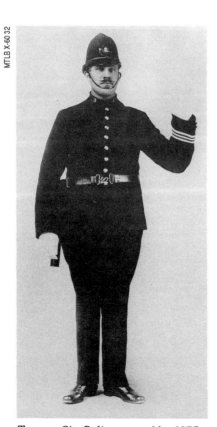

Toronto City Police constable, 1875.

Among the earliest and most basic laws of the province were those which charged districts and later counties with the "erection and maintenance of a gaol, a house of correction and house of industry." The gaols which were subsequently built (either connected to or close by the court houses of each county) became the dumping-ground for all victims of the law, child or adult, sane or insane, man and woman, poor and destitute. Some attempt was made from time to time to improve physical conditions but no real progress was made in treatment or classification until in 1859 the province established a Board of Inspectors of Prisons, Asylums and Public Charities. By Confederation, the board not only supervised the administration of provincial funds to houses of refuge, providence, and industry but also had overseen development of an asylum at Rockwood for the criminally insane, the expansion of the nearby provincial penitentiary at Kingston and the creation of thirteen new gaols.

A major recommendation of the inspectorate was the creation of an intermediate level of correction between the county gaol and the penitentiary. Chief Inspector John Woodburn Langmuir was a guiding force in this respect and when his urgings were heeded in 1874, with the building of the Central Prison in west-end Toronto, he sensibly entered into a contract with the neighbouring Canada Car Company works. This arrangement allowed prison labour to be used in the plant and was remarkably enlightened for the time. The scheme fell apart as the railroad boom climaxed and collapsed. Not all saw the Central Prison with such hope. Pelham Mulvany in his handbook to Toronto in 1884 echoed what must have been a typical view of the institution and indeed of the towering Don Jail on the other side of the city: he saw "a gloomy pile of grey stone, whose high-walled precincts and grated windows proclaim it to be one of those caravansaries of crime and misery which grow with the growth of our boasted civilization."

Also in West Toronto lay the great domed hospital known as "999 Queen Street," built by John Howard in 1846. Until the end of the century it was reputed to be the best-ventilated mental institution in North America and certainly its treatment of patients was a good deal more enlightened than the law's handling of criminals. The building was a noted and notorious landmark until demolished by the provincial government in 1976.

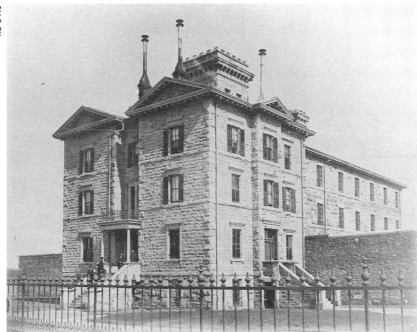

Wentworth County Court House and Jail, Hamilton.

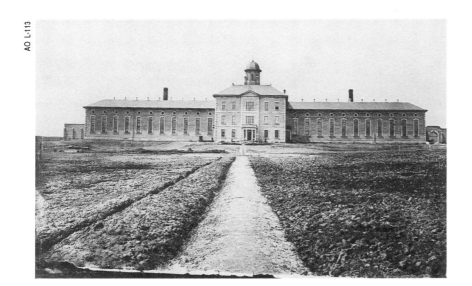

Central Prison, Toronto.

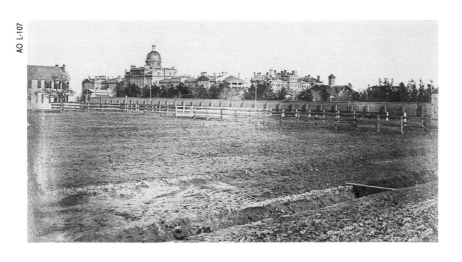

"999 Queen – The Lunatic Asylum," Toronto.

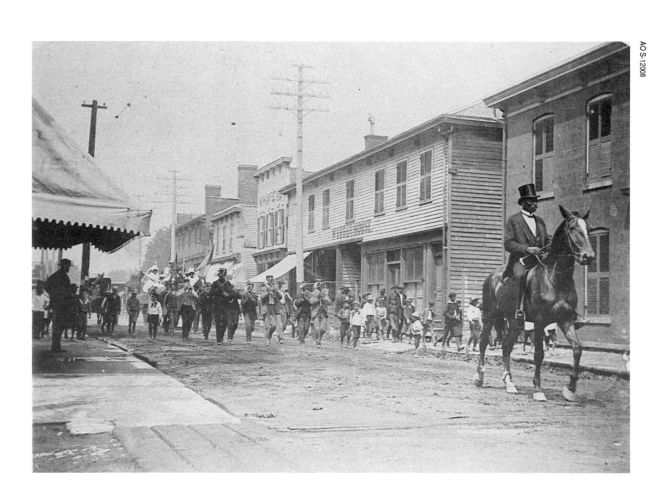

Amherstburg Parade, 1 August 1894. Emancipation Day is still celebrated annually to commemorate the day, 1 August 1833, when Britain and the Empire abolished slavery.

Fugitive blacks who made their way to Canada generally did not venture far into the country but stopped near the border. The first substantial settlement was at Amherstburg, near Fort Malden, which as early as the 1820s, was the centre of a substantial tobacco trade controlled by black farmers. Amherstburg later was an important terminus of the "Underground Railway," and continued to be a significant black centre in the province. Dissenting schools operated here until 1917.

N. Clarke Wallace of Woodbridge, in 1891 president of the Orangemen of the World, was the epitome of the enormously powerful Loyal Orange Association of British America. By 1878, the association had at least two hundred thousand members, most of whom were in Ontario where Orangeist dogma was at its strongest. The order's grasp on Protestantism made it a powerful force and it contributed substantially to the bitterness of Ontario's attitudes towards both Catholics and French Canadians. Celebration of William III's victory at the Battle of the Boyne in 1690 was a major annual event in Toronto and for many a small country town in Central Ontario the "King Billy" parade on 12 July was the event of the year when all that was British and Protestant could be reaffirmed.

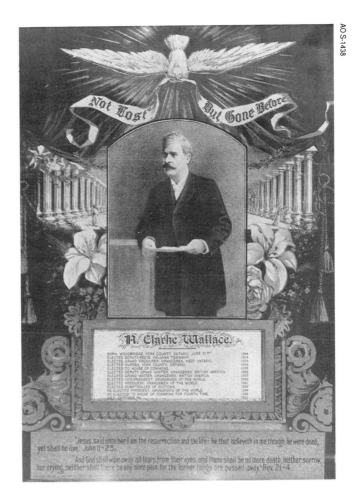

Right: *"Not Lost, But Gone Before," N. Clarke Wallace, Orangeman, Woodbridge, 1901.*

Below: *Orange Parade, Almonte, Lanark County.*

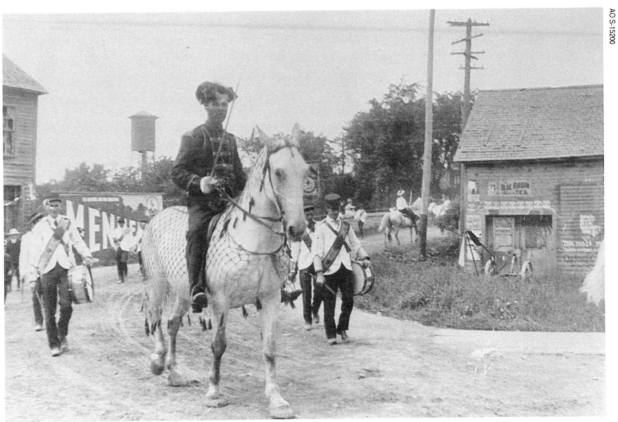

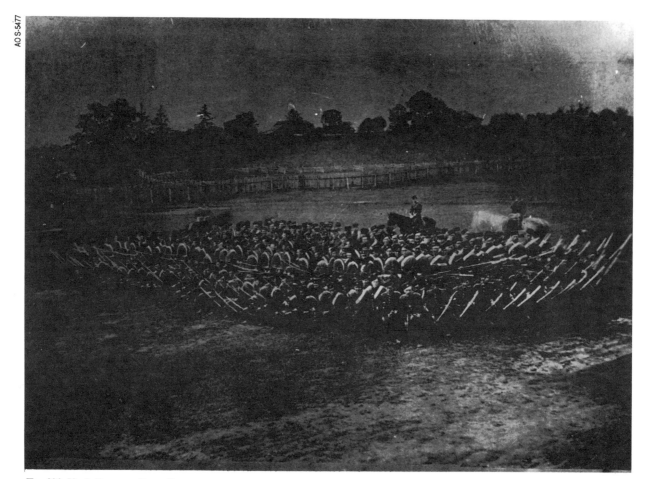

Twelfth York Rangers Battalion, 1890s.

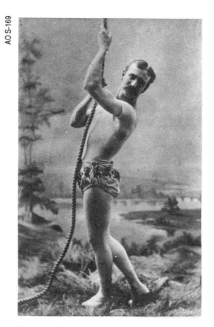

Farini of Niagara.

The Wellington or British Square was used effectively against French cavalry in the Napoleonic Wars, and Zulu warriors in Africa. Modern industrial warfare and precision artillery, first experienced by Canadians in the Boer War, proved inappropriate to the picturesque postures of the Canadian militia.

Ontario's reigning pangymnastikonaerostationist, Bill Hunt of Port Hope (born 1838 in Lockport, New York), was better known as Guillermo Antonio Farini, the dashing aerialist (funambulist, if you prefer). He thrilled audiences in circuses and over gorges like Niagara with stunts of great drama. As early as 1860 he repeated many of the great Blondin's feats on a slack rope stretched across the Niagara River (he cycled across, hauled his manager on his back, washed clothes, ate meals, etc.) and made famous descents by rope onto the deck of the *Maid of the Mist* as it churned into the boiling waters below the Falls. Less recognized have been Hunt's inventions, especially of the theatrical circus cannon, his paintings (exhibited with C.W. Jeffreys's work in 1908), his manuscript history of the First World War, and other works such as *Ladies' Hats* and *How to Make Yogurt*, a sequel to his successful *How to Grow Begonias*. He married Anna Muller, pupil of Franz Liszt and niece of Richard Wagner, in 1886.

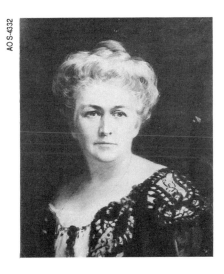

AO S-4432

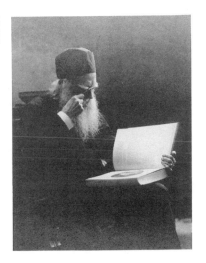

AO S-677

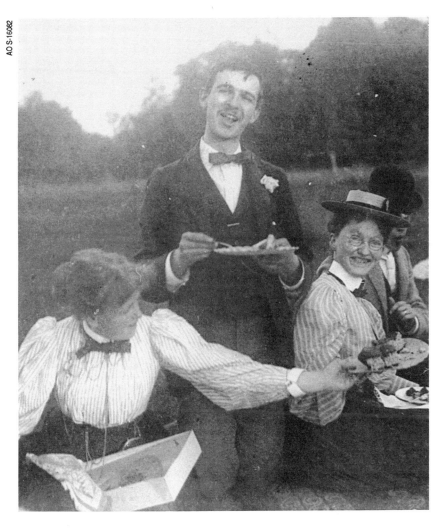

AO S-16082

Above left: *Adelaide Hoodless, 1857–1910, was the founder of the Federated Women's Institutes of Canada. The movement started in 1897 when Mrs. Hoodless, speaking to a meeting of the Farmers' Institute at Stoney Creek, suggested that farm women should have organizations of their own – to study homemaking. The movement caught on and Mrs. Hoodless widened her struggle to advocate the teaching of domestic science in schools. To this end she founded the Ontario Normal School of Domestic Science and Arts in Hamilton. She was also one of the prime movers of the National Council of Women and served as first treasurer, from 1893 to 1901.*

Above right: *The Reverend Doctor Henry Scadding was the son of one of York's first pioneers, John Scadding, former manager of Lieutenant-Governor John Graves Simcoe's estate in Devonshire, England. Rector of the Church of the Holy Trinity in Toronto (now surrounded by the Eaton Centre), Scadding is remembered as Toronto's most tireless early historian. Toronto of Old, his major work, was published in 1873. Scadding was also a president of the Canadian Institute, a founder of the York Pioneers, and first president of the Pioneer and Historical Association of Ontario.*

Below: *Picnic, Choates Wood, Northumberland County, 1897.*

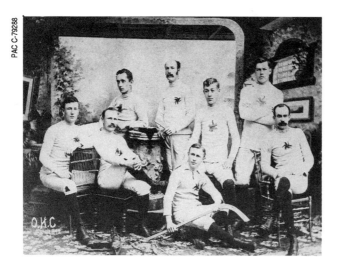

Ottawa Field Hockey Club, 1892.

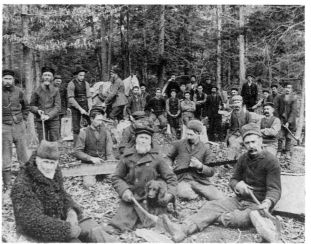

Wood bee at Salem, Cramahe Township, Northumberland County, 25 January 1899.

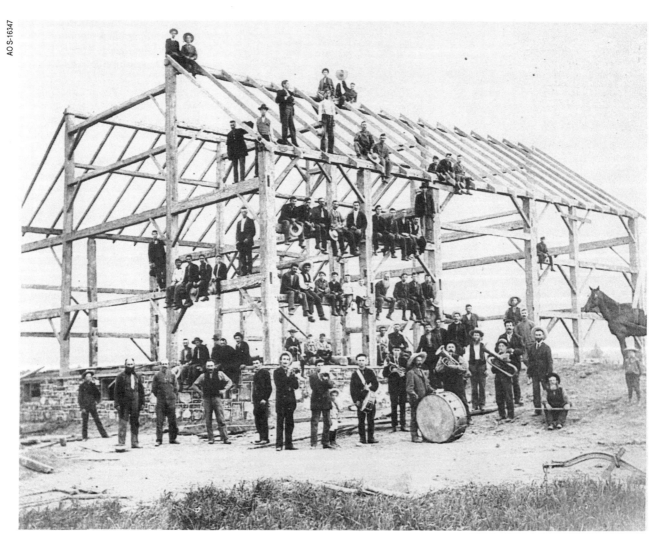

Barn raising, King Township, York County, 1901.

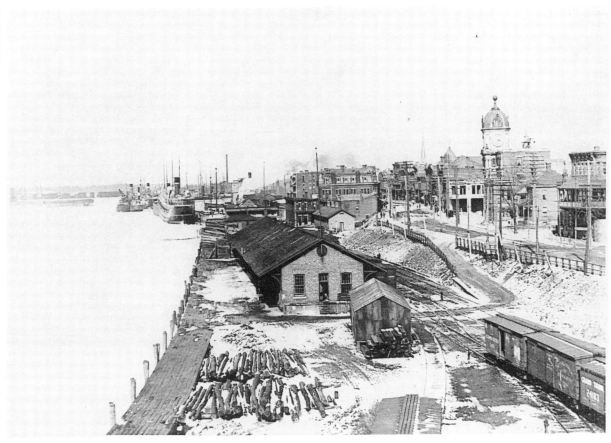

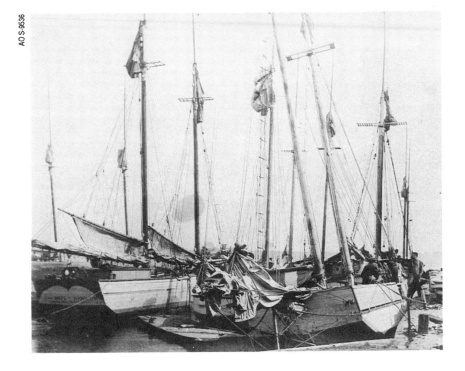

Above: *Sarnia waterfront,
c. 1905.*

Left: *Stonehookers, Toronto,
c. 1910. Flat-bottomed and
functional, these sailing barges
transported locally quarried
granite, lime, and sandstone to
urban construction sites.*

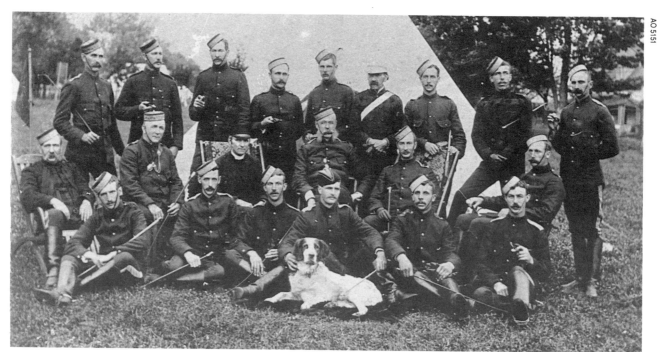

Officers of the Third Dragoons militia regiment, Belleville, Ontario, 1898.

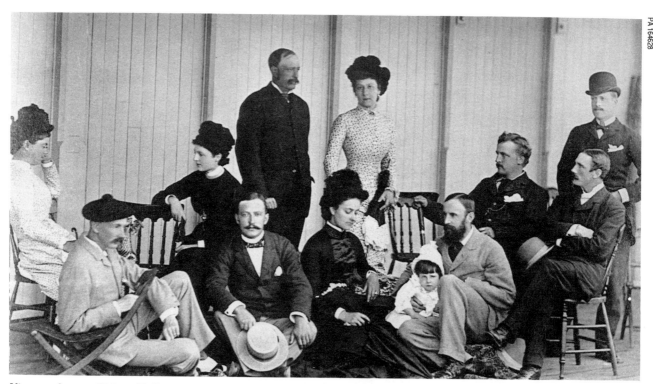

Vice-royal party, Rideau Hall, c. 1880. Princess Louise (standing at centre); her husband, the governor general, the Marquis of Lorne, seated at her left.

Robert McLaughlin was born in 1836 in the village of Tyrone in Durham County. With no technical training, in 1867, he went into the carriage business and built two cutters. Two years later, he established the McLaughlin Carriage Works at Enniskillen. The firm moved to Oshawa in 1877 where it became the largest carriage works in the British Empire. In 1899 a fire swept the Oshawa works and the firm took temporary refuge in makeshift quarters at Gananoque. A motor-car factory was founded in 1907 which merged with others in 1918 to form General Motors of Canada. Robert McLaughlin died in 1921 but his son, Colonel R.S. "Sam" McLaughlin, carried on the business.

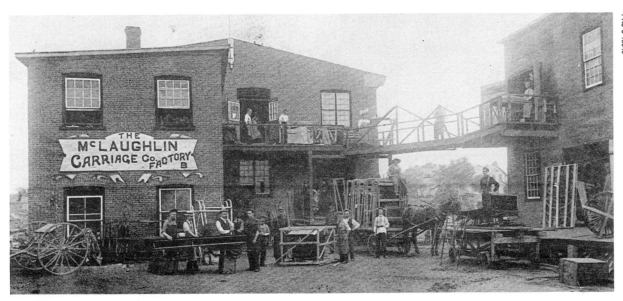

PAC C-19549

McLaughlin Factory, Gananoque, 1899.

The Ontario government made every effort to secure immigration. The late nineteenth century saw a great tide of boosting literature from Ontario flood the United Kingdom. Typical was *The British Farmer's and Farm Labourer's Guide to Ontario* as issued "By authority of the Government of Ontario." Ontario's vast agricultural opportunities were paraded on every page of the text and heralded by an introduction and "Summary of Advantages":

Up to this point, then, the British farmer will have lost nothing by the change from the British Isles to Ontario, while in some respects he will be an obvious gainer. He will secure:
(1) Free land, cheap land, and plenty of it, purchasable and transferable without trouble or any serious cost.
(2) Free schools, as good as any in the world, which his children may attend without any loss of caste or social position and leading up to the highest educational honours.
(3) Free churches – and no tithes or charges for any but his own – voluntarily supported.
(4) Not Quarter Sessions or County Boards rule, but the management of his own local affairs to the expenditure of the last sixpence.
(5) A free vote.
(6) All the protection and safety that British law itself can ensure.

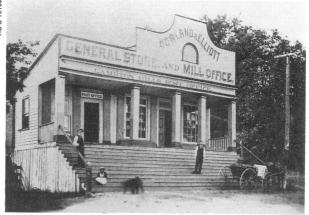

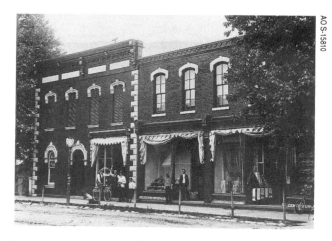

Howland & Elliott General Store and Mill Office, Lambton Mills, York County, c. 1890.

Norwich street frontage, Norwich, c. 1890s.

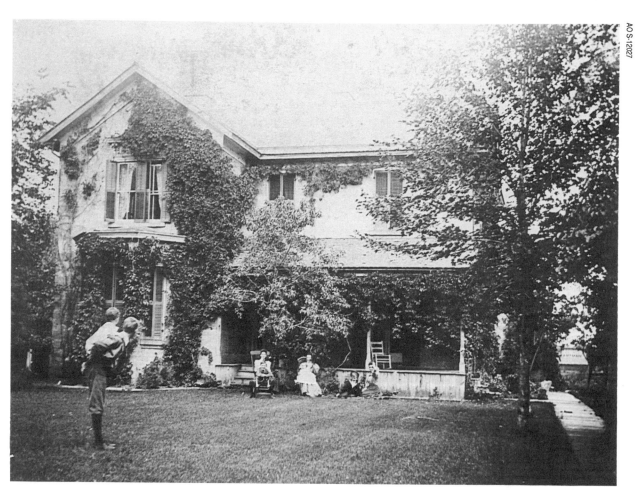

Anglican rectory, Amherstburg, 1896.

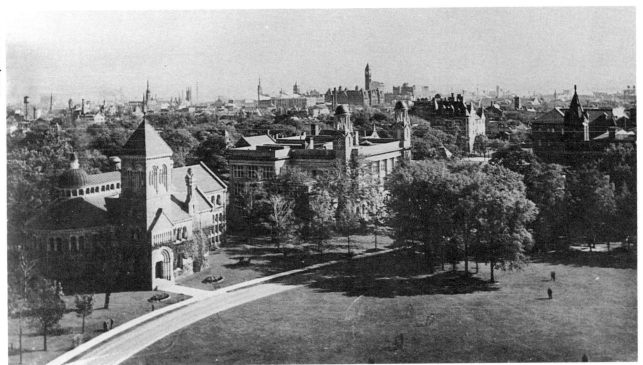

Toronto, from University College's tower, c. 1890s.

Turn-of-the-Century Toronto

Turn-of-the-century Toronto was proud of itself. A visitor reading the newspapers would think himself at the centre of the universe, privileged to be in a city of charm and culture, of man-made and natural beauties, pious, political, prosperous, wise, and witty. Rupert Brooke, the English poet, visited the place a dozen years later and saw it a trifle differently:

> But Toronto – Toronto is the subject. One must say something — *what* must one say about Toronto? What can one? What has anybody ever said? It is impossible to give it anything but commendation. It is not squalid like Birmingham, or cramped like Canton, or scattered like Edmonton, or sham like Berlin, or hellish like New York, or tiresome like Nice. It is all right. The only depressing thing is that it will always be what it is, only larger, and that no Canadian city can ever be anything better or different.

> If they are good they may become Toronto.

Toronto in fact was a typical North American city. It bustled, but so did Cleveland, Buffalo, and Cincinnati. And it was like those Yankee mid-western cities in most other ways as well. What made Toronto a little different was a vaguely British air.

And, of course, the continuing fact that it was a WASP fortress. About two-thirds of the two hundred thousand or so residents were native-born Canadians, and most of those were born in Ontario. Of the others, English or Welsh immigrants comprised sixteen per cent, Irish nine per cent, and Scots four per cent. Almost everyone else had come from the United States. These figures would change, but not dramatically. In the decade before the First World War, besides being white, and Anglo-Saxon, Toronto was undeniably Protestant. The Canadian census of 1891 showed over eighty per cent of the population was Protestant, with fully a third adhering to Anglicanism. Religious fervour filled the city, at least on Sundays, at any rate, because it was the only show in town.

Toronto had been a commercial centre for a century, but now it could, thanks mainly to Macdonald's National Policy, make a claim to being an industrial city as well. Both commerce, from Toronto's traditional hinterland up Yonge Street and from Ontario's ripening New North, and growing industry were changing the face of the city and making its waterfront and railway depots even uglier and more treacherous than they had been earlier in the century. If Toronto were ever to be con-

111

sidered picturesque, as the boosters continually boasted, the attraction was found in parks or the quiet, broad residential streets stocked with a fat, contented Victorian middle class.

In the 1880s these solid citizens had been roused to combat threats to civic virtue. Toronto had not been good – prostitution, gambling, and unlicensed drinking were identified as the chief offences, and W.H. Howland was elected mayor in 1886 to clear them out. He did so to the unrestrained applause of the city's church leaders. Toronto became Good and the reputation clung to the city like a clergyman's cloak. By 1900, to spend a week in Toronto on Sunday had become a standard Montréal joke.

"City of Churches" was one of the prouder boasts of Toronto's propagandists. John Ross Robertson's formidable catalogue of them in his celebrated *Landmarks of Toronto* numbered almost two hundred. "There is no city on the American continent of the size of Toronto," he declared, "that is to be compared with it in the number and magnificence of its churches. Their architectural beauty of construction, their elegance of furniture and decoration, and the convenience of all their appointments are justly not only matters of astonishment to the foreign visitor but matters of admiration and wonder." Not everyone agreed, and one observer, C.P. Mulvany, expressed his wonder in a different way:

> It has often formed a subject of reflection to philosophic observers that a vast amount of religious energy is wasted by the multifarious sub-divisions of the Protestant denominations in our city. Each sect must have its own minister, its own denominational college where that minister may be educated in all the narrowness of party lines. It is simply appalling to think of the money wasted in building so many church edifices, few of which can ever be said to be filled; in none of which do the poor of Toronto form an appreciable part of the congregation. Besides these evils, the working classes – the producers – who as a rule have small incomes, are burdened by the presence in their midst of a vast and constantly increased army of non-producers who live in rent-free palaces, and are totally free from taxation.

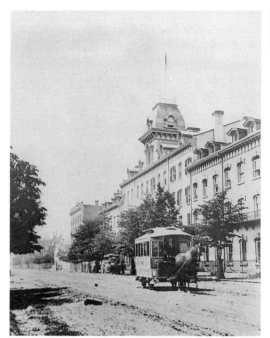

Queen's Hotel, Toronto, c. 1895.

The above building, or more properly buildings (since four attached townhouses made up the place), dated from 1838 and had been used first as private residences and then by Knox College until 1856 when they became Sword's Hotel. Re-christened Queen's in 1859, the building was a pleasant luxurious centre until 1927 when it was wrecked and the pompous Royal York put in its place. In 1891 G. Mercer Adam proclaimed its virtues:

> The Queen's Hotel has long held a leading place among the resorts of the travelling public in Toronto. The proprietors, Messrs. McGaw & Winnett, besides possessing great personal popularity, are experts in catering to the wants of their guests. Such distinguished visitors as the Grand Duke Alexis of Russia, Prince Leopold, Prince George, the Duke and Duchess of Connaught, the Marquis of Lansdowne, Lord and Lady Stanley, and Sir John Macdonald, have made the Queen's their home while in Toronto. The hotel, which for more than a generation has been identified with the growth and development of the city, commands a splendid view of Toronto Bay and Lake Ontario. It is elegantly furnished throughout, and is surrounded by beautiful grounds. It has an excellent cuisine and wine-cellar, and the ta-

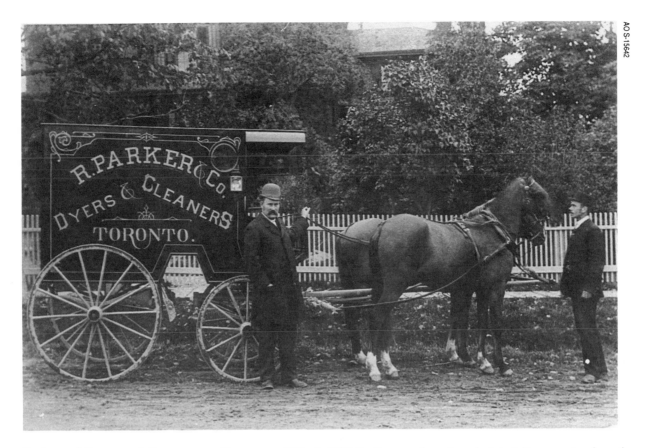

Parker and Company delivery wagon, Toronto, c. 1890s. In 1898 the firm purchased an electric delivery wagon from the Still Motor Company Limited – for a thousand dollars.

ble-attendance and general management are such as give unbounded satisfaction.

Streetcars were an explosive topic in Toronto in the 1890s. The question was the sanctity of Sunday, and whether the cars should be allowed to run on that holy day. The owners of the then-private street-railway system argued that the cars were useful, and would give a poor workingman a way to get to church, and then a breath of fresh air after. Any profits, of course, would be incidental. The protectors of Sunday's sanctity, dubbed "the Saints" by their detractors, opposed the cars vigorously and vehemently. The reputation of Toronto the Good was at stake. Eventually, a popular referendum gave the nod to Sunday cars, and Toronto survived.

The Board of Trade building, one of Toronto's first office buildings to be draped around a steel skeleton, eventually served as the headquarters of the city's public transportation service, the Toronto Transportation Commission.

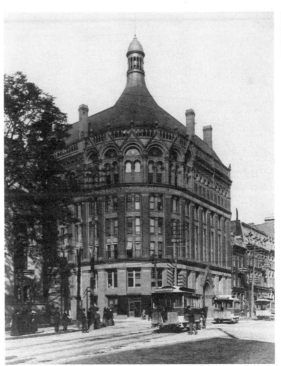

Streetcars at the Board of Trade building, Front and Yonge streets, Toronto, c. 1892.

Ceremonial Arch, Bay Street, south of the City Hall, Toronto, 1901. The arch was erected for the visit of the Duke of Cornwall and York (the future King George V), and is situated beside the headquarters building of the Independent Order of Foresters.

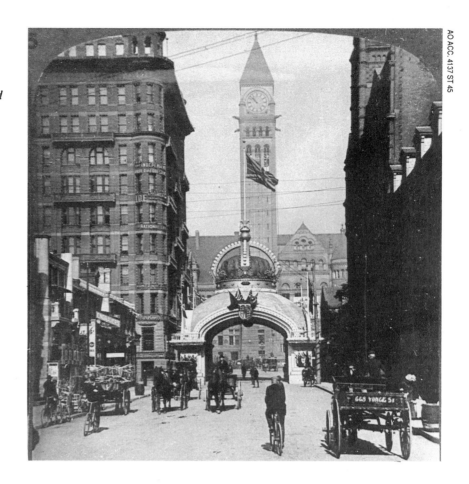

Toronto's Yonge Street wharf was the hub for commercial and pleasure traffic on Lake Ontario. Among the steamship companies represented was the Niagara River Line, which ran three ships, the *Chippewa*, the *Corona*, and the *Chicora*, between Toronto and Niagara. Six trips were made daily except Sunday; the duration of the journey was two hours and the price $1.55. The company literature was unyielding in its praise for Toronto, "the most progressive city of Canada," and urged Americans to lose no time in visiting their "cousins to the North." Links were also advertised for steam/rail traffic, and the company bragged of a connection via the New York Central Railroad's "Empire State Express" which would move a passenger from Manhattan to Toronto in twelve hours. A stopover on the Niagara River (with a cruise on one of the company's river boats, naturally) was also recommended to break the journey: "the exquisite moonlight effect on the water is beyond the descriptive power of the ordinary individual."

Another line operating from Toronto was the Richelieu and Ontario, the "R&O." The steamers *Kingston* and *Toronto* journeyed from Toronto to Kingston, through the Thousand Islands to Montréal and Québec, and then as far east as Murray Bay, Tadoussac, and the Saguenay River. The first leg of the journey, Toronto to Montréal, cost $10 and took 27 1/2 hours with stops.

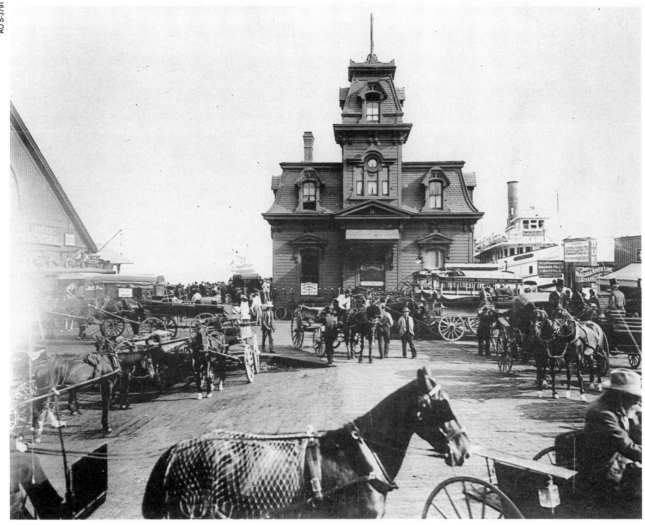

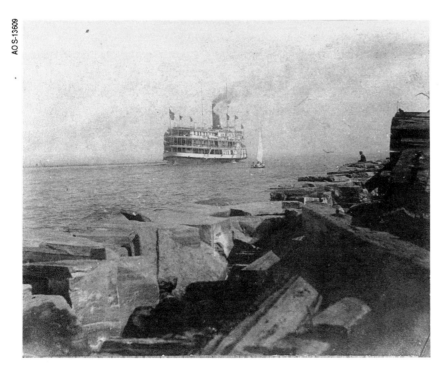

Above: *Yonge Street wharf, Toronto Harbour, c. 1902.*

Left: *S.S.* Toronto *leaving Toronto Harbour, c. 1900.*

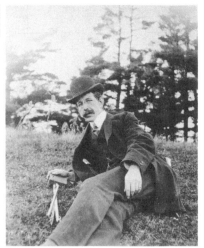

Although Victorian formality in dress had relaxed somewhat, the casual approach to clothing, even for leisure activities, was unacceptable to most Edwardians. A gentleman could expect to pay between ten and twelve dollars for a suit and as little as a dollar for his bowler hat.

The New Century

The complexion of Ontario had changed by the turn of the century. A fundamentally rural province was becoming predominantly urban. Some, but by no means all, of the province's politicians noticed it. Those who succeeded Sir Oliver Mowat in the Liberal saddle – first A.S. Hardy from 1866 to 1899, and then Sir George Ross (Mowat's former Minister of Education) from 1899 to 1905 – increasingly appeared out of touch with "modern" interests. The Liberal party still sang the temperance tunes of rural Ontario, and these were becoming increasingly discordant to town-dwellers. The Tory leader, James (later Sir James) Whitney, however, was as much a man for the times as Oliver Mowat had been: Whitney inherited a similar political savvy – a stubborn feel for what the voters wanted.

His party came to power in the election of 1905, and some part of his success can be explained by the prosperity of Canada at large. For Ontarians, Ontario was Canada and Canada was Ontario; the two easily became intermeshed. Whitney capitalized on this identification. Ontarians certainly approved of prosperity, and admitted that it coincided with the Liberals' being in office in Ottawa, but that didn't mean that most Ontarians liked Liberalism. "You cheer me," Sir Wilfrid Laurier, the prime minister, observed in 1904, "but you do not vote for me." Part of the reason was that the provincial Liberals were tired and worn out and, in the first years of the century, buffeted by much-publicized corruption. The most notorious event was the so-called "Gamey Affair." In 1903 the Conservative member for Manitoulin, Robert Gamey, rose in the house and flashily displayed three thousand dollars in banknotes. He went on to suggest that the Liberals had tried to buy his political support. Although a Commission of Inquiry dismissed the charge, enormous publicity resulted and the dark shadow of suspicion fell across the provincial Liberal party.

All this helped Whitney but cannot alone explain his success. Putting the "progressive" into conservatism was his major accomplishment, and he was aided in the task greatly by Sir William Meredith, the long-time Ontario Tory leader. Three achievements mark the Whitney years: public ownership of hydro transmission (later to be extended to ownership of the production itself); the creation of the modern University of Toronto; and the establishment, in 1914, of a Workmen's Compensation Act. Others could be mentioned as well, but all his innovative legislation served the growing urban population; the Liberal Opposition simply had no comeback. Even when Newton Wesley Rowell became Liberal leader in 1911 the party clung to the temperance issue. This was largely due to the influence of the Methodist church (Rowell's middle name was no accident), whose influence on leading Liberals was very much a mixed blessing. Methodists were becoming involved in urban reform, however, and viewed temperance as a critical issue as much in the cities as in the countryside.

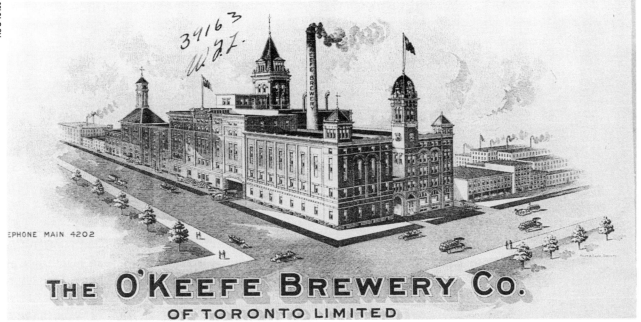

EPHONE MAIN 4202

THE O'KEEFE BREWERY CO.
OF TORONTO LIMITED

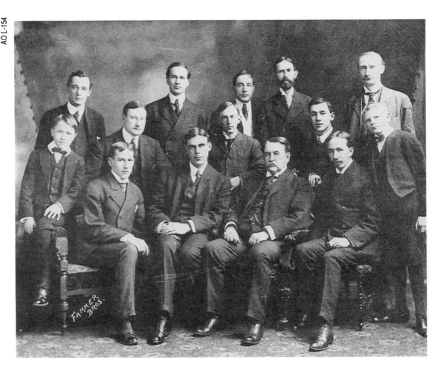

Above: *O'Keefe Brewery Company, Gould Street, Toronto. Letterhead, c. 1905. Eugene O'Keefe founded his Toronto brewery in 1862; it was the first in Canada to make lager as well as ale and porter.*

Sir James Pliny Whitney, premier of Ontario, 1905–14, seated among legislative pages and members of the press gallery, 1905.

Whitney was succeeded on his death in the autumn of 1914 by Sir William Hearst, who continued the broad trends of his policies through the war years. Those years, however, brought a new, or rather renewed, definition to the whole temperance issue.

117

Left: *Federal Post Office and Customs Building, Brantford, 1910.*

Right: *Union High and Public School, Port Perry, c. 1900.*

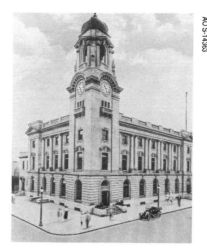

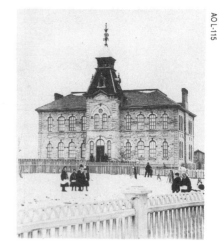

Toronto City Hall flashed with electrically generated light in October 1910, a victorious symbol that the battle over Niagara's waterpower had been won by the Whitney administration and its hero of the hour, Adam Beck. For more than five years Whitney and the Provincial Hydro Electric Commission (under the chairmanship of Beck) had attacked the great private power interests. "Cheap power" became Beck's watchword and that of the Municipal Power Union which clamoured for a publicly owned and operated provincial transmission

City Hall, Toronto, 1910.

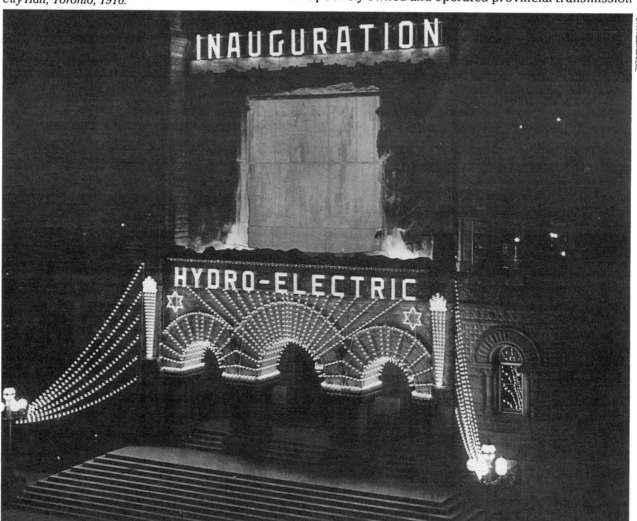

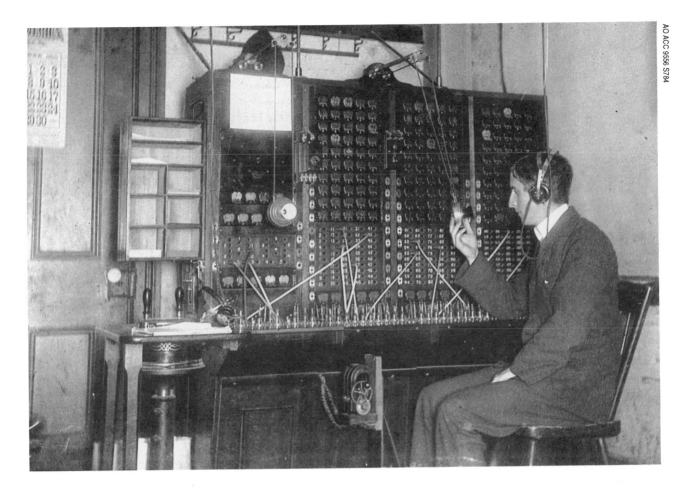

system. Toronto was a key target in Beck's program of government-owned power because the privately owned Toronto Electric Light Company had successfully resisted the City Council's attempts to take it over since 1895. The Toronto *World* in 1907 neatly encapsulated the spirit that characterized much of the contest:

> The greatest light that God gave to man is the pure white light generated by God's greatest masterpiece – Niagara Falls. Do not let the middlemen – the Gibsons, the Pellatts, the Jaffrays, the Nicholls – get between the people and this great blessing and make it dear and limit its use, so that they may be rich.

Alexander Graham Bell developed his idea of transmitting a human voice over an electrically charged wire in Brantford during the summer of 1874. Only four years later, Canada's first telephone exchange was operating in Hamilton with eight lines and forty subscribers. Under a Dominion government charter in 1880, the newly formed Bell Telephone Company (operated by the National Bell Telephone Company of Boston, a firm to whom Bell's father had sold his Canadian patent for $100,000) obtained exclusive rights to manufacture telephone equipment and sell telephone service in Canada – a virtual monopoly.

Bell Canada could barely cope with the enormous demand for service and was forced first by necessity, and in 1885 by statute, to reduce its monopoly and concentrate its services in Ontario and

Bell Telephone Company switchboard, Port Hope, 1898.

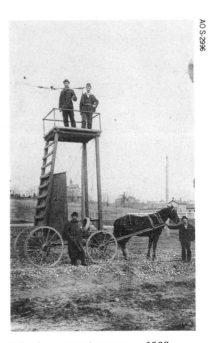

Telephone repair tower, c. 1902.

Québec. Ontario had a number of independent systems before 1900 – even in remote areas like that served by the Manitoulin and North Shore Telephone and Telegraph Company Limited. Ten years later, when regulation of telephone systems became subject to the Ontario Railway and Municipal Board, it was estimated that besides Bell there were nearly 460 independent companies in the province. In 1921 the number of systems peaked at about 690 companies. But competition from Bell's superior technology and sheer size has caused the number of independents to shrink to fewer than forty.

By the turn of the century the University of Toronto, the provincial university, required serious revamping. Financial problems had continued through the 1890s, but they were not the only source of concern. The university was completely under the control of the provincial government, and that government frequently made political decisions about faculty matters, especially appointments. As early as 1853 Francis Hincks, co-leader of the Canadian government, had seen his brother made professor of natural history in preference to the brilliant English scientist Thomas Henry Huxley. Toronto's resident intellectual, Goldwin Smith ("the seer of the Grange"), a former Regius Professor of Modern History at Oxford, argued continually that the University of Toronto should be liberated from governmental control and

University of Toronto Commission, 1905. Left to right: A.H.U. Colquhoun, Rev. H.J. Cody, Sir William Meredith, J.W. Flavelle, Rev. D.B. Macdonald, Goldwin Smith, B.E. Walker.

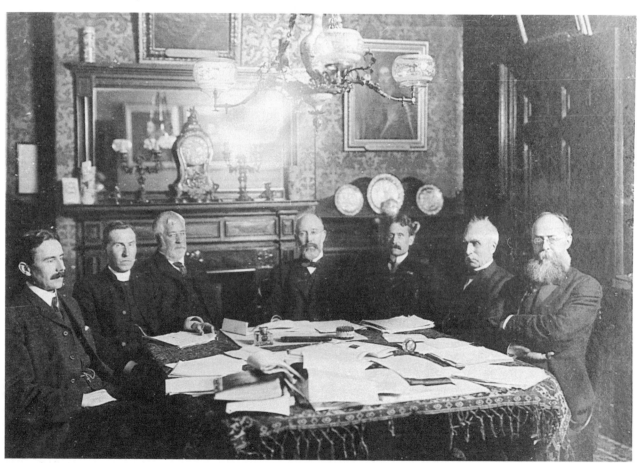

protected from party manipulation so that it "might serve both the state and scholarship more effectively." The progressive impulse was playing an important part in reshaping American universities – why not the University of Toronto?

That was the primary intention of James Pliny Whitney and his new Progressive Conservative government. Whitney, upon taking office, lavished government grants on the university, and, in the autumn of 1905, established a commission to look into the whole question of university government. The membership was distinguished: Goldwin Smith, Joseph (later Sir Joseph) Flavelle, Sir William Meredith (the university chancellor), Byron E. (later Sir Edmund) Walker, the Reverend Canon Cody, the Reverend D.B. Macdonald, and A.H.U. Colquhoun (of the Department of Education). They held seventy-seven meetings and paid visits to leading American universities. Their recommendations would chart the U of T's course for decades to come. A Board of Governors was to be appointed, the president would be the chief executive officer, academic affairs were to be governed by a Senate, university faculty councils would control uniformity in teaching, and the schools of medicine and engineering were to be given full faculty status. The commissioners took the trouble to arrange their recommendations in the form of a government bill which passed early in 1906. The modern University of Toronto has been the result, and the procedures established were followed by many other colleges and universities within and without Ontario.

David Boyle, archaeologist, ethnologist, and curator of the Old Normal School Museum. Museums were a consideration of the University Commission as well. They recommended the establishment of a general museum as a necessary part of any university. In 1912 the legislature established the Royal Ontario Museum and the University of Toronto was given a loud voice on its Board of Trustees.

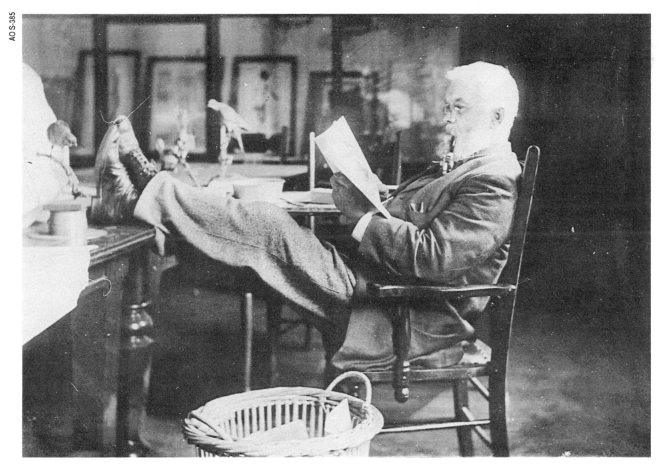

AO S-385

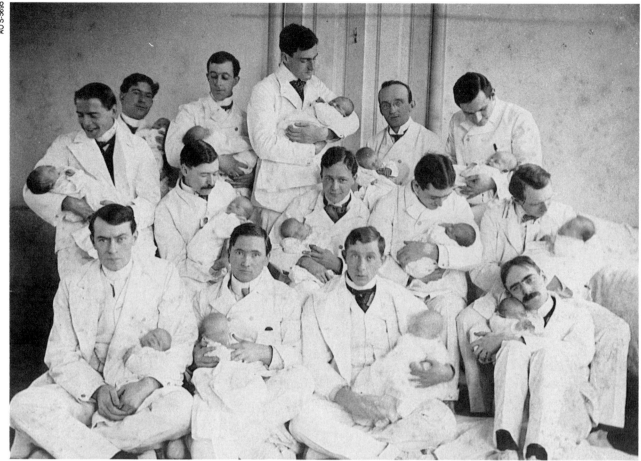

Interns and a new generation, Toronto General Hospital, c. 1900.

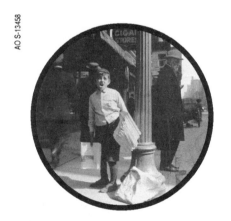

Toronto newsboy, 1905.

Ontario established a good many royal commissions to look into aspects of its society and government in the late nineteenth and early twentieth centuries. None was more important than the 1890 Report of the Royal Commission on the Prison and Reformatory System of Ontario. Backed by impressive evidence, J.J. Kelso, newspaperman and president of the newly formed Toronto Humane Society (1887), testified to provincial neglect of children's needs and rights. In 1891 Kelso founded the Children's Aid Society and in 1893 the legislature passed an "Act for the Prevention of Cruelty to, and better Protection of Children." And that same year Kelso became the first Ontario superintendent of neglected and dependent children.

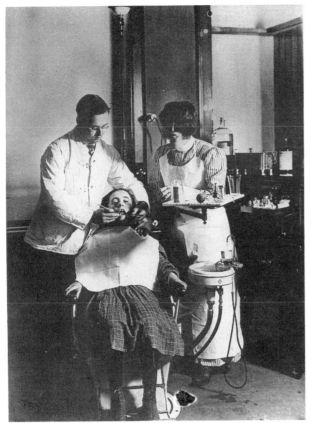

Dental inspection, c. 1900.

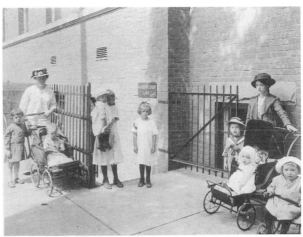

Whooping cough clinic, Hospital for Sick Children, Toronto, c. 1912.

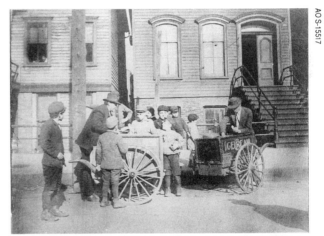

The Ontario Board of Health, in this official photograph, cautioned against buying ice cream from street vendors.

Another Board of Health photograph showing the happy results of good health care.

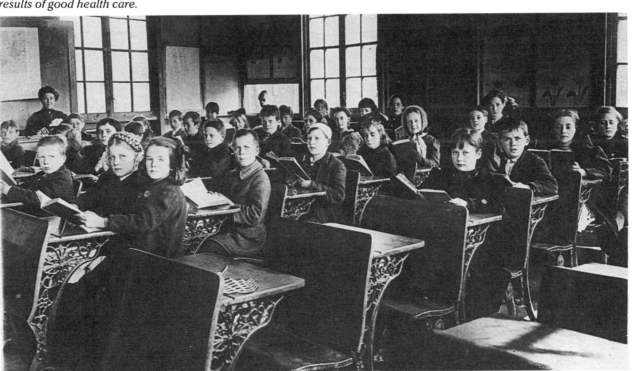

Garment workers, Toronto, c. 1910.

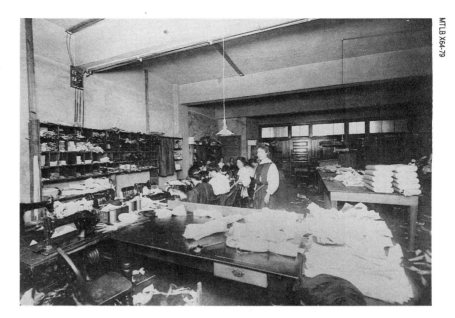

Urban Issues

The turn of the century is frequently remembered as a time of unbridled free enterprise. Captains of industry and railroad barons are pictured as ruling the economic roost with a snapping, snarling individualistic zeal. There were, indeed, such creatures, even in Ontario, but they were exceptions. In fact fears of the social and economic consequences of industrialization and urbanization (and also of the massive increase in immigration) caused Ontarians to join together as they never had before. And the response wasn't made solely by working men and women. Businessmen banded together, so did manufacturers: it was the great age of voluntary associations, church groups, and clubs of every sort.

But working men and women had more reason than ever to support unions; not only were their workplaces frequently massive and impersonal, but the management frequently was "international" (generally meaning American). Immigration posed a great threat too, as it

Pneumatic tube system, Eaton's Cash Office, Toronto, c. 1904.

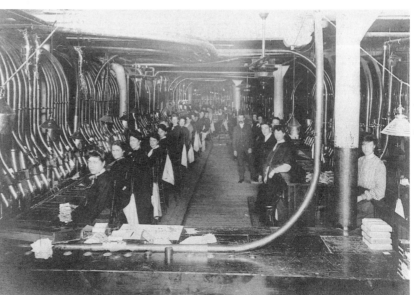

no longer meant simply farmers, but also industrial workers to compete for jobs in the new areas of Northern Ontario or the industries of the southern cities. And immigration and industry had transformed the face of those cities. Toronto's population of 181,215 in 1891 became 209,892 ten years later, and 381,833 in 1911. The upsurge was the same in most other Ontario and Canadian cities. Industrial Hamilton almost doubled to 81,869 in those same years, and an expanding civil service caused the same thing to happen in Ottawa (87,062 in 1911). The changed cityscapes also showed that there was a human cost to prosperity and expansion. To a casual eye cities were the reserves of the well-off or the poor, with few in between. To be middle class was to be well off. Richmond Street in London and St. George in Toronto were showcases of manicured prosperity, but a few blocks away the urban poor clustered in dingy alleyways or back streets, tucked not completely out of sight of the grand new hotels, federal buildings, and department stores.

Municipal reform meant not simply the squeezing-out of corrupt politicians from City Hall, but also addressing a new problem – what specific shape should reform take? Up to the 1890s initiatives had

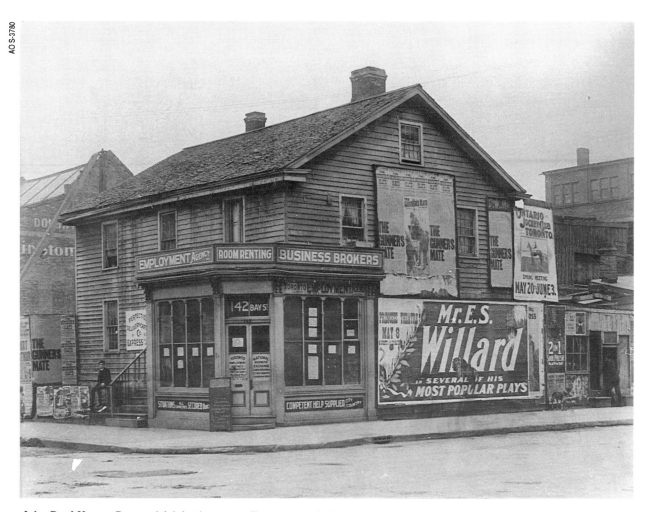

John Doel House, Bay and Adelaide streets, Toronto, c. 1900. Originally the building was a brewery, and Mackenzie and his followers planned much of the abortive 1837 rebellion within its walls. It underwent a number of incarnations: carpenter's shop, planing mill, and, at the turn of the century, employment agency.

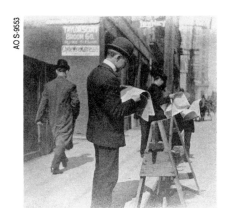

Unemployed, Toronto, c. 1905.

been private, with concerned individuals and churches working almost independently to relieve social distress. This response was soon seen as hopelessly inadequate; the sheer size of the new cities dwarfed well-meaning individual efforts. It was only slowly that reformers grasped the idea that a collective problem demanded a collectivist solution.

Drawing on American experience, Canadians organized a Union of Canadian Municipalities to discuss similar urban problems. New, larger, voluntary associations became popular avenues for reform, and the whole movement was championed by the newspapers. Most important, churches, especially in Ontario, wrapped themselves up in a new "Social Gospel" and saw their roles in society not just as caring for individual souls or promoting the afterlife, but as addressing the social problems of the here and now. The Salvation Army and the Methodist church were examples of such progressive thinking.

Many of the advocates of urban reform were rural apologists who longed for a lost way of life. To these observers the new city must be the City Beautiful, the Garden City, resplendent with parks, trees, boulevards, and green vistas. Others were more concerned with practical issues such as public ownership of municipal utilities, or the new concept of town planning, or reform of municipal government.

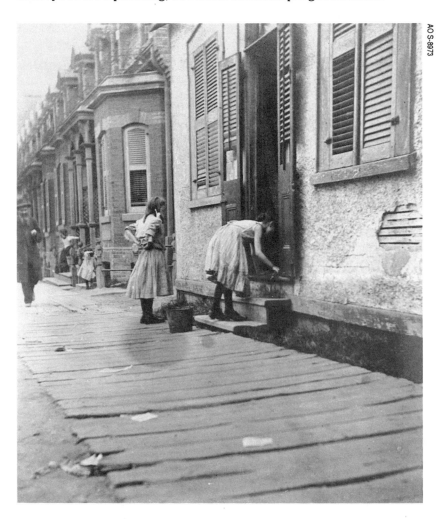

Child labour, St. John's Ward, Toronto, 1905.

The plight of the poor working girl was a familiar refrain during the two decades before the First World War. During that period more women joined the urban work force than ever before. Women were considered to be "suitable" for different jobs from men and, of course, received different wages. The typewriter, in a sense, was woman's liberator and enslaver at one and the same time. Social critics also failed to see women in the workplace as anything but women, and so completely overlooked class issues, and blinded themselves in the process to the need for real equality for women's work. Even trade unions tended to differentiate between male and female workers. "We think that women should not be allowed to work in the foundries," one prominent labour organization observed, "as it has a tendency to degrade them, to lower the wages of the men, and to keep a number of young men out of work." Attitudes towards women at work changed very slowly, although the First World War (despite the fact that it did not radically alter female working patterns) caused a shift in attitudes: both men and women began to feel that a woman's place was not in the home unless she wanted it that way.

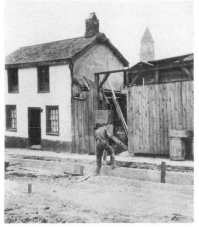

Toronto, 1905. Serving the poor was clearly not yet a priority of city management. In the face of unpaved streets, open sewers and ramshackle housing, Toronto's City Fathers in 1899 spent the lavish sum of two and a half million dollars in the construction of a new city hall.

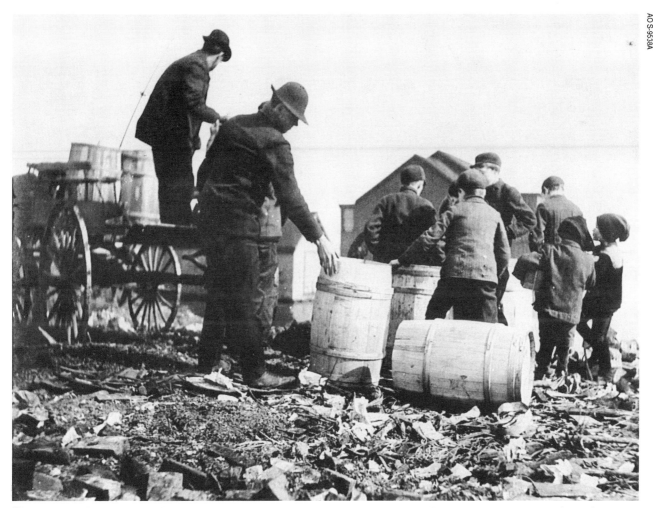

Toronto waterfront, March 1910. Often entire families were reduced to the level of scavengers, scouring garbage dumps along the harbour to salvage anything of value.

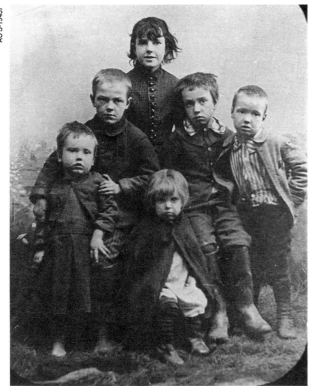

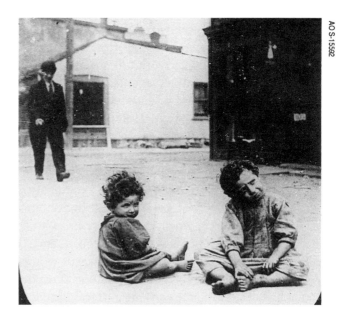

Above: *Slum children, Toronto.*

Left: *Poor family, Toronto, 1905.*

Below: *Sleeping out, Toronto, 1911.*

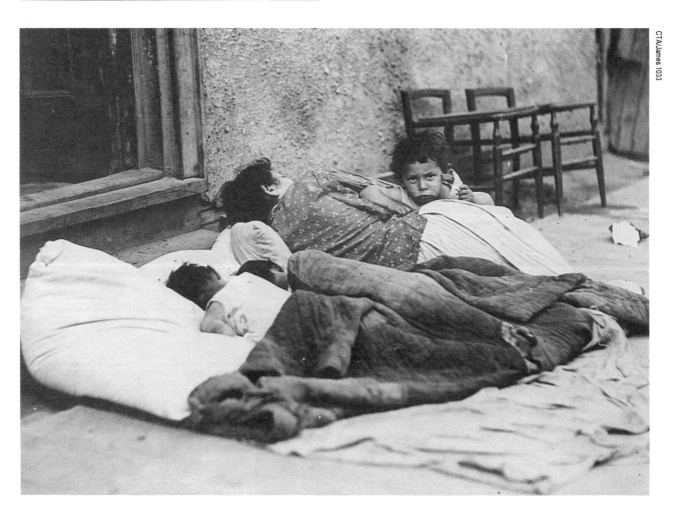

The Salvation Army – the Sally Ann, with its blood and fire, red shields, drums and tambourines – had its start in Toronto in 1882. The movement spread quickly throughout the province, but it was not until the 1890s that the Army's "Social Wing" became a significant and independent part of its whole Christian philosophy. "Soup to salvation" clearly had not been enough and in the first years of the new century three programs emerged which were a distinct response to social needs: Grace Maternity Hospitals, increased immigration work, and active guidance in the police courts and prisons.

Grace Hospital in Toronto started in 1905, and was much more than a rescue home for "scarlet ladies" as many of the public thought. From 1905 to 1914 the Army assisted more than a hundred and fifty thousand emigrants to leave what its founder, William Booth, had called "Darkest England." Many went to New Ontario, especially the Cobalt region. "I am convinced," declared Premier Whitney, "that the Salvation Army is by far the best immigration agency which ever worked in this country." In penal work, the Army took a lead. Brigadier W. Archibald of Toronto, a long-time advocate of parole and rehabilitation, in May 1905 resigned from the Army (with its permission) to become Canada's first Dominion parole officer.

William Booth, commanding general of the Salvation Army, visited the Canadian Corps four times: 1886, 1894, 1902, and finally in 1907.

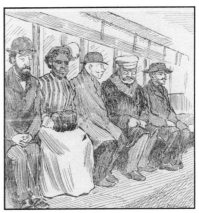

"Anglo-Saxon Toronto." Front-page illustration, Saturday Night, *3 December 1904. "Nativist" declarations were not restricted to people of different colour or language. "No English need apply" was a common sign in Toronto in the decade before the First World War.*

Salvation Army, Toronto, 1907. Banners proclaim a welcome to Booth.

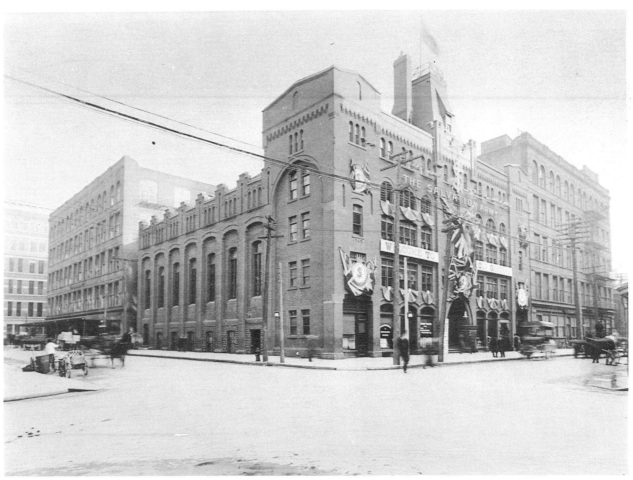

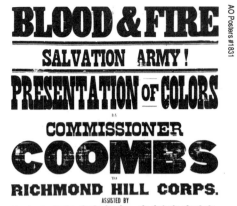

*Salvation Army poster, Richmond Hill,
c. 1886.*

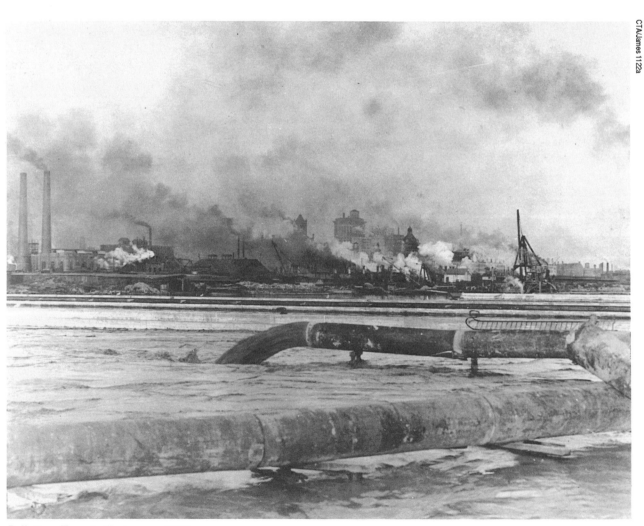

Pollution, Toronto Harbour, c. 1912.

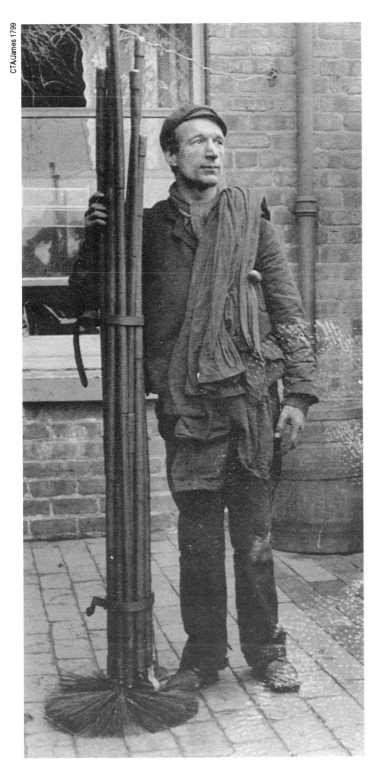

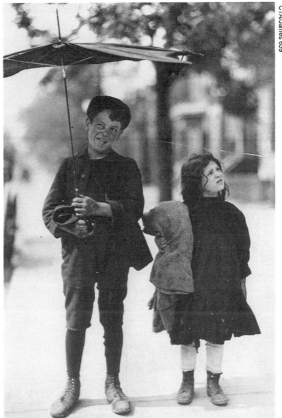

Chimneysweep, Toronto, c. 1900.

Toronto, c. 1908.

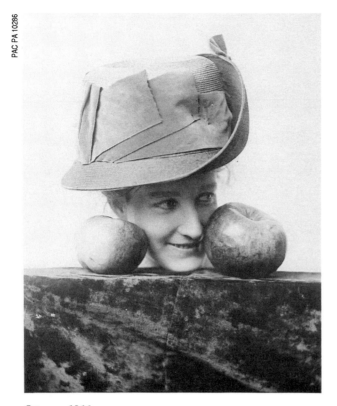

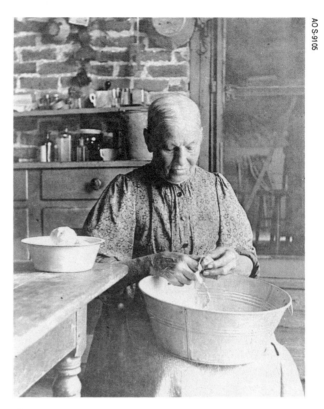

Ottawa, 1911.

Rainham Township, Haldimand County, July 1906.

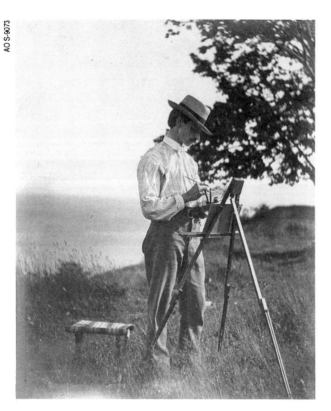

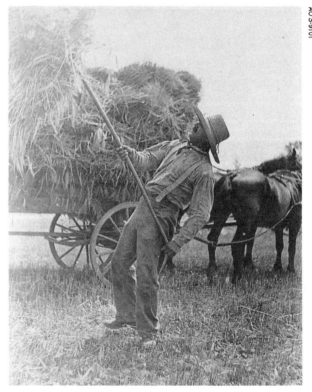

Scarborough Bluffs, near Toronto, 1906.

Rainham Township, Haldimand County, 1906.

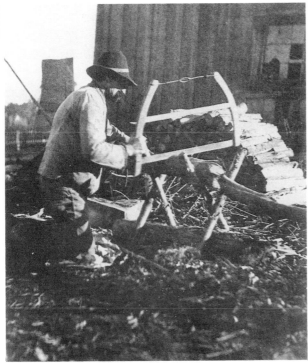

Davisville, near Toronto, 1906.

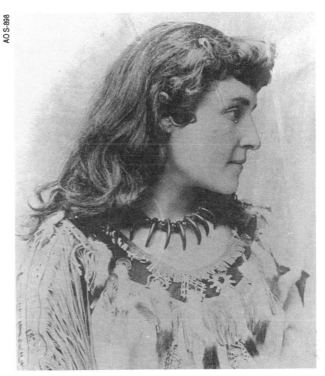

E. Pauline Johnson, "Tekahionwake," Mohawk poetess. "And up on the hills against the sky,/ A fir tree rocking its lullaby,/Swings, swings,/Its emerald wings,/Swelling the song that my paddle sings."

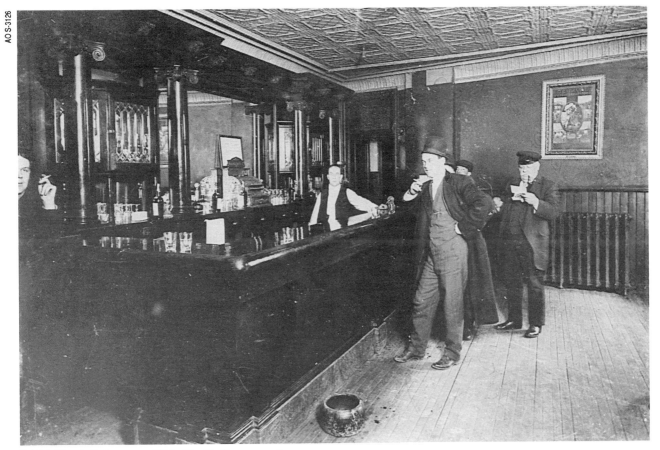

British Hotel, Cobourg, c. 1910. Charlie Casey tending.

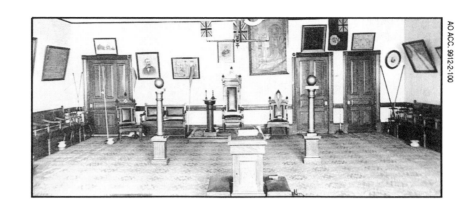

Interior of Masonic Hall, Sarnia, c. 1900.

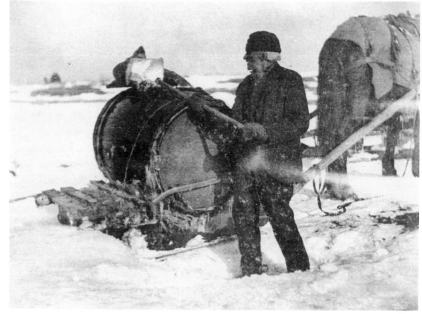

Ottawa, 1906. As late as 1906, Ottawa's water supply was supplemented by independent vendors who made deliveries of relatively unpolluted river water from large wooden casks (called puncheons) fixed on a sled or two wheels and drawn by a single horse. Prices doubled in winter when it became necessary to chop through the thick ice.

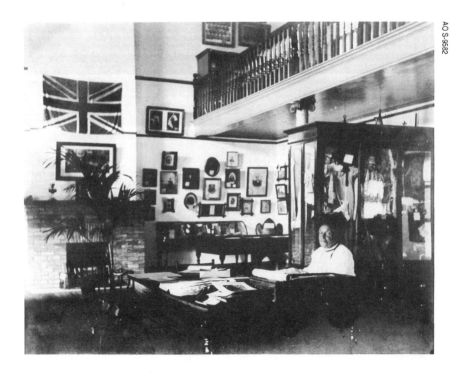

Niagara-on-the-Lake, Ontario, 1906. Janet Carnochan, president of the Niagara Historical Society and curator of its museum. The collection contained such bizarre items as a battle-axe extracted from an Ayrshire bog, a treasured map of Sebastopol, Louis Riel's Labrador seal coat, and General Isaac Brock's cocked hat.

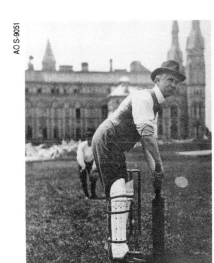

Speaker of the House of Commons, Robert Franklin Sutherland, at cricket on the parliamentary lawn, Ottawa, June 1906.

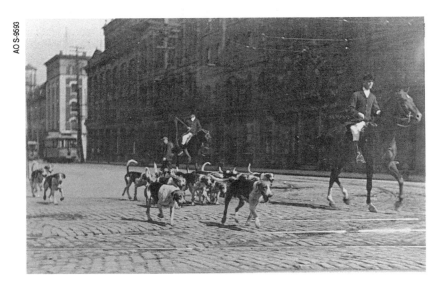

The hounds out on Front Street, Toronto, c. 1905. Introduced by British officers shortly after the Conquest, the "genteel" sport of fox-hunting remained a class phenomenon. The Toronto Hunt was organized in 1843 and was active in areas well within the city limits until after the First World War.

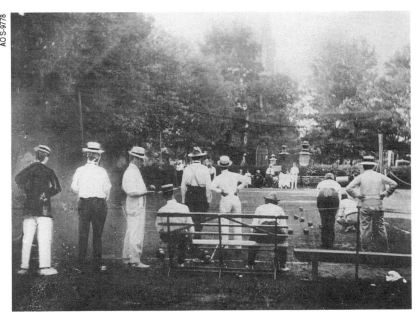

Lawn bowling, Port Dover, 1913.

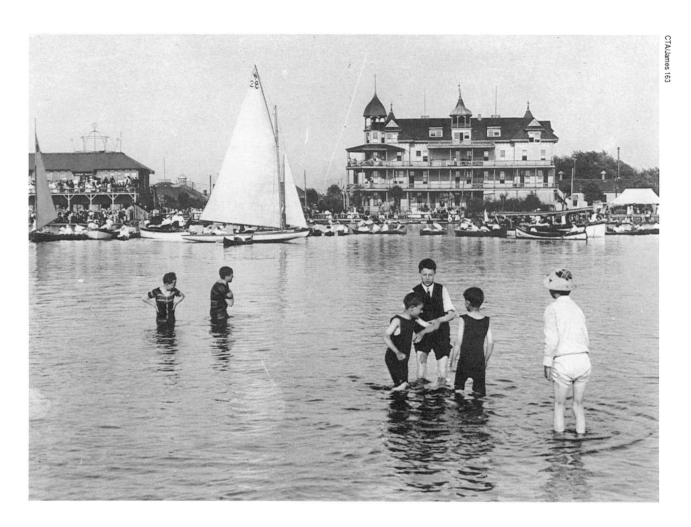

Above: *Hotel Hanlan, Toronto Island, 1907. The hotel on the peninsula that became an island in 1858 was built by John Hanlan in 1874. His son, Ned, champion oarsman, operated the building in the last decades of the nineteenth century when it grew rapidly into a recreational centre surrounded by a roller coaster, merry-go-round, and a baseball stadium before fire consumed most of the site in 1909. City boosters were swift to compare Hanlan's Point to New York's Coney Island.*

Right: *Scarborough Beach Park, 1907. Operated by the Toronto Railway Company, forerunner of the Toronto Transit Commission, until 1926, the Beach Park offered a midway, athletic field with large grandstand, and "the chutes" waterslide.*

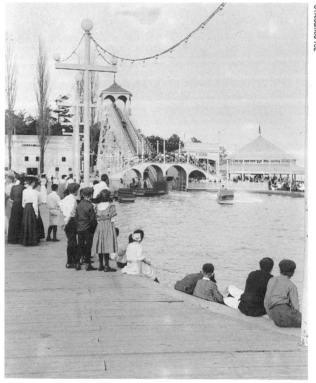

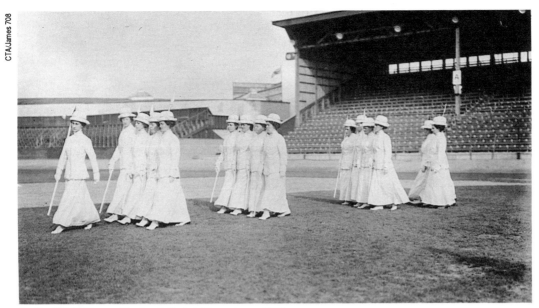

Ladies' Drill Team, Hanlan's Point, Toronto, c. 1908.

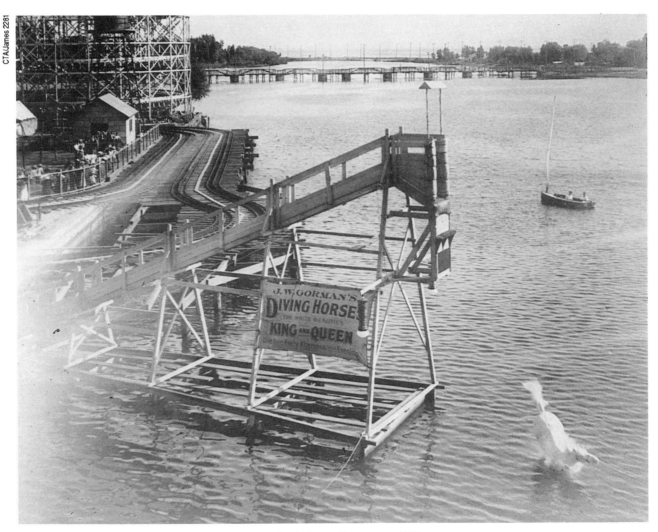

King or Queen? J.W. Gorman's Diving Horses, Hanlan's Point, Toronto, c. 1908.

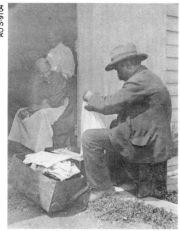

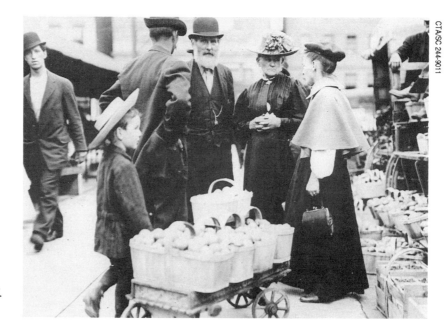

Above: *"Pedlar's Visit," Rainham Township, Haldimand County, 1906.* Right and below: *Hamilton Market, 1909.*

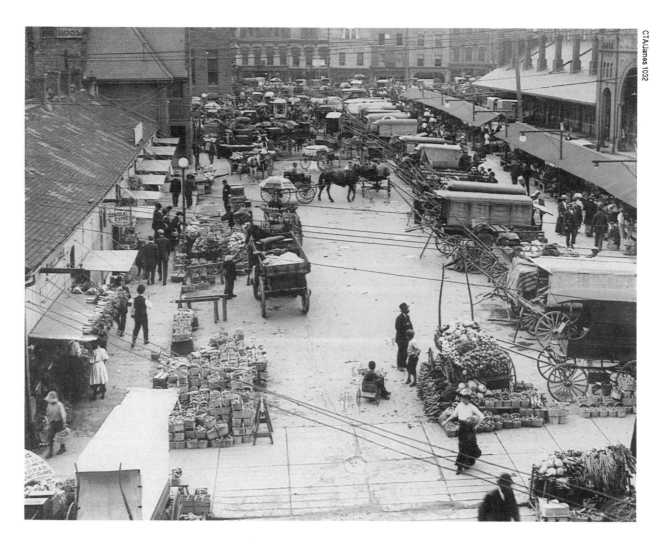

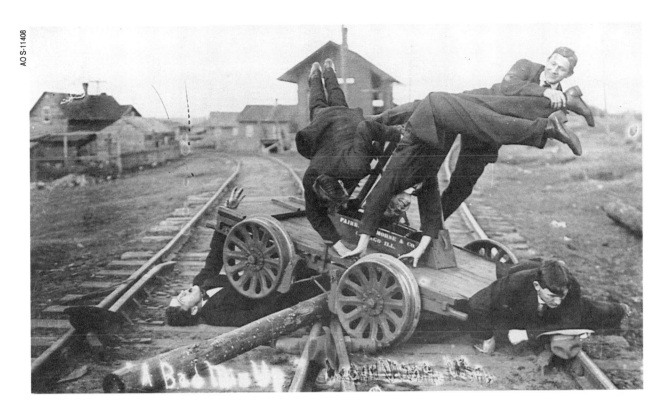

Fort Frances, 1904.

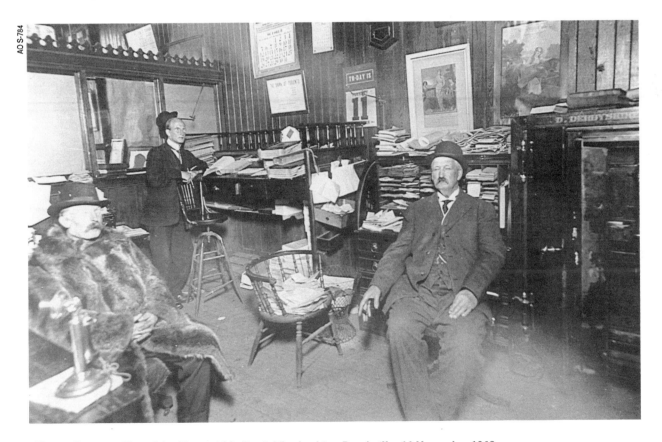

Cheese Factory office of the Honourable Daniel Derbyshire, Brockville, 11 November 1913.

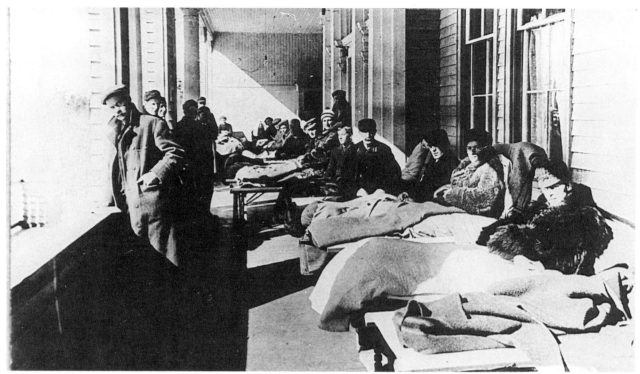

Muskoka Free Hospital for Consumptives, Gravenhurst, c. 1904.

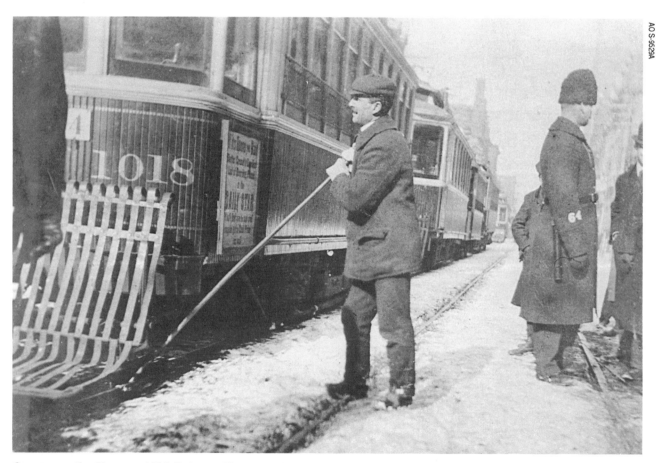

Streetcar strike, Toronto, 1910. Before public ownership of transportation in 1921, Torontonians coped with nine different systems and nine separate fares. A trip through city cost anywhere from two to fifteen cents. Stoppages were not uncommon and further disrupted service. In 1910 over thirteen hundred employees struck the Toronto Street Railway Company.

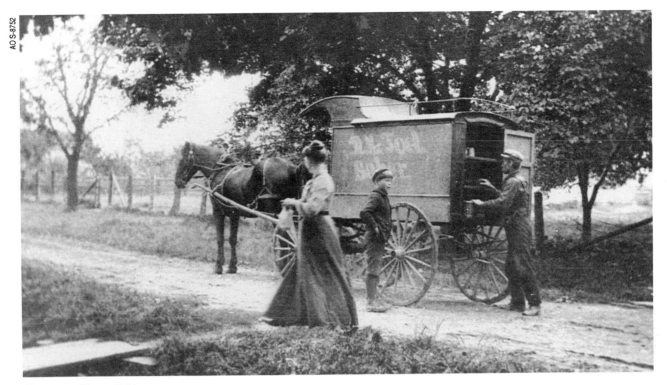

Bowmanville, c. 1904.

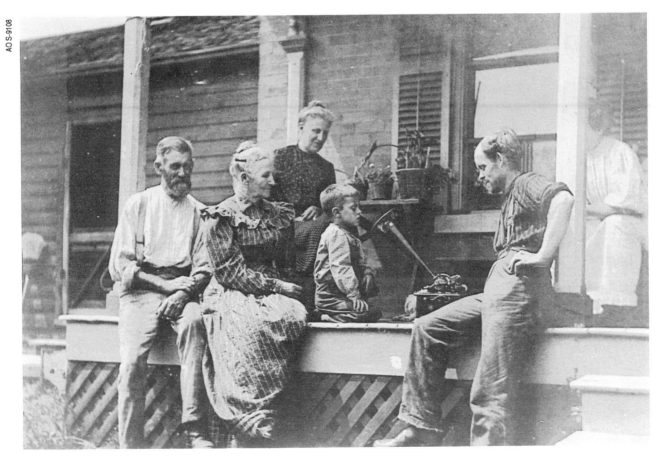

Clarkson, Ontario, 1906.

Port Dover, August 1911.

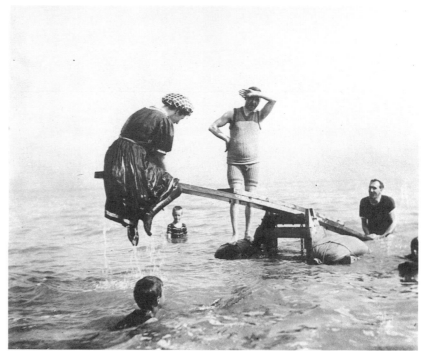

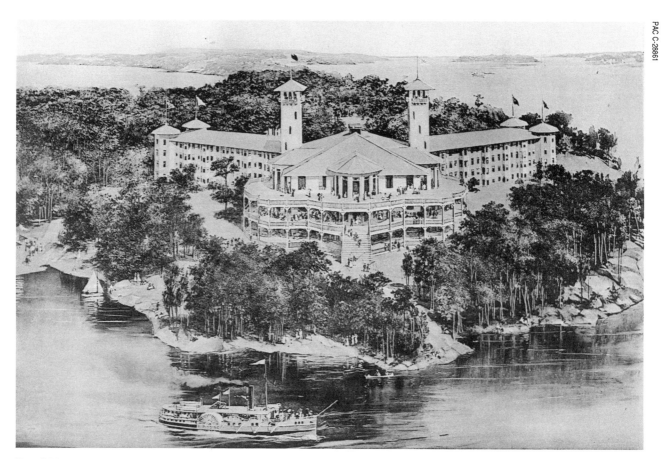

Royal Muskoka Hotel, Lake Rosseau, c. 1910.

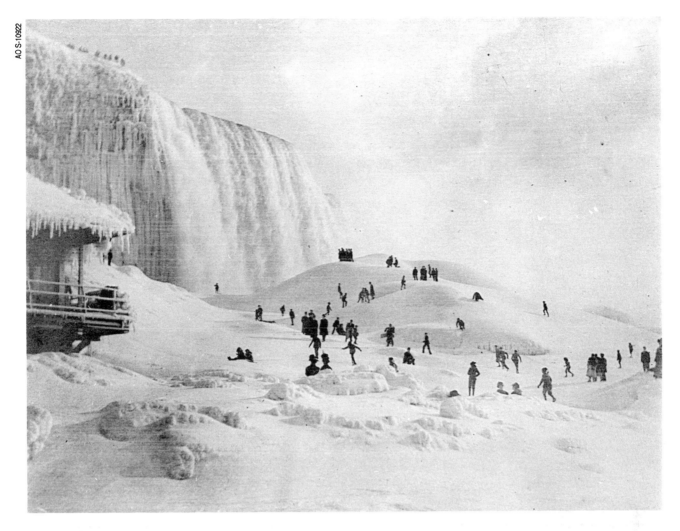

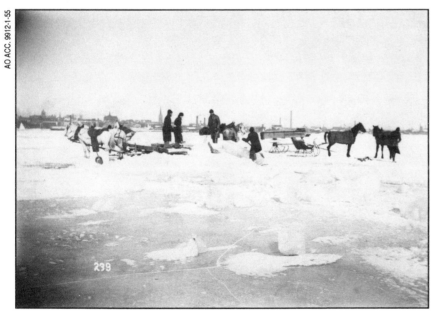

Above: *Niagara Falls, c. 1905. Enormous chunks of ice and slush often unite to form an ice bridge from Canada to the United States across the Niagara River below the Falls. Until 1912, when the bridge was closed to the public because of a triple drowning, the site was visited daily by hundreds who tobogganed on the slippery slopes or took refreshments at numerous temporary shanties.*

Ice-cutting, Toronto Bay, c. 1900.

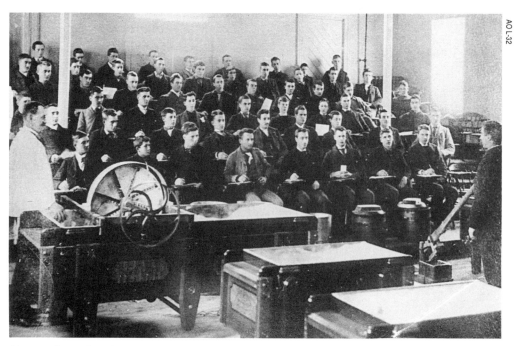

Ontario Agricultural College, Guelph, c. 1900.

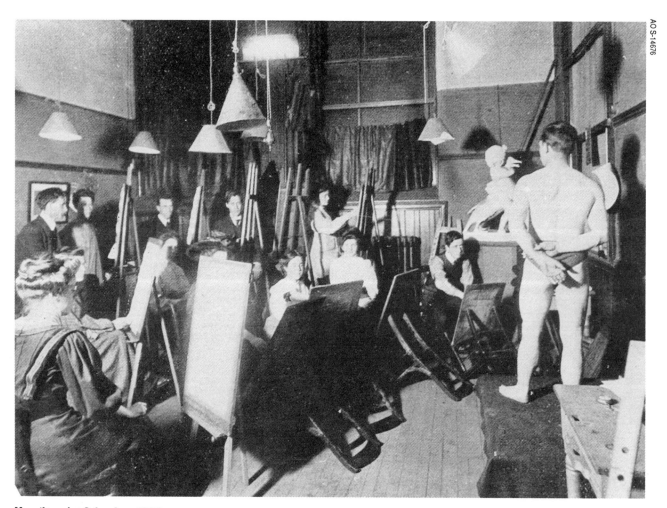

Hamilton Art School, c. 1907.

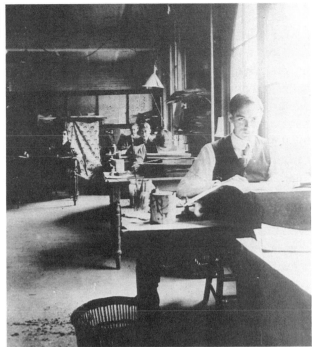

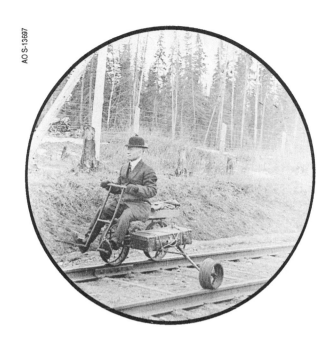

Tom Thomson at Grip Limited, a Toronto commercial art house, 1911. The Grip office at one time employed five of the future Group of Seven artists in addition to Thomson. J.E.H. Macdonald can be seen in the rear right corner of the office.

The Reverend Neil Morrison en route, Timiskaming, c. 1910.

Below: *Gas explosion, Brantford, 1909.*

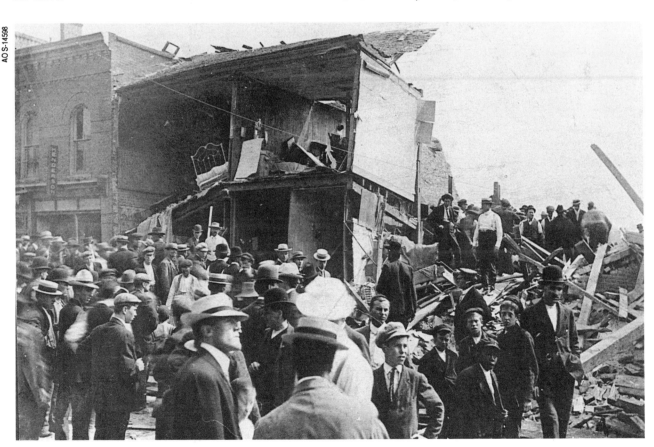

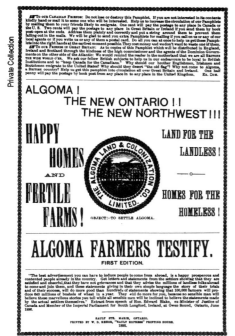

Algoma Land & Colonization Compony brochure, Sault Ste. Marie, 1892

The North

Northern Ontario, for the first hundred years of settlement in the south of the province, was a remote land of Indians, fur traders, and lumbermen. By the mid-nineteenth century, native British North Americans were challenged by American interests to look northwestwards to the vast tracts of forest, rock, and lake beyond most people's experience (and imagination). French Canadians feared its effects on the balance of political power, but there was no doubt that the inheritance of territory from the Hudson's Bay Company in 1870 would force exploration and the definition of a northern frontier – an "Empire of the North" as government railroad brochures later called New Ontario.

The Ontario government in 1870 needed little prodding to jump at the prospect of immense revenues from northern mineral and timber resources, especially with American markets and technical enterprise lying handy to the south. Taste for the riches to come was particularly sharpened by the discovery of silver on a storm-battered island in Lake Superior near Thunder Bay. Silver Islet Mine was to anticipate the character of much of Ontario's mineral exploitation – it was financed and operated by Americans, it showed rapid and substantial profits, and then suddenly it collapsed absolutely.

A decision by the Imperial Privy Council in London in 1888 gave ownership of the vast area west of Lake Superior to Ontario and in so doing squashed the federal government's view that the lands belonged to the Indians and were relinquished to Ottawa through treaties. The council maintained that the Crown had always had proprietary title and that "the Indian title was a mere burden." Other concessions followed and in 1912 Ontario's modern boundaries were established; the extensions gave the province effective responsibility over territory three times the extent of the old province.

Administration of the newly acquired districts was designed to encourage orderly development of resources – lands and licence agencies were established, townships opened up, colonization encouraged by roads, school grants, police divisions, and even a pioneer dairy farm at Lake Wabigoon (later, Dryden). One agricultural commission reported on settlement as early as 1881; another, on mineral resources, in 1890 sparked government creation of a Bureau of Mines to regulate and direct mining; yet others in 1892 investigated fish and game resources and forest reserves. The finite symbol of the concern for proper land use came with the creation of Algonquin Park in 1893.

The Bureau of Mines' geological researches in the 1890s acted as catalysts to the gold and silver discoveries of the next decade, and the government directly subsidized the enormous steel empire of F.H. Clergue at Sault Ste. Marie – clear evidence of how far beyond educational and promotional campaigns it was willing to go under new "business is business" maxims. By 1896 the Northern Railway had reached the CPR transcontinental track at Nipissing Junction. Motivated by the same drive northwards, Premier Ross chartered the Temiskaming and Northern Ontario Railway in 1902. It took only six years to connect Toronto with the National Transcontinental Railway route at the new township of Cochrane. During construction of the line in 1904, silver was accidentally struck at Cobalt; gold discoveries at Timmins, Porcupine, and other places attracted T.&N.O. branch lines and subsidiaries, like the Nipissing Central which actually operated sophisticated urban streetcars between Cobalt and Haileybury on the shores of Lake Timiskaming.

The Cobalt experience, though itself shortlived, did more than any government promotion ever could to establish the worth and attractions of the Canadian Shield in Ontario's north. It is without question too that the mixture of government and private enterprise which so swiftly pried open the riches of New Ontario laid the basis for Ontario's domination of the Canadian economy. As a Liberal party election pamphlet of 1905 shrewdly observed, "it depends on the development of 'Northern Ontario' whether Ontario itself shall retain a place second to that of no other Province, or shall subside into a second or third rate position."

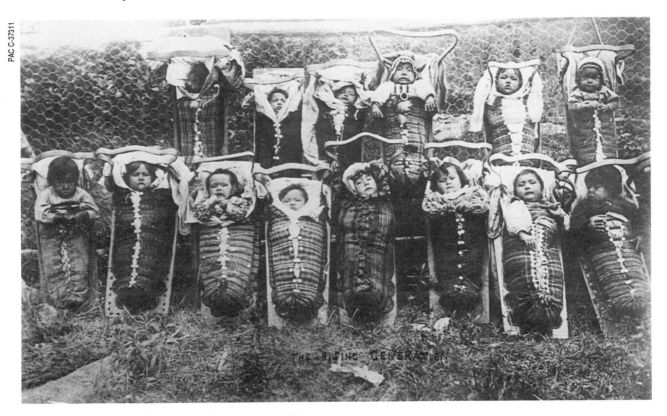

"The Rising Generation," Montréal River area, c. 1904.

Gerald Campbell, resident engineer, Grand Trunk Pacific Railroad, Englehart, c. 1908. The purpose of the Grand Trunk Pacific, a subsidiary of the Grand Trunk, was to complete the line from Winnipeg to Moncton via Québec City and thereby drain some of the prosperity of flourishing New Ontario, notably the Cochrane area.

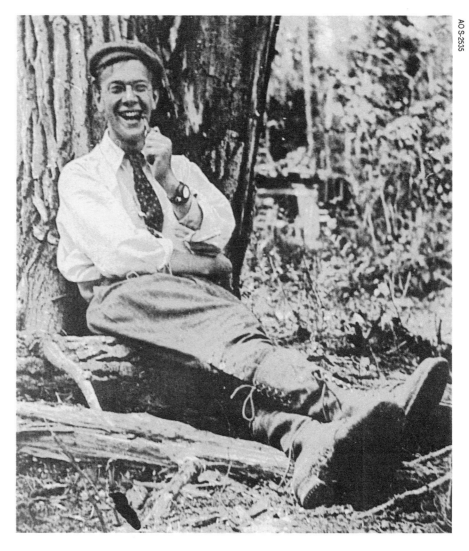

Grand Trunk Railway Station, Haliburton, 1897. The recreational north that most urban tourists still know – hunting, shooting, fishing, and camping – was another important feature of Northern Ontario life at the turn of the century.

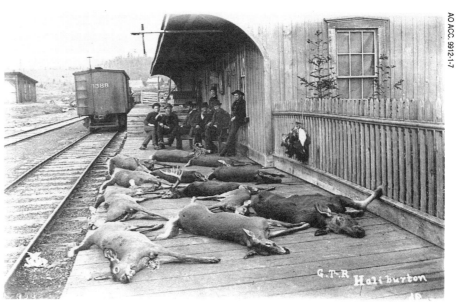

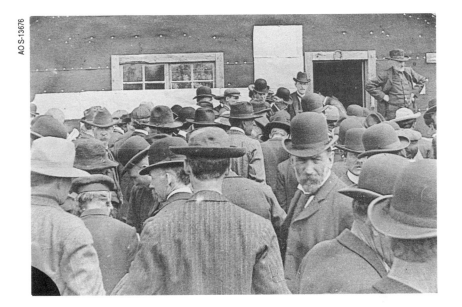

*Land office, Englehart, c.1906.
J.L. Englehart, chairman of the
Temiskaming & Northern Ontario
rail line (now the Ontario Northland
Railway), gave his name to this
junction in the "Great Clay Belt,"
twenty miles west of New Liskeard.
The railroad was financed by the
Ontario government to facilitate
settlement.*

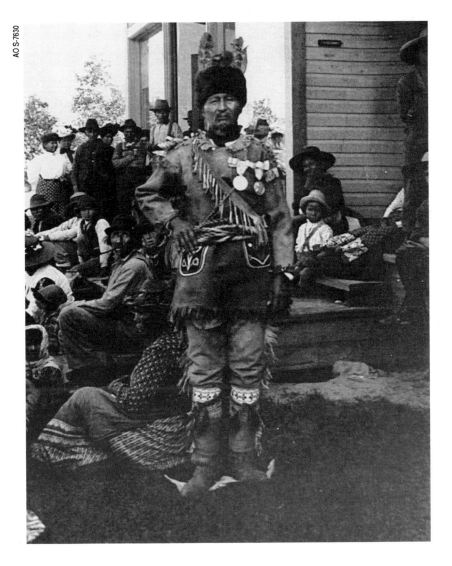

*Chief "Espaniol" at Hudson's Bay
Company Post, Biscotasing, 1906.
The local name was and is "Bisco."
When the CPR moved through here
the town was a typical frontier fur
post. The fur trade took over once
again after the CPR left and the town
returned to its slumber. In 1908,
however, a large lumbering concern
located there, and the boom-bust
cycle started up again.*

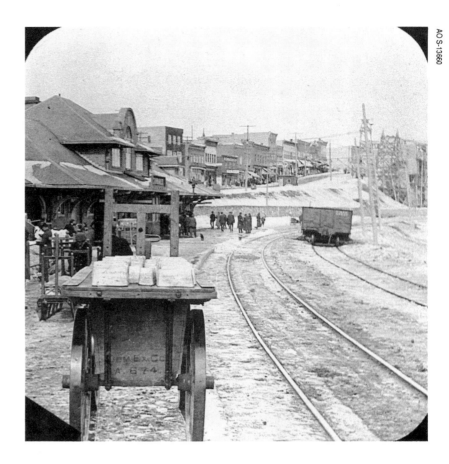

Right: *Silver shipment, Cobalt Station, Temiskaming and Northern Ontario Railway, c. 1910. Cobalt had sprung up in six years from nothing to a bustling "boomtown" – a condition which was not to last. Silver was the base, and its discovery had been an accident of the construction of the railroad. Eventually, forty mines operated in the area, and by 1908 the population exceeded seven thousand. Fires, however, and a great drop in the value of silver on world markets after the First World War, initiated a decline from which Cobalt has never fully recovered.*

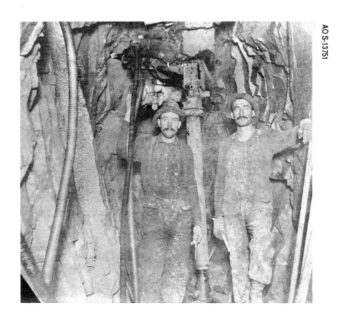

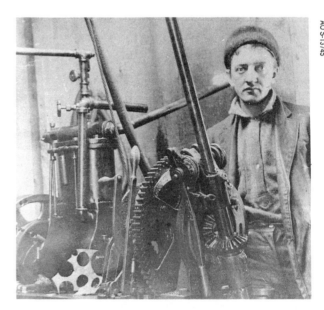

In the mine drift, South Porcupine area, c. 1910.

Mining machinery, South Porcupine area, c. 1910.

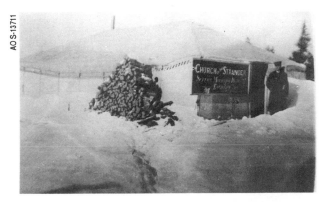

Tent chapel for itinerants, Golden City, Porcupine Lake, c. 1905.

Before money could be made in Ontario's north, men's bellies had to be filled, their souls saved, and the sheer ordeal of labour drowned in liquor.

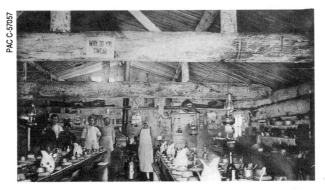

Interior of a lumber-camp mess hut, 1910.

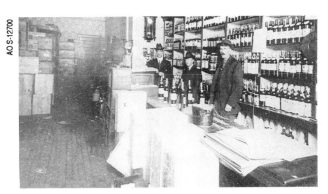

Liquor store, New Liskeard, c. 1900.

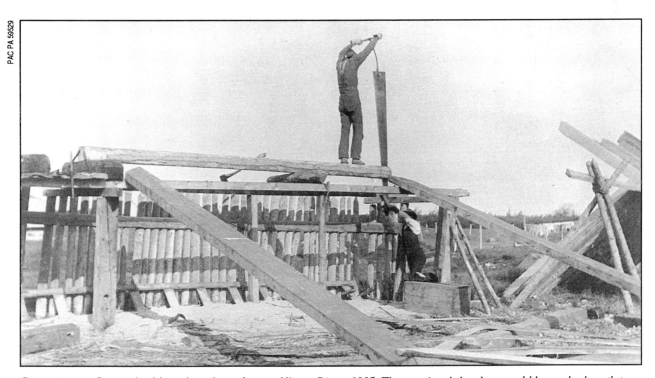

Pit-sawing on Ontario's old northern boundary at Albany River, 1905. The province's borders would be pushed north to their present extent in 1912.

151

"Brush" cut, 1897.

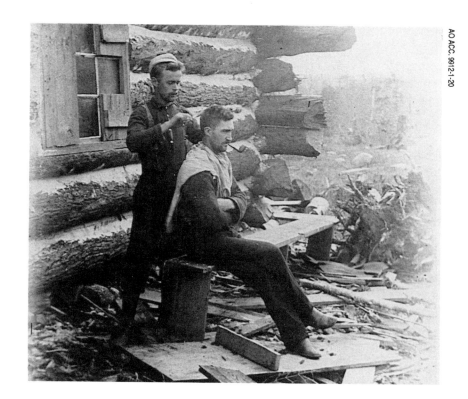

Below: *South Porcupine Miners' strike, 1913–14. Parade outside Western Federation of Miners union office.*

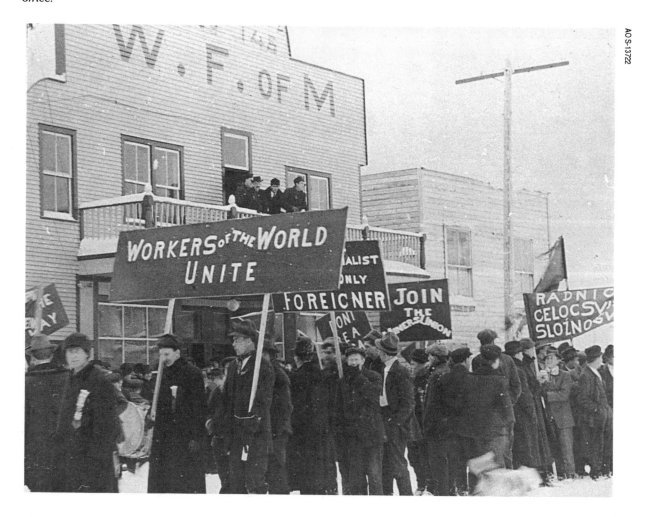

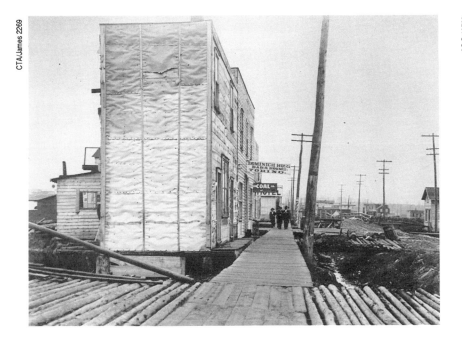

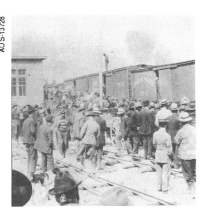

Above: *The first relief train from Toronto arrives at South Porcupine in late July 1911.*

Above left: *Main Street, South Porcupine, c. 1912.*

Fire ravaged the mining towns of the north time after time – and still does. Before the start of the provincial fire-fighting service at the end of the First World War little could be done to stop the devastation, and survivors were usually obliged to restart their communities from scratch. The great Cochrane fire of July 1911, for example, killed over seventy people and shattered fifty stores, fifteen hotels, four churches, and two schools; in 1912 and 1914 the towns of Timmins and Haileybury were razed. Nevertheless, under vigorous provincial promotion of colonization roads, railroads, and agricultural settlement in the Great Clay Belt, the Temiskaming census division could report a tenfold increase in population from 1901 to 1911.

Below: *Timmins after the fire, 1913.*

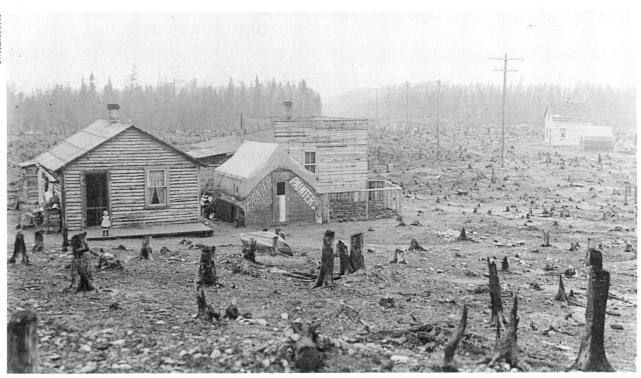

Main Street, Cochrane, c. 1910. Frank Cochrane, James Whitney's minister of lands and forests, had close links with the mining entrepreneurs of the New North. The Ontario government worked hand-in-glove with the companies to ensure systematic, profitable exploitation of mineral wealth. Strikes, of course, were not wanted by either government or business.

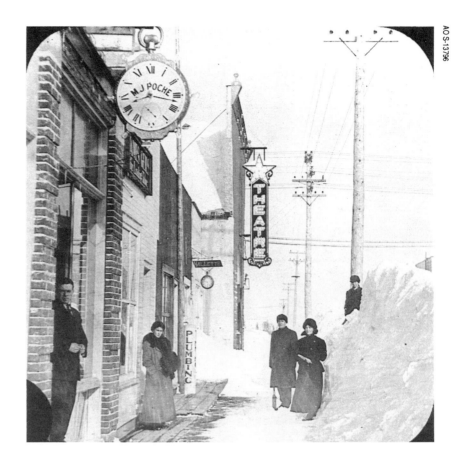

A dramatic and extensive wilderness of forest, rock, and water inhabited since the seventeenth century only by Indians and fur traders formed that part of Ontario known as the Northwest. Until the Canadian Pacific Railway arrived at the twin settlements of Prince Arthur's Landing (later Port Arthur) and Fort William (the North West Company fur-trading fort since 1804) in the late 1870s, the whole vast area was one of vague and difficult jurisdiction. By the last two decades of the nineteenth century, provisional districts had been staked out (Thunder Bay, Rainy River, and Kenora to the west; Cochrane, Temiskaming, and Nipissing to the east) and Queen's Park was encouraging land settlement along with the lumbering and new mining operations. The population fluctuated seasonally; sometimes, as in Kenora or Keewatin, summer cottagers increased it by almost half. Though the grand settlement notions harboured by the government never materialized, because so much of the land was unsuitable, the towns on the railroads flourished admirably and sometimes offered as much in variety, vigour, and sophistication as many of their sister towns in the settled south.

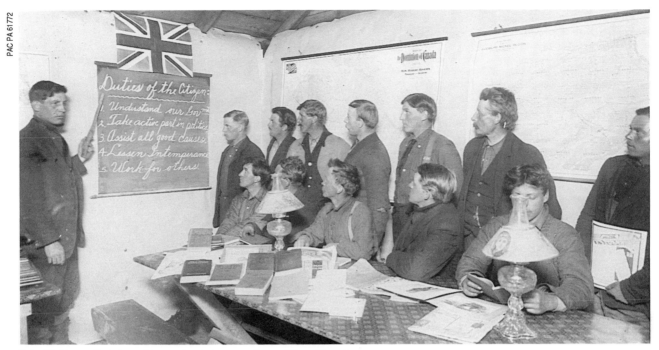

D.L. McDougall giving a lesson in civics to a class of Scandinavians at Larchwood, near Sudbury, 1913.

The Frontier College movement, organized in Toronto in 1899 by the Rev. Alfred Fitzpatrick, a Nova Scotian Presbyterian, was at first called the Reading Camp Association. The aim was to give men in work camps some form of rudimentary education which would enable them to move into better employment. But another goal was more calculated – to assure that men in the camps would be protected from radical agitation by a healthy dose of "Canadianization." Field teachers and correspondence courses became the backbone of the pedagogical effort. The voluntary organization was incorporated by Act of Parliament in 1922.

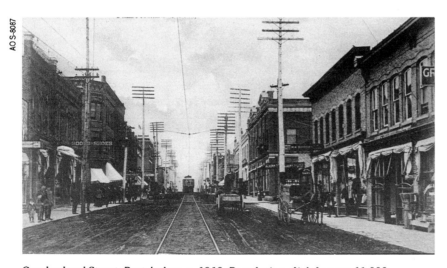

Cumberland Street, Port Arthur, c. 1910. Population slightly over 11,000.

The Patriotic Column, T. Eaton Company, Toronto, 1900.

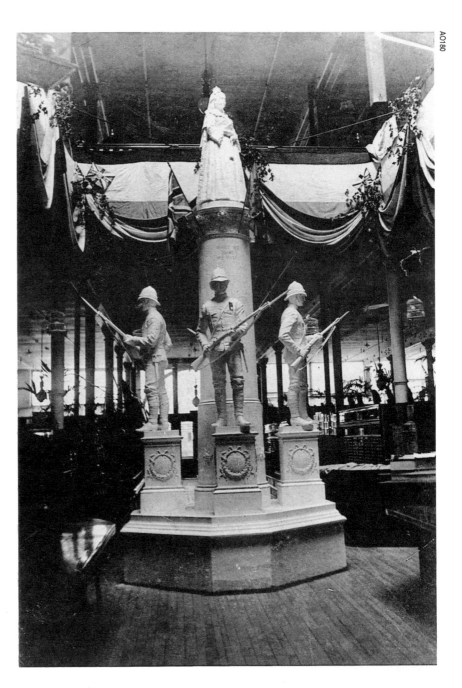

AO180

Always in the van when Easter decorations are concerned, as in everything else, The T. Eaton Co., Limited, have this year prepared a patriotic surprise for visitors to their establishment . . . This particular piece of work is called a "patriotic column." It consists of an octagonal base over eight feet across, from the centre of which rises a magnificent Grecian pillar, on the top of which stands a life-sized figure of Her Majesty, attired in her robes of state, and wearing on her breast a spray of shamrock. The shaft and figure are twenty-three feet in height, and the base of the shaft is three feet in diameter. The cap of the pedestal on which the figure of the Queen stands is finished in a Gothic effect of maple leaves. The base of the pillar, which is three feet in diameter, is surrounded by a decoration in broken armament, drum, and banner effect, with maple leaf and beaver, and bears the figures, "1899" and "1900." Above this is the motto: "United we stand; divided we fall," and further up are inscribed, "What we have we'll hold," and "Soldiers of the Queen." From the cap float four flags: the Union Jack, the British ensign, the Canadian flag, and the Irish flag.

Extract from Mail and Empire, *7 April 1900.*

Marching to the Imperial Drummer

Ontarians considered themselves, unflinchingly, to be part of Greater Britain. Not a few thought they might, potentially at any rate, be greater Britons. A fierce sense of loyalty still gripped the province in the late nineteenth century. Sir Charles Dilke, the Imperial statesman, noted in 1890 that the English spoke of "Her Majesty's Opposition" but that the Conservatives of Ontario had attempted to better the phrase, and styled themselves "Her Majesty's Loyal Opposition." The crusade for Imperial federation was popular in Ontario, but had to be weighed against Canadian autonomy and independence. As well, the Americans were casting covetous eyes on the place, a reality which had been a constant backdrop for Ontarians since 1792.

The Boer War, 1899–1902, caused many Ontarians to feel the call of the blood, but Sir Wilfrid Laurier recognized the immense threat to national unity that the war offered: French Canada was overwhelmingly opposed to the adventure and to any Canadian commitment at all. French Canadians were quick to point out a superficial similarity between the racial divisions of South Africa and those of Canada. Laurier cleverly sidestepped the issue by compromise. He authorized a volunteer corps to serve under Imperial command – ultimately seven thousand Canadians took part. In the next federal election, the result was clear – the Liberals lost a few seats in Ontario, and picked up a few

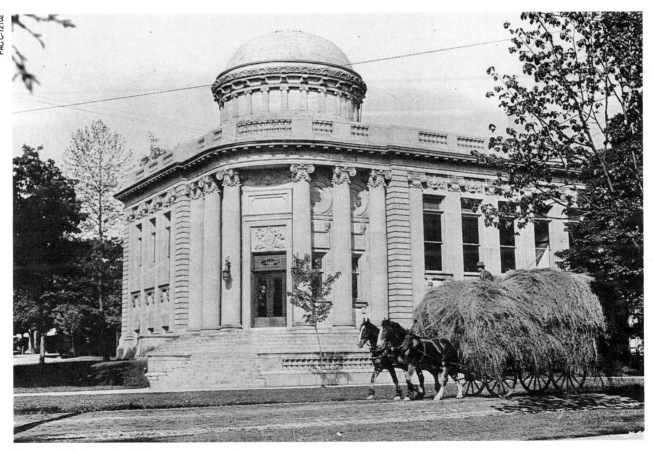

The Public Library, Guelph.

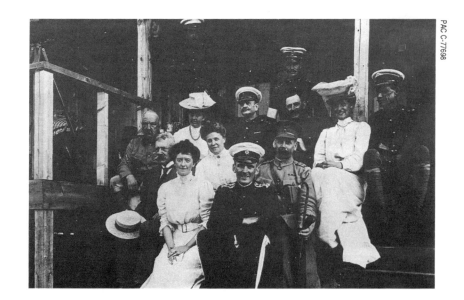

Officers and wives, Camp Petawawa,
August 1906.

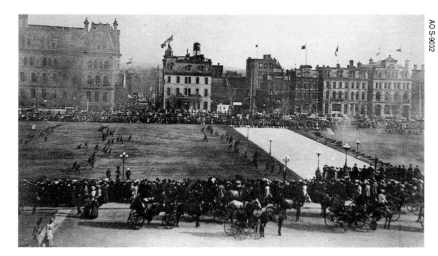

Sham fight, Parliament Hill, Ottawa,
19 April 1906.

Pretoria Day celebrations, Yonge
Street, Toronto, 5 June 1901.
Torontonians filled the streets to
celebrate the first anniversary of
Lord Roberts's capture of Pretoria
from the Boers, 5 June 1900. The
Globe *scarcely noticed the celebra-*
tion, however, merely observing a
day later, on 6 June 1901, that "We
wish somebody would notify the
Boer leaders that in the columns of
the Globe *we declared the South*
African War closed a year ago." By
the spring of 1901 British and
Imperial troops occupied most of the
main cities but the Boers began
extensive and effective guerrilla
operations and the war dragged on
until the end of May 1902.

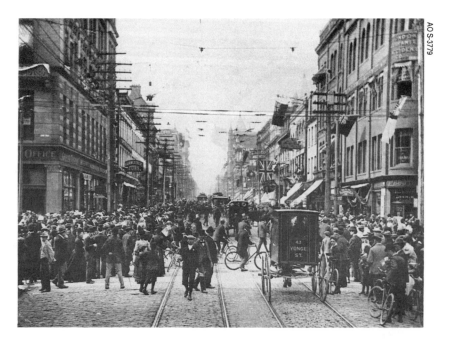

in Québec.

The Alaska boundary award of 1903 provided another time of testing. It was widely felt that under American pressures Britain had yielded Canadian interests. That shook Imperial federationists, but for most Ontarians it didn't really mean too much; they were pleased to bask in Britain's Imperial sunshine and enjoyed "the sense of power" that it gave to them. But Imperial entanglements were drawing Britain and her colonies, and Canada was still a colony in many ways, inexorably towards war.

Prime Minister Laurier, by 1909, found that the pressures of the European armaments race were intruding into Canadian affairs. Would Canada support Imperial naval efforts? Instead of a commitment to the Royal Navy, Laurier suggested the creation of a Canadian navy: four cruisers and six destroyers to form the core. His bill became law in 1910, but to no avail as the Liberals were defeated in the election of 1911. For the moment the issue was shelved. But the political lesson was clear. Laurier and his Liberals were defeated in Québec because he had gone too far with his naval act; in Ontario because he had not gone far enough. Besides, another issue had split the voters. Once again in 1911 the Liberals promoted the idea of reciprocity. But it was a different country from what it had been in the 1890s, and any commitment to reciprocity would have to be highly qualified and advanced by careful degrees. The National Policy, with its east-west axis, after a rocky start in the 1880s had proven to be a boon, especially during the Laurier years. Westerners might look for an escape from the tariffs that forced them to buy Eastern Canadian manufactures,

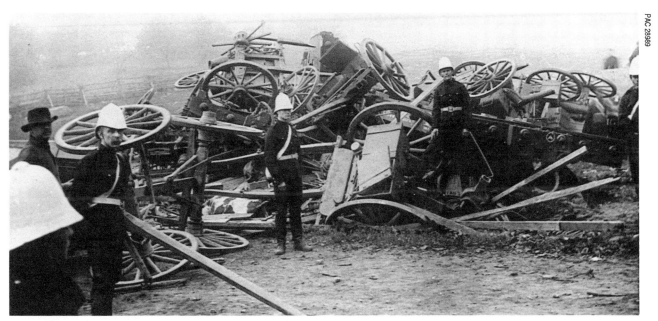

Artillery train wreck, Enterprise, Lennox and Addington County, 9 June 1903. Until Camp Petawawa was established in 1905 militia units held artillery practice every summer at Deseronto. Batteries usually brought their own equipment. The Globe *reported on the tenth of June 1903 that "the 11th and 16th Field Batteries, which were due [at Deseronto] to-day, [were] detained at Enterprise on the Bay of Quinte Railway by an accident, in which they lost a number of guns and a quantity of shells and baggage. One horse was killed and sixteen more or less seriously injured, two of which will have to be destroyed. The batteries will proceed to Deseronto from Enterprise to-morrow morning."*

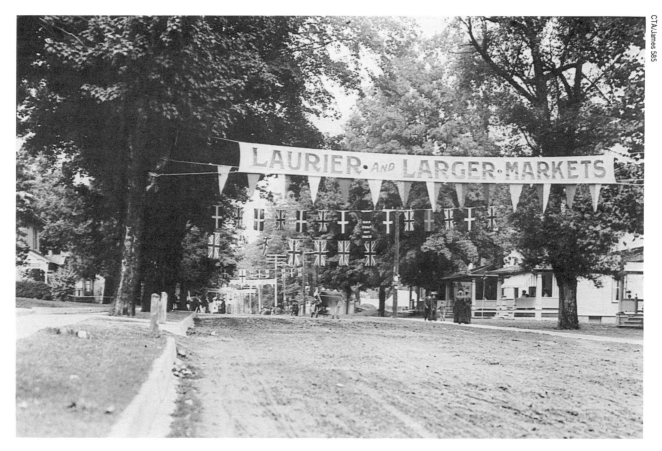

Simcoe, Norfolk County. Campaigning, 1911.

but Ontarians saw the "N.P." as their very bread and butter. Besides, the old saw was revived that reciprocity was the first step to domination by Americans – stout Ontarian hearts bridled at that suggestion.

The sounding of the old loyalty theme, however, was not the only explanation for Laurier's downfall. Sir James Whitney's superb Conservative political organization revealed much about the Tory win in Ontario. And almost a century after the War of 1812 anti-Americanism was definitely still alive in rural Ontario. Ontario farmers might have seen clear advantages from reciprocity in the marketing of their crops, but they were definitely anti-Yankee. And perhaps old-fashioned Ontario bigotry (admittedly in Loyalist clothing) had something to do with Laurier's downfall as well – the rout of Laurier meant the end of a Catholic French régime in Ottawa. In any case the federal results were clear enough in Ontario – seventy-three Tories elected as opposed to thirteen Liberals. The country, largely, followed suit.

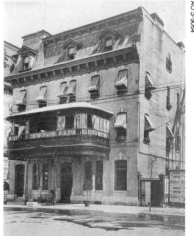

Rideau Club, Ottawa, 1906. The Rideau Club, haven for Canada's politicos, and directly across from the Parliament Buildings on Wellington Street, was incorporated in 1865. Among the charter members were Sir John A. Macdonald and Sir George-Etienne Cartier. There were many smoke-filled rooms.

The Liberal *Toronto Star* (whose circulation was and is the largest of any Ontario newspaper) had been a firm supporter of the Empire and Canada's careful nationalistic role within it throughout the period of the Boer War. But in 1903, when the Alaska boundary settlement gave advantage to the United States, the *Star* thundered "that Britain has an Empire she would protect only against weak aggressors." So the paper turned and became a skilful opponent both to Canadian contributions to an Imperial navy and to the creation of a Canadian navy. In the bitter federal election of 1911 the *Star* supported Laurier and reciprocity. It wasn't a question of loyalty or treason as Robert Borden's Conservatives shouted; rather, the *Star* explained patiently, it was a class issue – between "the privileged few and the unprivileged mass." More than words were necessary: the newspaper filled its front windows with foods bought in Toronto and Buffalo to show how reciprocity would mean lower prices for the average Ontarian. The rival *News*, a Tory evening paper, made the same effort and got precisely the opposite results.

Actually, food prices generally were (and have remained) higher in Ontario than in New York State, and the *Star* was accurate in its exhibition. Not that it helped the Liberals very much; the *Star*, although it remained a Liberal paper, never again advocated reciprocity.

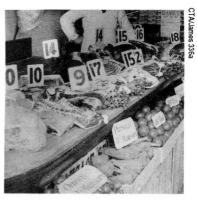

William Davies storefront, Queen Street West, between Bay and Yonge streets, Toronto, 1911. One of the first chain-stores in Canada.

Toronto Star *building, 1911.*

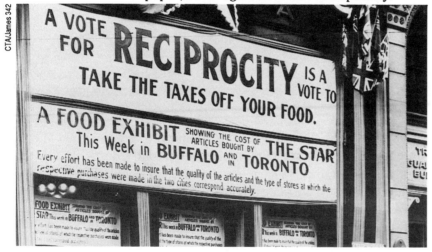

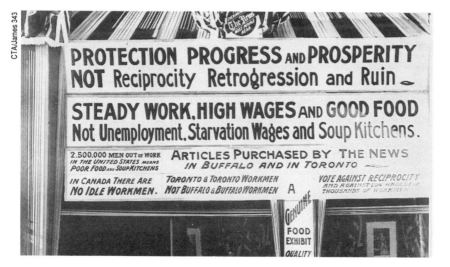

Toronto News *building, 1911.*

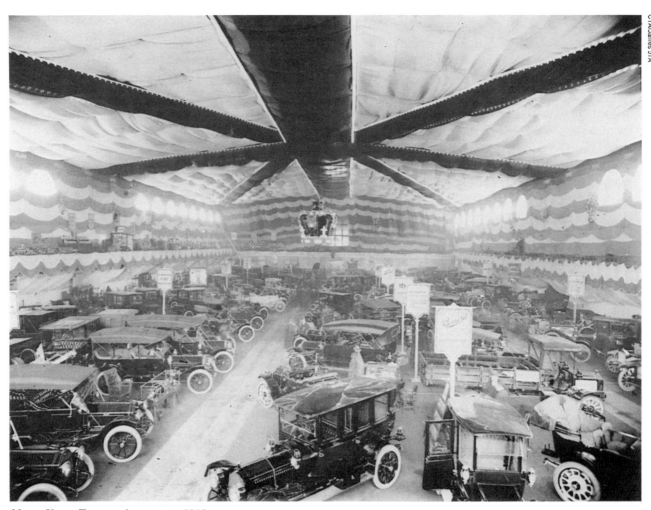

Motor Show, Toronto Armouries, 1912.

Ontarians began their love-hate relationship with the automobile be-fore 1900. The province's first motorist was John Moodie of Hamilton, who in 1898 imported a gasoline-fired Winton from the United States (and paid twenty-five per cent duty – charged on the basis that it was a locomotive). Moodie, who handed over $1,000 for the car, gained a substantial reputation for running tollgates. Occasionally he travelled to Toronto; one tedious puncture-filled trip took him eighteen hours.

Roads were the great enemies of the early automobile. Few were paved, and spring and fall brought traffic to a halt.

The province's first motor show was held in Toronto in 1906 and soon became an annual affair. The automobile by then had sponsored the growth or expansion of many related industries, and certainly was no longer considered a rich man's toy. It would not be until after the First World War, however, with the advent of the cheap production line, that the car would move within the grasp of nearly everyone and become a powerful agent for social change.

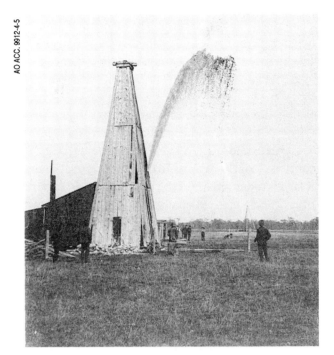

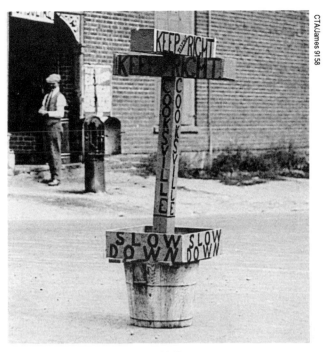

"Shooting an Oil Well," Lambton County, c. 1903.

Traffic indicator, Cooksville, 1912.

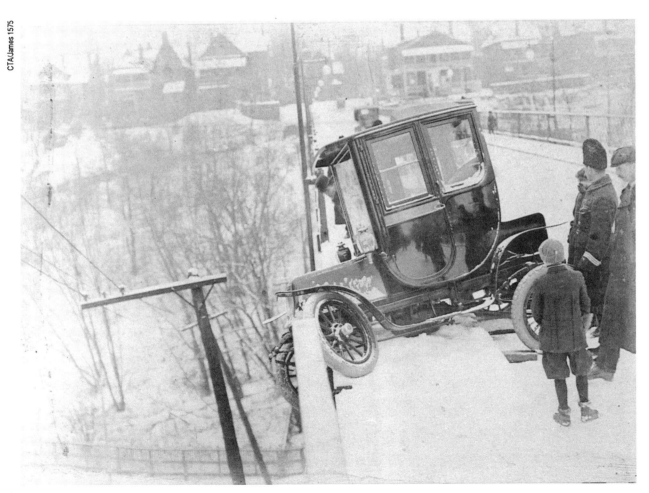

Electric car crash, Glen Road bridge, Toronto, 1912.

163

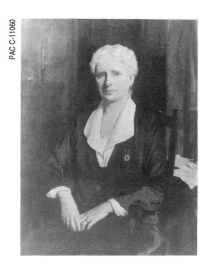

Mrs. Clark Murray, founder of the Imperial Order Daughters of the Empire (IODE). Motto: "One Flag, One Throne, One Empire."

The year 1912 was a suitable time for Ontarians to take stock of themselves. As fears of a general war grew in Europe, Ontario was at one and the same time intensely concerned, because of its Imperial connections, and detached, because of distance and an involvement with its own internal affairs – "progressive" politics and the exploitation of the north. The increasing influx of British immigrants to the province, however, in part the fruit of the Ontario government's massive immigration machinery, kept British ideas and events in the forefront.

It was also the centenary of the War of 1812, and a revival of pro-Imperial, anti-American sentiment marked the occasion. In October of that year, at Queenston Heights, a great celebration of the victory was held. James Hughes, a Department of Education inspector, used the occasion to wave the flag:

We should teach other lessons from the War of 1812. We should fill each child's life with a splendid courage that can never be dismayed, by telling how a few determined settlers scattered widely over a new country successfully repelled invading armies coming from a country with a population of twenty-fold larger. We should teach reverence not only for manhood but for womanhood by recounting the terrible hardships endured willingly by Canadian women generally, as well as by proudly relating the noble work done by individual women, of whom Laura Secord was so conspicuous an example.

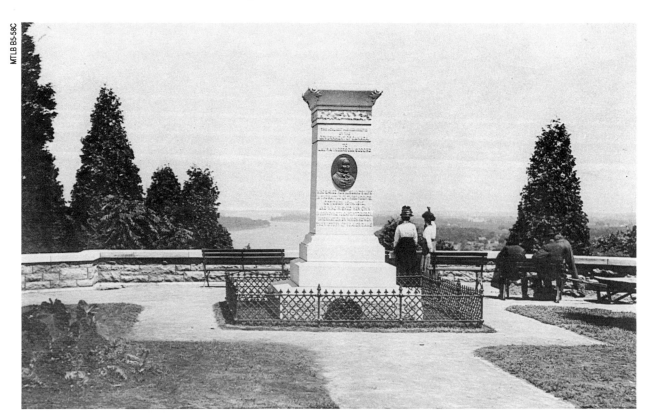

Laura Secord Monument, Queenston, c. 1912.

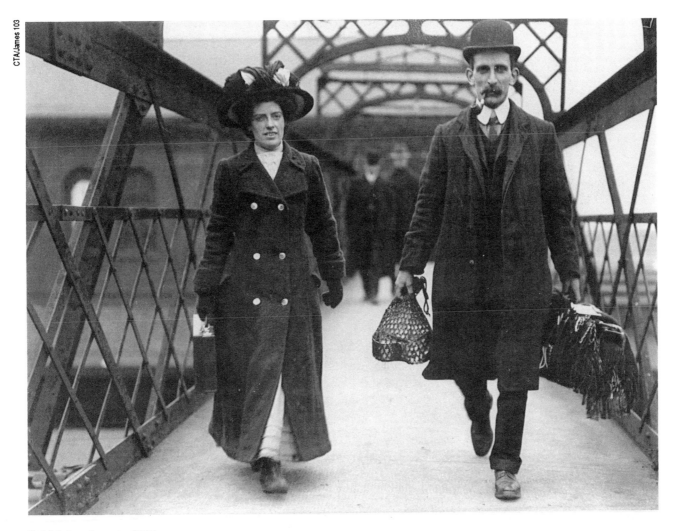

British immigrants, 1912.

A certain class of thoughtless people call us "flag-wavers" if we strive to give our young people a true conception of the value of national life, and of their duty to have a true love for their country and for their Empire. If a flag-waver means one who is proud of a noble ancestry, and determined to prove worthy of the race from which he sprung; one who knows that his forefathers gave a wider meaning to freedom, and who intends to perpetuate liberty and aid in giving it a still broader and higher value; one who is grateful because his Empire represents the grandest revelation of unity yet made known to humanity and who accepts this revelation as a sacred trust – then I am a flag-waver, and I shall make every boy and girl whom I can ever influence a flag-waver who loves his flag and waves it because it represents freedom, and honour, and justice, and truth, and unity, and a glorious history, the most triumphantly progressive that has been achieved by any nation in the development of the world.

Ontarians were moved by more than rhetoric to remember the provincial past; for some it didn't seem so long ago. Michael O'Neil, an Uxbridge blacksmith, was 104 years old in 1912. Most of Ontario's past was measured in his life-time:

Born:	1808
War of 1812:	4 years of age
Rideau Canal:	19 years
Rebellions:	29–30
Union of the Canadas:	32
Responsible Government:	41
Reciprocity:	46
Confederation:	59
Pacific Scandal:	64
John A. Macdonald's death:	83
Boer War:	91
Ontario Hydro:	100

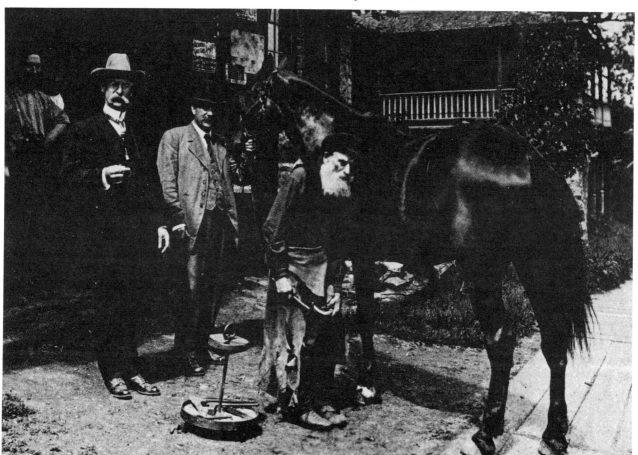

AO S-15404

Michael O'Neil's blacksmith's shop, Uxbridge, July 1912.

Some Ontarians, on the eve of the First World War, resisted as best they could the intrusion of the twentieth century with its motorcars, crowded cities, women's suffrage, and labour problems. They advised a return to a simpler life and celebrated the romance and virtues of small towns and the countryside. Ralph Connor, the novelist, published a string of emotional rural idylls, most notably *The Man from Glengarry* (1901) and *Glengarry Schooldays* (1902).These stories idealized rural life and emphasized the worth of the moral education which country living supposedly brought. The same lessons were being recommended elsewhere in the country by other writers: Lucy Maud Montgomery's *Anne of Green Gables* could have been set in Ontario rather than Prince Edward Island; in fact, Montgomery lived in Leaskdale, north of Uxbridge, for much of her life. Nellie McClung produced similar escapism for the prairies, for instance, in *Sowing Seeds in Danny.*

Stephen Leacock succeeded in sending up the whole genre and immortalizing it at one and the same time in his *Sunshine Sketches of a Little Town.* Leacock's book is an essential and hilarious primer for understanding Old Ontario, for although more and more Ontarians lived in large cities like Hamilton or London, their roots (and those of Leacock himself) were still locked in the countryside. He wrote in the preface:

> In regard to the present work I must disclaim at once all intention of trying to do anything so ridiculously easy as writing about a real place and real people. Mariposa is not a real town. On the contrary, it is about seventy or eighty of them . . .

> The inspiration of the book – a land of hope and sunshine where little towns spread their square streets and their trim maple trees beside placid lakes almost within echo of the primeval forest – is large enough. If it fails in its portrayal of the scenes and the country that it depicts the fault lies rather with an art that is deficient than in an affection that is wanting.

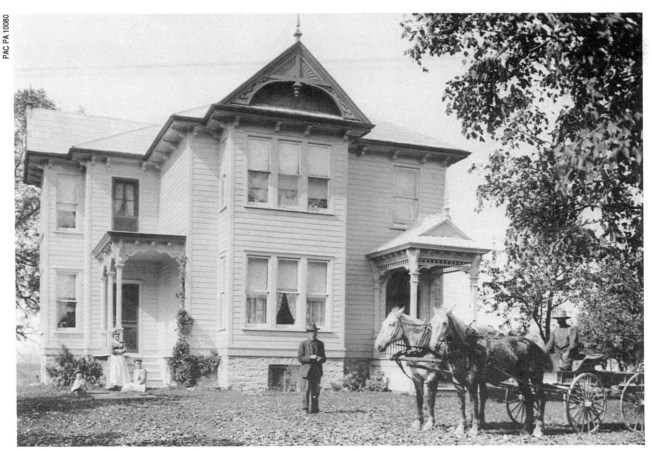

PAC PA 10080

Farmhouse, Prince Edward County, c. 1911.

*County road, southwestern Ontario,
c. 1901.*

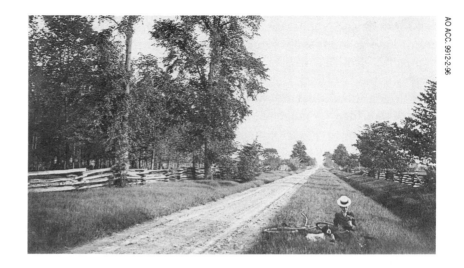

Tay Township, Simcoe County, 1908.

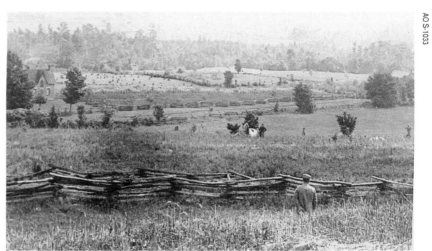

The Don Valley, near Toronto, 1906.

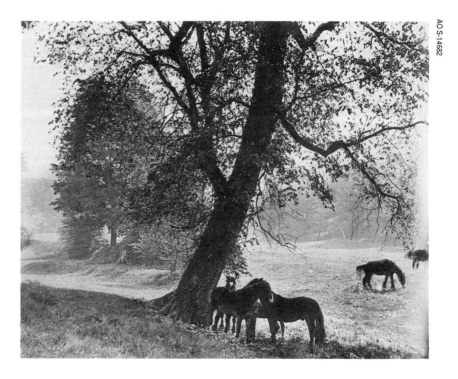

War 1914–18

The Civic Holiday weekend in August 1914 ended with the news that Great Britain and the Empire were at war. With a surge of patriotism people rallied to the flag, prompted at least in the larger towns by constant rallies, and the sudden appearance of militia units guarding public buildings, bridges, and "vulnerable" points. Men hastened to enlist, farmers soon doubled wheat production, donations poured in for equipment, supplies, and, later, relief, and before the month was out the government of Ontario gave half a million dollars to the Imperial War Fund.

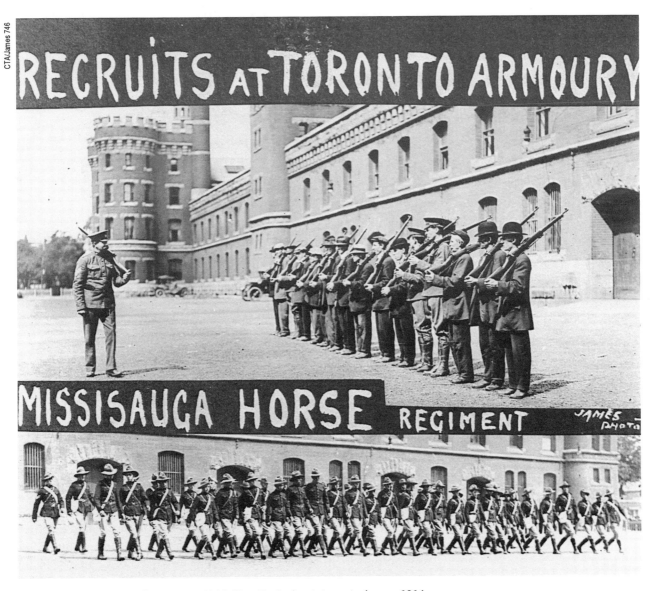

Recruits at the Toronto Armouries, 1914. Men flocked to join up in August 1914. Some were experienced in military service but most were not. Spectators crowded armoury galleries to view the drilling of raw recruits and cheered wildly at railroad stations as men entrained for the muster-camp at Valcartier, Québec. The first Canadian contingent was filled without the slightest trouble and was in fact over seventy per cent British-born.

169

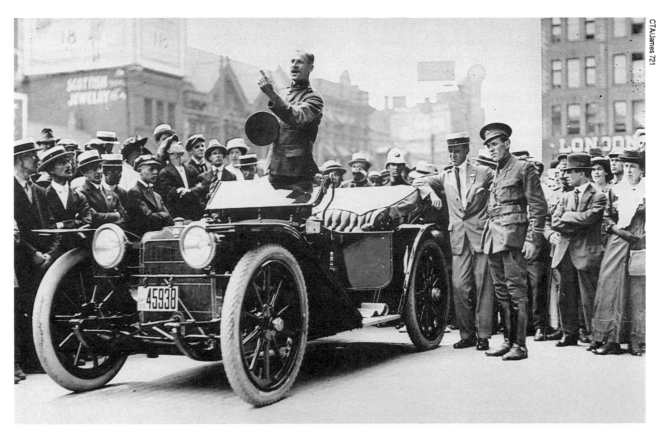

Recruiting: Mayor T.L. Church (straw hat) with J.W. Geddes and the Rev. J.D. Morrow, 1916.

By the end of the year, recruiting had slowed down as the realities of war spread across the front pages of newspapers. Bitterness against Ontario farmers for not encouraging their sons and labourers to join up erupted in headlines such as "Is rural Ontario losing its Imperial spirit? Must the stalwarts of the breezy uplands, the vigorous manhood of mountain and plain be branded as laggards in the Empire's shoulder-to-shoulder march to the trenches?" (*Globe*, 22 January 1915). The sobering news from Ypres and the sinking of the *Lusitania* in the spring of 1915 temporarily increased enlistment, but it soon fell off again. In desperation, that summer, the government permitted civilians to work on the recruiting campaigns and they took off with zest, frequently to the strains of songs such as "Why Aren't You in Khaki?", the official ditty of the Recruiting League.

Prohibitionists gained momentum during 1915 amid arguments that liquor would weaken the army's fibre and prolong the war. By November soldiers were forbidden to visit liquor stores, and in March 1916 a parade of ten thousand people in Toronto petitioned Premier Hearst with the chant: "Ontario will be dry by the first of July." Recruiting picked up again with astonishing strength. Another successful recruitment ploy was the "shaming" tactic, such as handing white feathers to young men wearing civilian clothes on the street. "Harvest leave" made enlistment attractive to rural men and lessened the manpower crisis somewhat. Meanwhile Ontario women and children went on stitching, bandage-rolling, and packing comfort parcels. In May an Ontario Organization of Resources Committee was hurriedly established to keep supplies coming and morale in high gear.

Nearly 190,000 Ontario men volunteered between 1914 and the introduction of conscription in the summer of 1917. Local tribunals set up under the Military Service Act were flooded with claims for draft exemptions, and the old urban-rural suspicions resurfaced as the tribunals seemed to favour the farmers. In reply to the calls for heightened food production, spring-grown crops were increased in acreage, and organizations and firms encouraged townspeople to join the harvest and thereby lessen the drain on labour forced by compulsory military service. Shortages in food, power, and war supplies were common by the end of 1917; in the following spring a campaign called "Soldiers of the Soil" signed up 16,700 Ontario boys to work on the farms. Food prices soared and it looked as if 1918 would be every bit as bad as 1917. To make matters worse, an influenza epidemic struck down thousands of people towards the fall of 1918 and killed at least five thousand by November. But on 11 November the Great War was over and armistice declared.

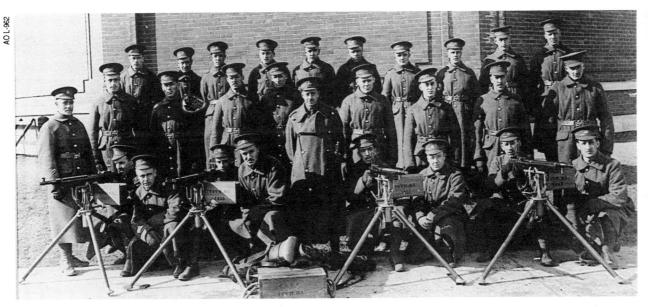

A platoon of the 19th Battalion, Canadian Expeditionary Force, c. 1915.

Returning soldiers were a severe social and economic problem, as well as a medical one. Often crippled or disabled from gas poisoning or shelling, Ontario's soldiers came back to tightened belts and scarce jobs. It wasn't until the relative boom of the 1920s that this typical war-induced situation was relieved. The social upset of those four brutal years had a remarkable effect on Ontario women as well. In the first months women generally backed the war effort and packed their husbands and sons to the front; until 1916 wives had to give permission before their husbands could go. Fairly quickly, women moved into the labour force, picking up service jobs vacated by men or working in the munitions factories. The suffragettes still hung tightly to their principle of getting women the right to vote, while supporting the war effort without question, and to their astonishment (and many others, too) Premier Hearst introduced a suffrage bill in early 1917 which passed without hitch. This abrupt reversal of the Ontario government's position on female suffrage greatly eased tensions and encouraged support for the great thrift and conservation campaigns begun later in the year. Even the starchy *Globe* expressed its admiration for women's part in the war and admitted that "during this period of testing the Canadian women have developed a capacity for leadership and for organization which has set the pace for men."

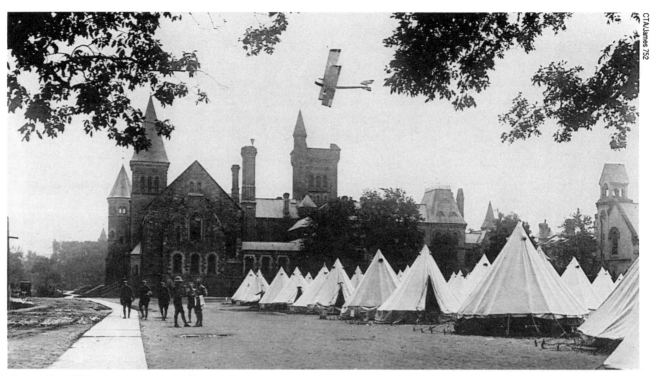

CTA/James 752

University of Toronto at war, c. 1915.

The provincial university, Toronto, leapt swiftly into war support. A Canadian Officers Training Corps (COTC) was started in October 1914 and nearly two thousand men were drilling on campus twice a week by the end of the fall term. Many students left Ontario with university-sponsored hospital units, artillery batteries, or the Canadian University Company which had been established to reinforce Princess Patricia's Canadian Light Infantry. Universities and colleges – notably Toronto, Ottawa, Queen's and Western – granted special annual credits to volunteers. Most of the faculty were caught up in related work. At the University of Toronto, instruction was given to Royal Flying Corps cadets at a special campus training centre and a clinic was set up to treat neurological injury. Connaught Laboratories, the university's research centre in drug production, generated supplies of antitoxins and serums.

At the outbreak of war the Ontario government gave fifteen thousand dollars to the Belgian Relief Fund. By 1918 that sum had grown to three million, mostly in carloads of foodstuffs. The Red Cross ambulance from Fort Frances was one such gift to the Fund. Ontario was very generous to other funds, including the relief fund after the disastrous explosion at Halifax, N.S., in 1917.

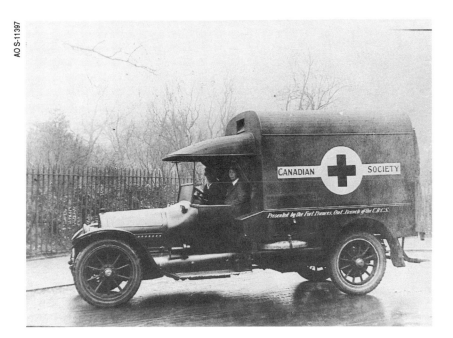

Fort Frances gives to Belgium, c. 1915.

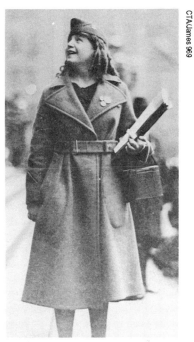

Kathleen Herbert selling bonds outside Toronto City Hall, 1915.

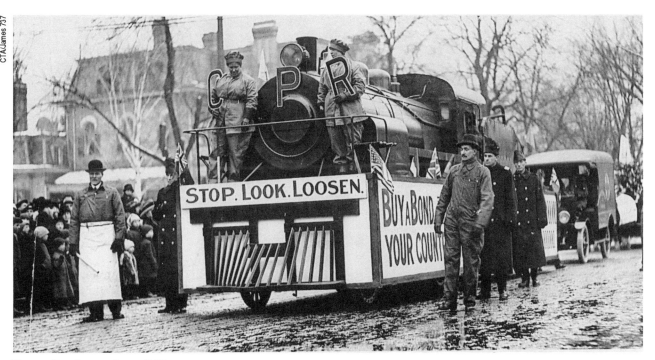

Victory Bonds parade, c. 1915.

173

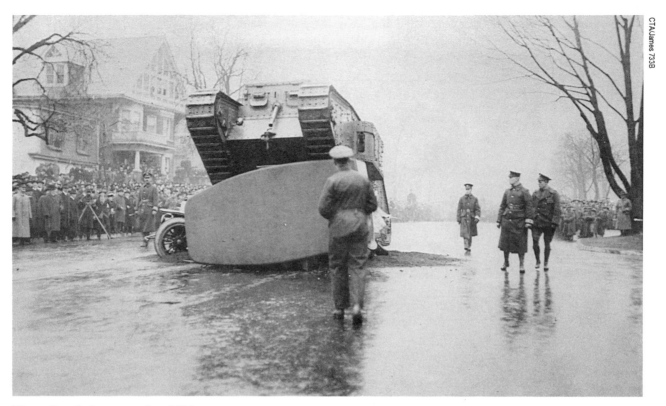

Victory Bonds demonstration, 1916.

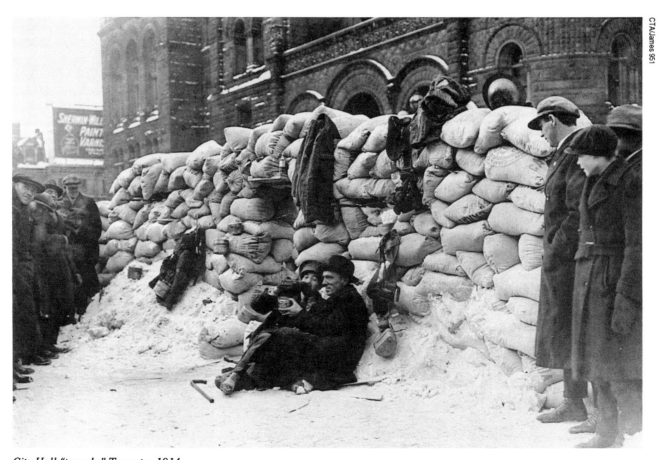

City Hall "trench," Toronto, 1914.

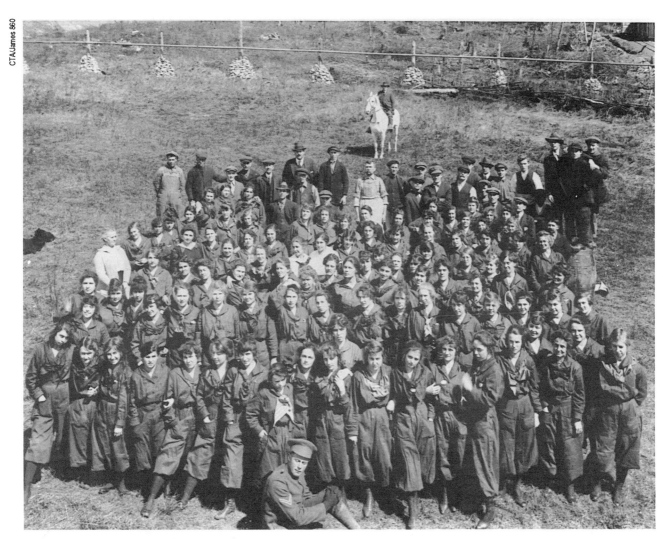

Women workers at Nobel Cordite plant, 1915.

For Canadian national unity the war years were catastrophic, and Ontario was responsible for much of the division. When war broke out, however, the unity question did not appear significant. Canadians marched off together – even Henri Bourassa, the French-Canadian nationalist leader, argued for loyal support of Britain.

Appearance was not reality. English Canadians, especially Ontarians, soon began to feel they were shouldering the major burden of the war. Specifically, Ontario complained that low French-Canadian enlistment figures were helping to prolong the conflict. In Québec, Bourassa now argued that the war effort was putting British interests ahead of Canadian ones. By late 1916 he had turned violently against the war, and reminded the readers of his influential Montréal paper, *Le Devoir,* of certain simmering, unresolved racial issues like Regulation 17 of the Department of Education in Ontario (which since 1912 had limited the teaching of French in schools), and the continuing shabby treatment of French-speaking troops – why, he asked, did supposedly bilingual Canada have an army that spoke and fought only in English?

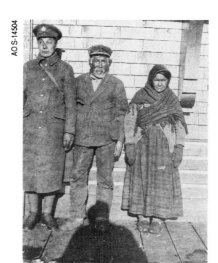

Jimmy Oscheckimick with his parents, Biscotasing, 1917. As wards of the Crown, Indians were not at first considered eligible for enlistment. Nevertheless, thirty-five per cent of military-age Indian males did get into the army. With the exception of the Six Nations, who believed their allegiance was directly to the King and not through the Canadian government, most Indian bands participated, some even financially. In January 1918 an order-in-council specifically exempted Indians from combatant military service.

Meanwhile, conscription became the issue of the day as it became increasingly apparent that more and more men were needed at the front. Prime Minister Robert Borden returned in 1917 from a meeting of the Imperial War Cabinet absolutely convinced that compulsory military service must be driven through if the war were to be won – and despite the bitterness it would provoke amongst French Canadians.

He was convinced as well that a coalition government, a Union government as he called it, must be created to represent all Canada in the struggle. Not all Liberals – and particularly not those in Québec, who included Sir Wilfrid Laurier, the leader of the Opposition – were convinced of either of these needs. As it turned out, the federal election of 1917 was the most bitter and racist poll in Canadian history. Laurier's Liberals were abandoned by their western and Ontario divisions, who flocked to the Unionist banner. Further, in Ontario, promotional groups like the Citizens' Union Committee vigorously campaigned for the Borden position, shouting along with the Toronto *News* and the *Mail and Empire* that a vote for Laurier would be a vote against Ontario's fighting men and the British Empire and in favour of Germany and the Kaiser. The wounds of Québec could not heal in this climate. Borden and the Unionists, through the devices of the Military Voters and Wartime Elections acts (which provided votes for servicemen and their close female relatives) skipped to a landslide victory – everywhere but in Québec. French Canada was left isolated and Liberal, and with another grievance against the English to add to a long list.

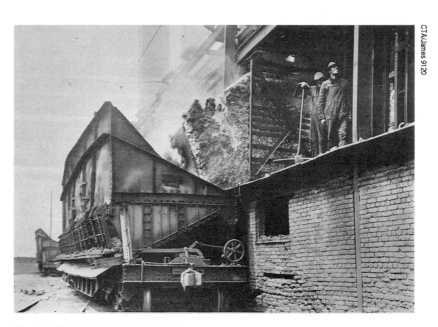

Steel mill, Sault Ste. Marie, 1916.

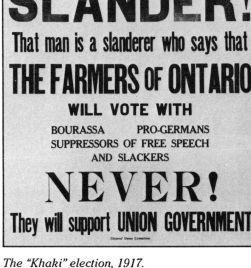

SLANDER!

That man is a slanderer who says that

THE FARMERS OF ONTARIO

WILL VOTE WITH

BOURASSA   PRO-GERMANS
SUPPRESSORS OF FREE SPEECH
AND SLACKERS

NEVER!

They will support UNION GOVERNMENT

Citizens' Union Committee

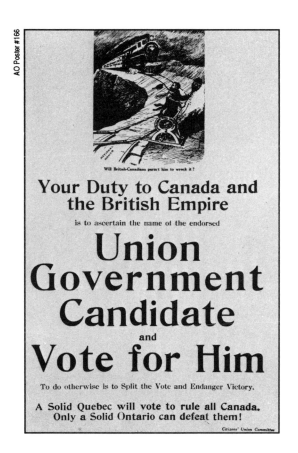

Will British-Canadians permit him to wreck it?

Your Duty to Canada and the British Empire

is to ascertain the name of the endorsed

Union Government Candidate

and

Vote for Him

To do otherwise is to Split the Vote and Endanger Victory.

A Solid Quebec will vote to rule all Canada. Only a Solid Ontario can defeat them!

Citizens' Union Committee

The "Khaki" election, 1917.

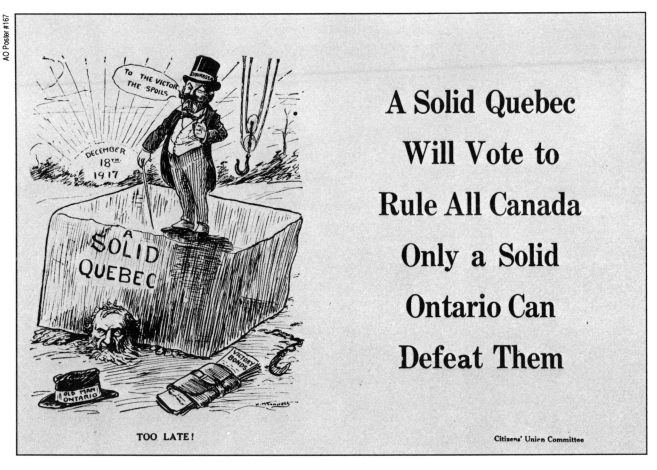

A Solid Quebec Will Vote to Rule All Canada Only a Solid Ontario Can Defeat Them

Citizens' Union Committee

Dominion experimental farm,
Ottawa, n.d.

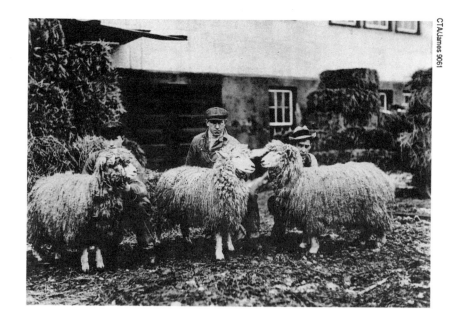

"The man who enlists to go to the front is making the supreme sacrifice that it is possible for a man to make. He is offering his life for his country. The man who is eligible to give similar service but feels that his call to duty is to stay at home and help his country with increased products should also be prepared to make many and great sacrifices. He is not offering his life and therefore should not stint in offering his means. If the young men who avoid military service do so because they think that during war times farming will yield them quick profit they must expect to take their profits with a share of public contempt."

Peter McArthur in the Toronto *Globe*, 30 January 1915.

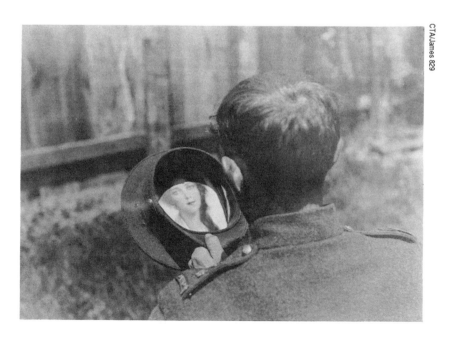

"While the downfall of Kaiserism was being signalized by the people of Germany in red revolution, the glorious victory of Liberty and Right was being celebrated by one hundred thousand Canadians in a solemn service of Thanksgiving in Queen's Park yesterday afternoon. There in the heart of a great city on the shores of Lake Ontario the throbbing heart of Canada's wide Dominion was focused. The soul of the high cause for which the civilized world had been contending for four fighting years."

Toronto *Globe*, 11 November 1918.

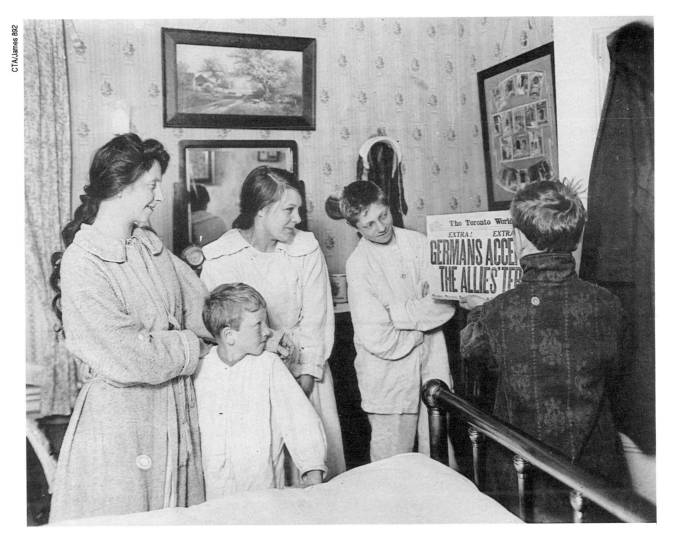

Armistice, 1918.

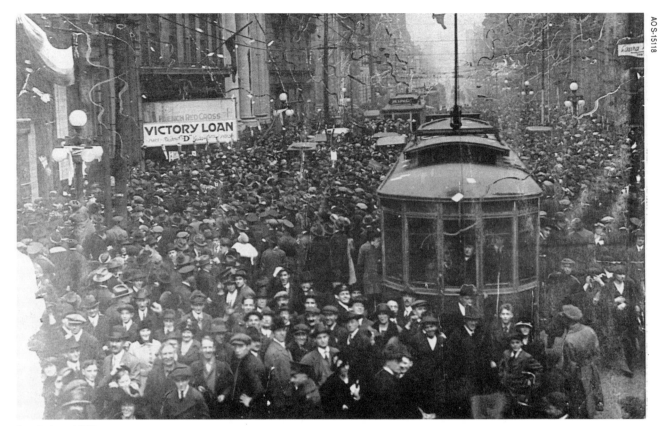

Armistice, 1918.

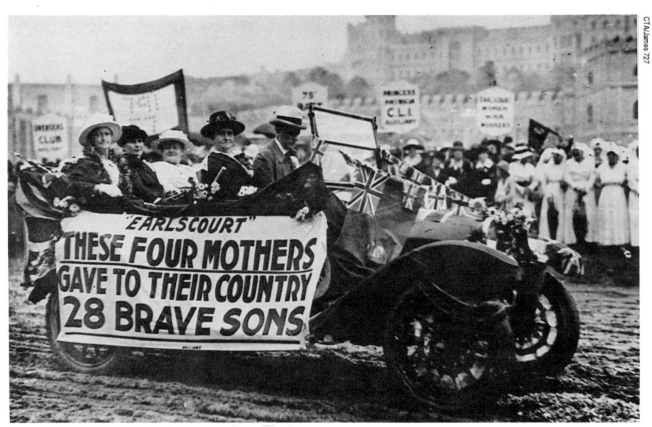

Warriors' Day parade, Canadian National Exhibition, 1920.

Ontario emerged from the First World War much sobered by the conflict's length, its losses, and its revolutionary effect on society. When the inevitable problem of "returned soldiers" and their employment loomed, the very basis of Ontario's livelihood was questioned. No longer would it be possible, for example, to accept as sacrosanct the capitalist economic system. Already the conscription issue had severely inflamed feelings of munitions workers who had declared through the Trades and Labour Congress that they would not be sent to the front to protect profiteers and tricky politicians. By 1918, the Industrial Workers of the World, the "Wobblies," with their cry for the One Big Union, were bringing about frequent strikes in coal fields and lumber camps as worker solidarity and Marxist literature and oratory made themselves felt. Men who before the war never would have challenged the prime source of their daily bread were emboldened to declare their newfound strength publicly. Nevertheless, just as Ontario had been distinctly unsettled (at times malevolent) towards German residents during the war, when the Communist "red scare" raised its head in the United States in 1919 shadows of revolutionary fear were cast across the border to highlight post-war labour unrest, inflamed by the lack of jobs and steeply rising prices.

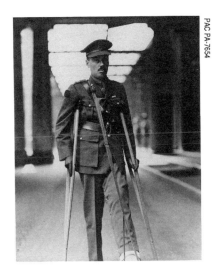

Returning soldier, Lieutenant G.H. Ferguson, M.C., 1918.

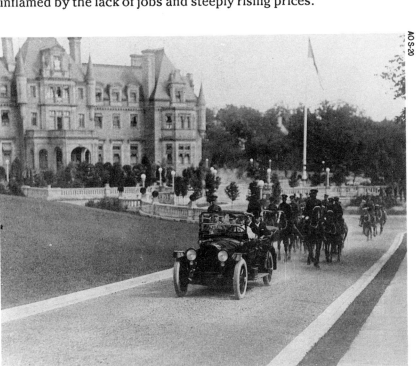

The war had been over for less than a year when HRH Edward, Prince of Wales, visited Canada. Imperial sentiment, understandably, had waned somewhat when the costs of Imperial warfare were reckoned. But the young Prince saw a tumultuous turnout in Toronto; the occasion being less one of royalty than the glamour of an attractive, eligible young heir. The Prince is seen here on the morning of 25 August 1919 leaving Chorley Park, the baronial home of the lieutenant-governor (then Sir John Hendrie), escorted by a detachment of Royal Canadian Dragoons.

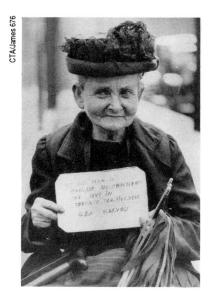

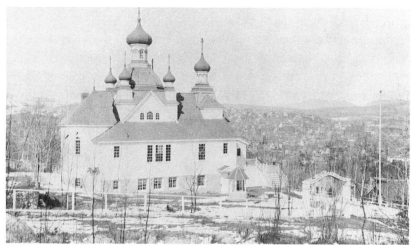

Above: *Russian Orthodox church, Kitchener, 1922.*
Left: *Woman selling pencils, 1918.*
Below: *Demonstration at Queen's Park, 1919.*

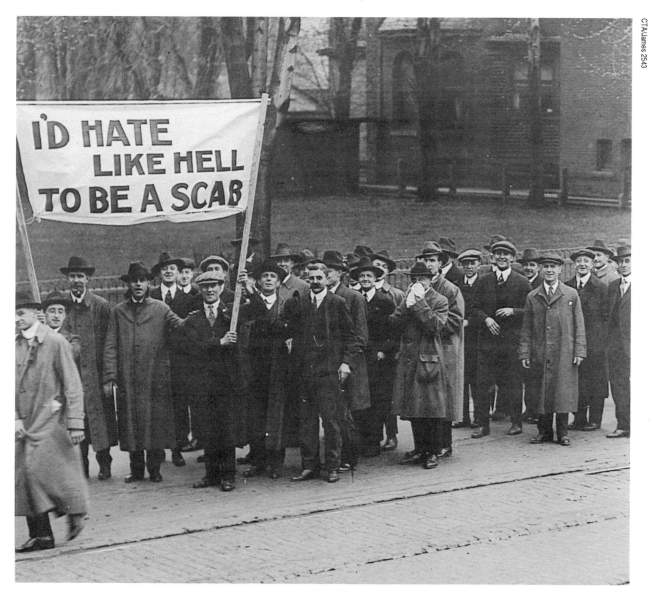

Keeping Them Down on the Farm

"Everything a farmer does," Sir Andrew Macphail told the Empire Club in 1920, "is done in his spare time." Canadian farmers must have had plenty of leisure after the First World War because they seem to have given up the plough for politics. Three Canadian provinces, Manitoba, Alberta, and Ontario, had farmer governments in the early 1920s, and the impact of the rural revolt at the federal level was just beginning to be felt.

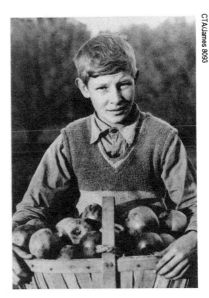

Sir William Hearst's "Progressive" Conservatives had survived the war intact; they expected no substantial difficulty in the 1919 provincial election. The Liberals were badly split after the "Khaki" vote of 1917, and the only other challengers were farmer and labour candidates. Farm organizations had never been a successful political force in Ontario and there was little reason to think the U.F.O. (the United Farmers of Ontario, an umbrella group organized in 1914) would be any different. The war, however, had pushed farmers too far. Not only the armed forces but industry as well gobbled up manpower, and the shift of young men and women from country to city was greatly accelerated from 1914 to 1918. Besides, farmers realized they were a waning power in the province's economy and government. In 1919, however, they were in a strong position to strike a conclusive blow at the Tories. Sir William Hearst, the Tory leader, was an amiable, agreeable man but

From Sir William Mulock's orchard, Aurora, n.d.

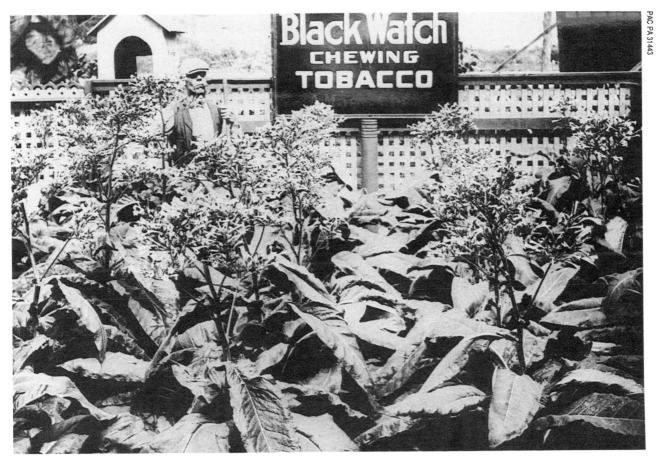

Tobacco, Leamington, 1923.

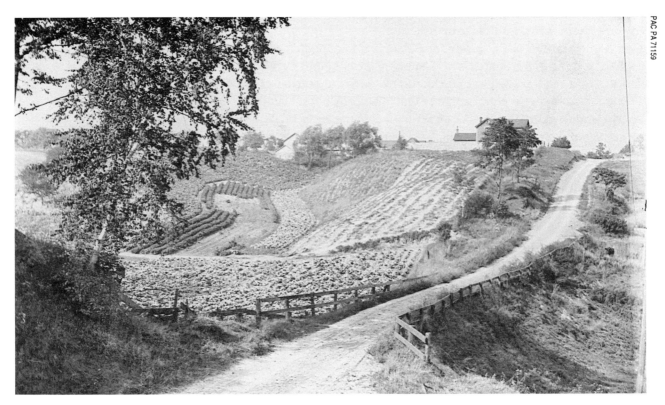

Humber River area, 1918.

he failed to keep the party machinery effectively oiled throughout the war. The results were not exactly decisive but close enough. When the votes were counted no party had won a clear majority, but the U.F.O. had more seats than any other. The Toronto *Globe* was astonished: "In 1905," the front-page story ran, "Ontario witnessed a political upheaval. Today she experiences a political revolution. At an early hour this morning [21 October 1919] the returns indicate that the coalition of Agriculture and Labour hold the largest representation in the new Legislature. In urban centres Labour made remarkable gains. In rural districts Agriculture all but swept the boards." Even the Liberals had done better than anyone had expected – they placed second.

And so the U.F.O., which had a president but not a leader, was called upon to form a government. E.C. Drury changed hats, stepped down as president and became leader; he then scrambled to attract Labour and Liberal members to support his government.

AO ACC 2120 0437-17

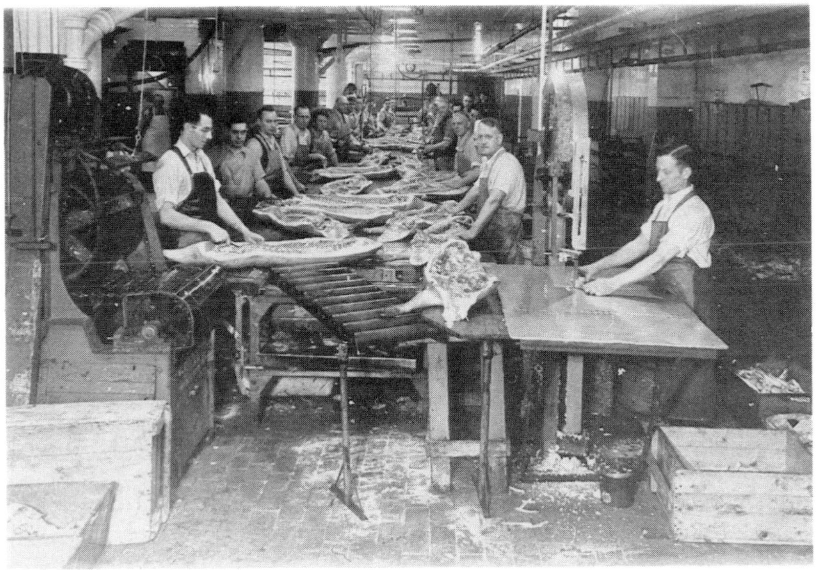

That government, when it was finally fashioned, cannot be viewed as a great success. It was honest government, cheap government, enthusiastic government, but woefully inexperienced. No one in the organization had ever held office before. A substantial number of reforms were made, however. Government in Canada before the war had been much concerned to grapple with the problems of opening the country, to the detriment of social-welfare issues. In Ontario the crusade had been to open the North and tap its vast wealth. The Drury government moved closer to home. A minimum-wage board was established, mothers' allowances extended, and party patronage abandoned; emphasis was laid on developing local roads rather than grand thoroughfares, and a determined effort was made to enforce the restrictions of the Ontario Temperance Act of 1916. Arthur Meighen, the federal Tory leader, called the Druryites "Bolshevists."

PA C-12112

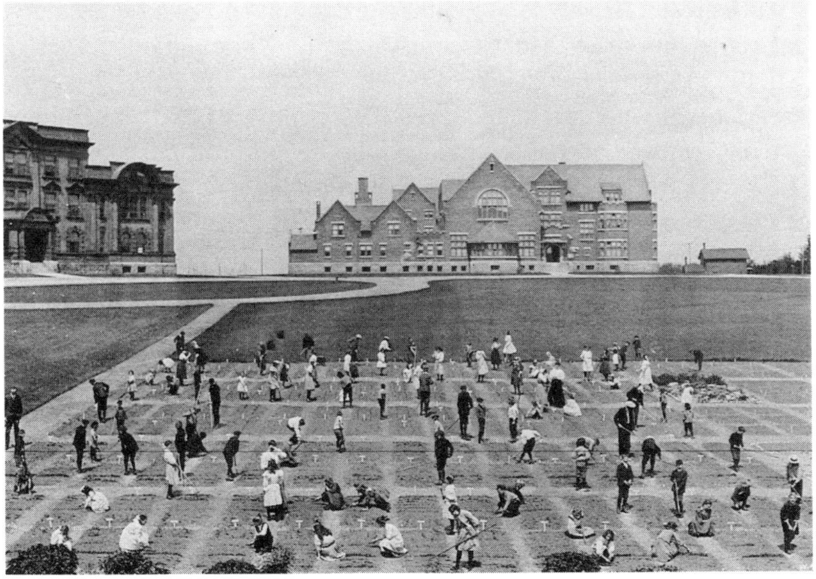

Garden plots, Consolidated Schools, Guelph. c. 1920.

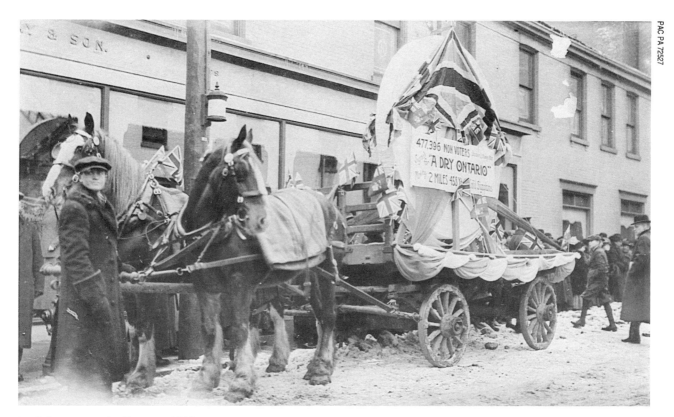

477,396 NON VOTERS
"A DRY ONTARIO"
2 MILES 458 Yd.

Prohibition parade, Toronto, 1916.

W.E. Raney, Drury's hard-working attorney-general, certainly was no Bolshevik. He was committed passionately to the politics of moral "uplift" and was unyielding in his efforts to cleanse Ontario of alcoholic infection. But his zealous efforts and heavy-handedness created much adverse publicity, and suggested to the public that the U.F.O. government was much more radical than it actually was. In any case, as the 1923 election loomed, it became increasingly evident that the U.F.O. was badly fragmented. J.J. Morrison, the secretary, argued vigorously against Drury that the party should retreat to being a rural pressure group. He refused to enter the cabinet and as a result much grass-roots support was lost among the farming population.

In the election of 1923 it became obvious that the Tories had corrected Sir William Hearst's mistakes. The provincial party machinery had been restored and was running smoothly under the leadership of G. Howard Ferguson – unlike Drury, a politician's politician. The Tories swept the province.

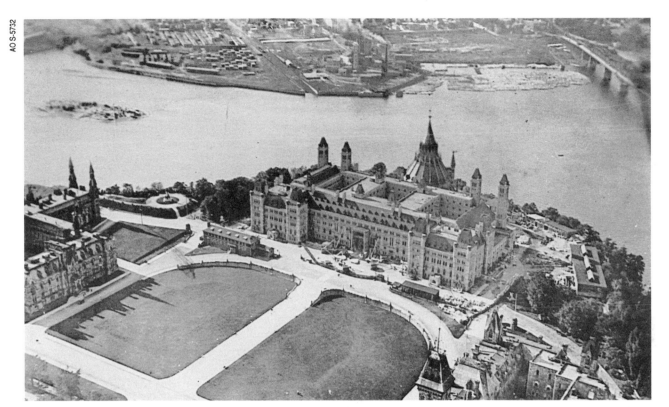

Parliament without the Peace Tower, Ottawa, 1920.

Back to Normal?

"Nation-building" had been a prime concern of the Dominion government before the First World War. During the Laurier years a new definition for Canada was made in terms of the national wheat economy and the seemingly never-ending stretches of prairie land to be taken up, peopled, railroaded, and marketed. During the war Canadians became used to a strong federal government directing the war effort, but afterwards it seemed that the federal government had moved into eclipse. National objectives had largely been filled, and in any case the war had savaged federal fortunes regarding unity with the alienation of Québec following the conscription crisis. The federal election of 1921 brought Ontario's Mackenzie King and his Liberals a nominal majority only, and westerners, through their endorsement of the maverick Progressive party, openly challenged the National Policy specifically and other national policies in general.

The 1920s and 1930s were a period of provincial ascendancy in Canada. One of the prime reasons for this was that Canadians were anxious, after having fought a war to make the world safe for democracy, to enjoy some of its advantages. New

social policies were demanded and according to the B.N.A. Act, social and government services were largely the constitutional concerns of the provinces. The only substantial federal foray into social assistance was the government's financial support for old-age pension schemes.

So it fell to the provinces to serve public welfare by building more hospitals, assuring community assistance, developing public utilities, constructing new highways, and extending education. But how was it all to be paid for? New services meant that provinces and municipalities had to find $173 million more in 1930 than they had in 1921. The chief sources would be massive provincial taxes on some of the very items the provinces were making desirable – revenues swelled as taxes poured in from liquor control, automobile licences, and gasoline. The danger was that these were luxury, or at least "semi-luxury," items. If the demand for them dried up in a recession or depression, where would revenues come from? And the problem was all the greater because in a recession social services would be all the more necessary.

G. Howard Ferguson's success as premier is not difficult to explain. He spoke with the voice of Old

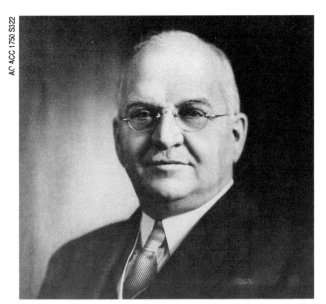

G. Howard Ferguson.

Ontario: Orange Protestant, British, stable, and rural. Besides, unlike Sir William Hearst, he spoke loudly and authoritatively, and was backed by a fine party organization to guarantee that he would be heard. He was also lucky. The 1920s were a time of open prosperity in Ontario and Canada. Also, political opposition in the province had been routed; farmers, Liberals, and labour were all too weak to pose any threat and too disorganized to form any coalition.

Ferguson is a kind of colossus in Ontario political history. Although he had one foot firmly entrenched in the old Tory past, another found less certain footing in the modern province. Ferguson believed in making government run like a business, and the civil service and administration were both made to conform with business structures, to the detriment of the power of individual MPPs (which in the past had been considerable). During Ferguson's premiership social problems were addressed. But frequently the answers that were found were technological – the rule of the experts had begun.

Ferguson also inherited and practised a good grass-roots politician's feel for his electors – as had Mowat before him. Ferguson was closely attuned to what people wanted, and he gave it to them with verve. In 1927 the old wartime Ontario Temperance Act gave way to the Liquor Control Act. Ontario was now effectively "wet," but control of sales and distribution was tightly held by the government.

Ferguson also renewed the province's interest in northern development, and Ontario mining stocks played a large role in the stock-market boom of the 1920s. And the Twenties did roar in Ontario, as they did everywhere else in North America. Airplanes, radios, cars for everyone, movie stars, beauty contests, flappers, and "razzle-dazzle" journalism enraged the older generation, who felt that the very fibre of Christian society was threatened. Where, they asked, would it all end?

Consistency for Ferguson took second place to opportunity. In his backbench days he had been a major force behind the adoption of Regulation 17, the restrictive legislation adopted in 1912 against the use of French in Ontario schools. He had reiterated his position, but with an Imperial tone, in 1916:

> This bilingual question is the greatest of the issues before us. It entirely overshadows nickel and booze and every other question. It touches the vitals of our province and our Dominion. If it is not dealt with the whole national fabric will be destroyed. The government I represent upholds British traditions, British institutions and one flag and one language for this Dominion. Unless something is done to meet this French-speaking invasion, this national outrage, this Dominion will be stricken to its foundation as this war has not stricken it.

These were strong words, and the conviction was seemingly strong too, but by 1925 Ferguson sensed that a compromise was necessary to mollify important Catholic (and French) opinion. He even persuaded the Orange Order that compromise was desirable. So he argued just the reverse of what he had said in 1911, 1912, 1916, and 1917. And the sweet talk worked. Regulation 17 was quickly watered down and Ferguson was readily applauded throughout the country as a great unifier. At the same time, realizing the opportunities the times offered, he took a strong provincial-rights stand against Ottawa which, if not making him a unifier in the way Sir John A. Macdonald had wanted, certainly brought him closer to the other provinces, especially Québec.

By the late 1920s, moreover, it was clear that Liberalism in Ottawa was likely to go the way of Liberalism in Ontario. When R.B. Bennett's Tories formed the federal government in 1930, Ferguson accepted the post of high commissioner to Britain, and the Ontario premiership, plus the growing Depression, was passed to "Honest" George Henry. He quickly demonstrated that he hadn't the showy talents of a Ferguson.

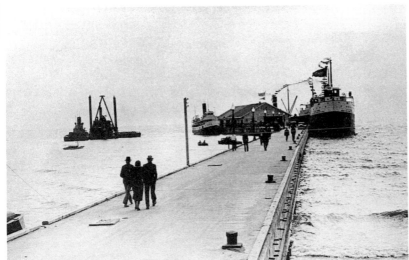

S.S. City of Windsor *and sisters, probably at Windsor, c. 1931.*

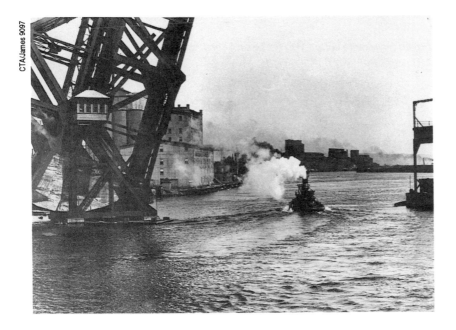

The Bascule bridge, Fort William, c. 1916.

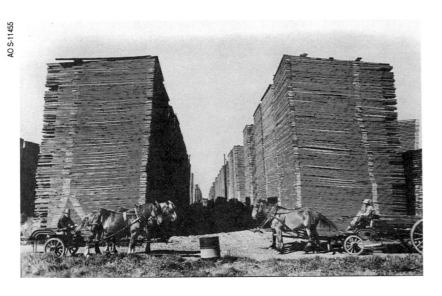

Shevlin-Clarke lumberyard, Fort Frances, c. 1920. Shevlin-Clarke was one of two Minneapolis groups of lumber manufacturers who had acquired extensive pine limits in northern Minnesota and in Ontario along the border lakes. Its mill was the largest in Fort Frances.

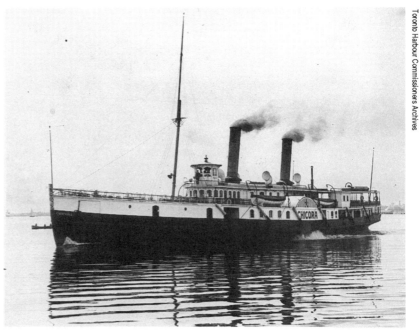

S.S. Chicora, *on Lake Ontario, n.d. The* Chicora, *a regular sight on the Toronto-Niagara route at the turn of the century, had one of the most swashbuckling histories of any vessel on the Great Lakes. Built in Liverpool, England, in 1864 as the* Let Her B, *she cut her teeth gun running between the Bahamas, Bermuda, and Confederate ports in the American Civil War. Subsequently sold to a firm in Pictou, N.S., she was brought in two pieces (to get her through the St. Lawrence canals) to the Great Lakes as the* Chicora *in 1868. Reassembled, she took Sir Garnet Wolseley's Red River Expedition from Collingwood to Fort William during the Riel Rebellion. In 1874, the governor general, Lord Dufferin, used the* Chicora *to tour the Great Lakes, after which the ship fell into disuse at Owen Sound. The Niagara Navigation Company started her up once again in 1878 to work the Toronto-Niagara run. There she stayed until her engines collapsed en route to Niagara in 1911. Not yet finished,* Chicora's *hull was pre-*served as a barge called* Warrenko *and carried coal in Kingston harbour until a freighter rammed and sank her in 1942.*

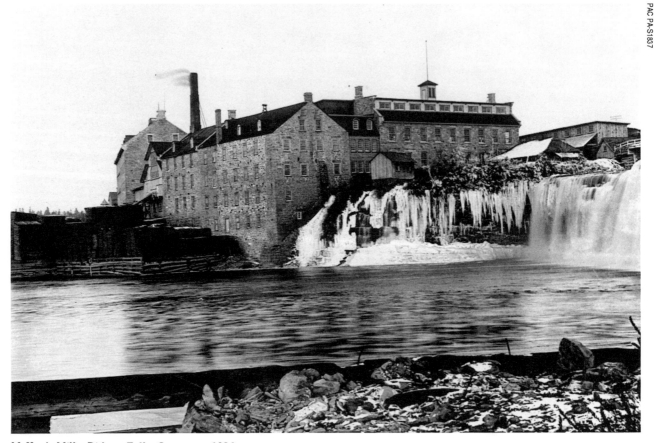

McKay's Mills, Rideau Falls, Ottawa, c. 1921.

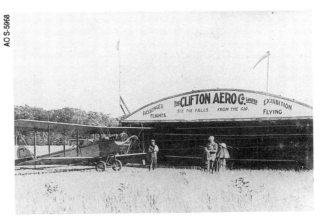

Radio pavilion, Canadian National Exhibition, 1920.

Clifton Aero Company, Chippawa, c. 1920. "Seeing the Falls" from the air fast became a steady attraction at Niagara in the early days of flying. Despite its undeniable excitement, a jaunt over the Falls was a long shot from the remarkable bush flying in Ontario's north where remote mining and lumber camps and newly instituted forest-fire patrols demanded aerial skills of the highest calibre. Not surprisingly, a good many bush and stunt pilots were First World War veterans.

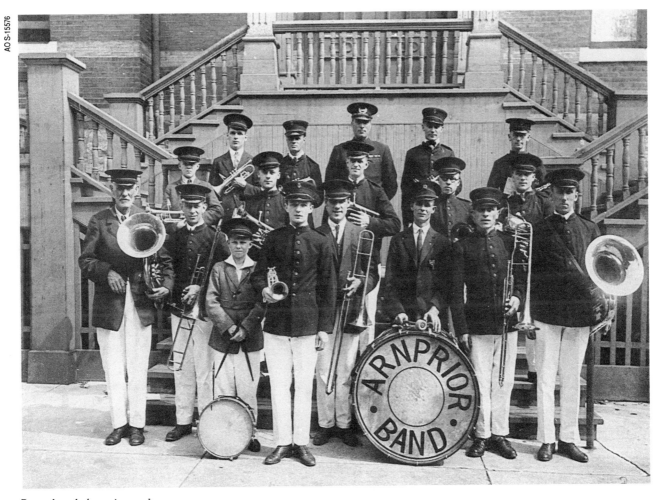

Brass band, Arnprior, n.d.

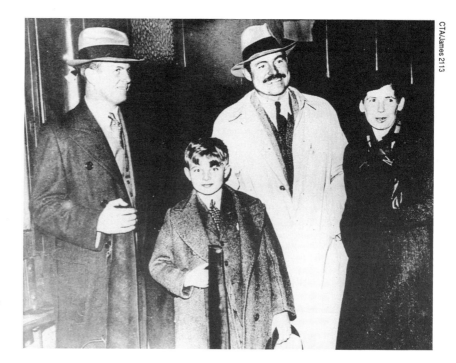

Ernest Hemingway and family, Toronto, c. 1923. Hemingway worked for a number of years for the Toronto Star *both in Toronto and in Europe as a roving correspondent. He didn't like the city very much, and appears to have liked newspaper work even less. He once told Toronto journalists that the trouble with newspapers was that "always the questions are who, where, when, how, but never why, which is the most important question of all."*

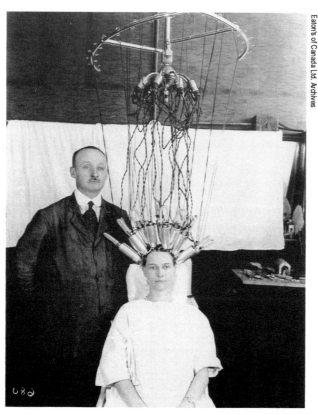

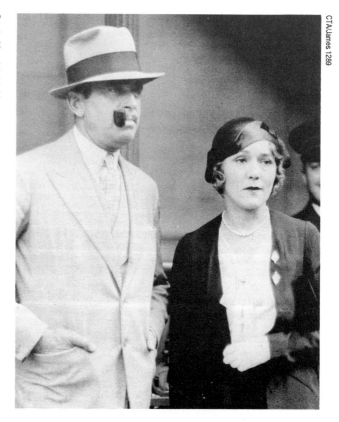

Ontario's "New woman," July 1920. The permanent wave in the T. Eaton Company beauty salon.

Mary Pickford (born Gladys Smith) and her husband, Douglas Fairbanks, visit her birthplace, Toronto, 1930. Pickford – "The world's sweetheart" – left her University Avenue house to go on Broadway, and later to film with D.W. Griffith. She was co-founder of United Artists Films.

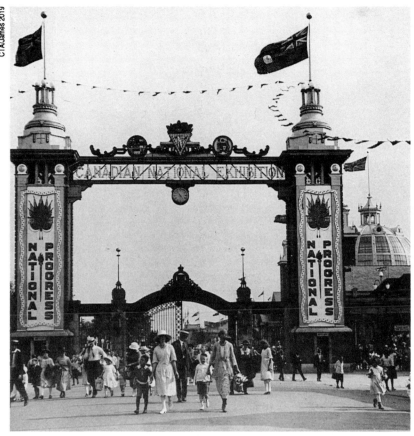

Canadian National Exhibition, 1923.

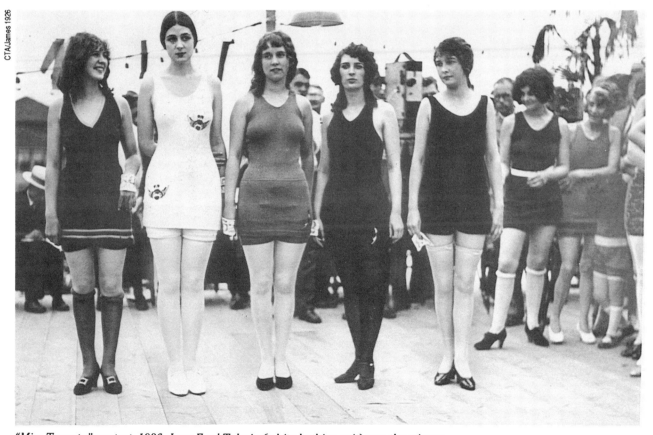

"Miss Toronto" contest, 1926. Jean Ford Tolmie (white bathing suit) was the winner.

Charles G.D. Roberts and Bliss Carman, poets.

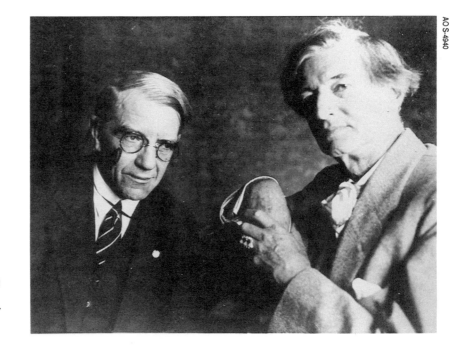

Below: *Arts and Letters Club, Toronto, c. 1921. Seated at the table from left to right are artists Frederick Varley, A.Y. Jackson, Lawren Harris, Barker Fairley, F.H. Johnston, Arthur Lismer, and J.E.H. MacDonald.*

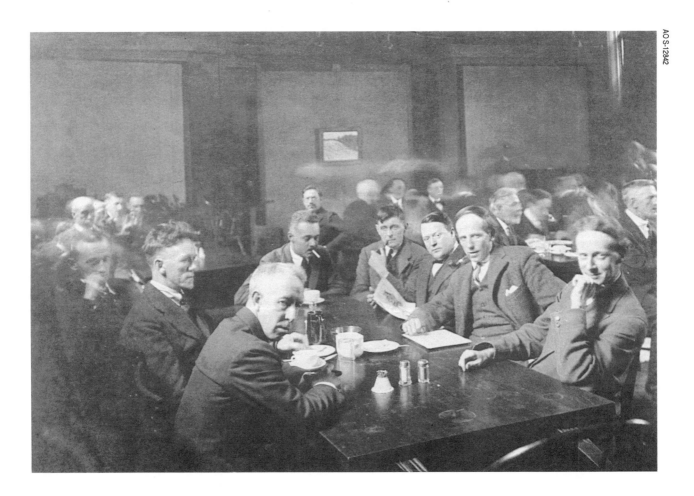

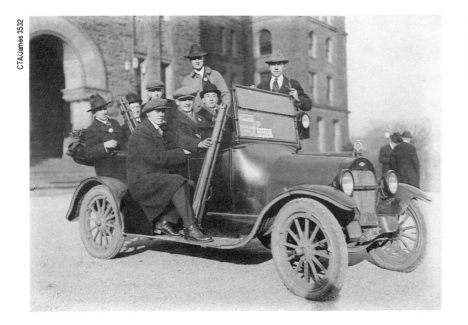

Press corps, Queen's Park, 1919. Press and movie photographers crowd for a "snap" in a Chevrolet bearing the hood-crest of the Ontario Motor League.

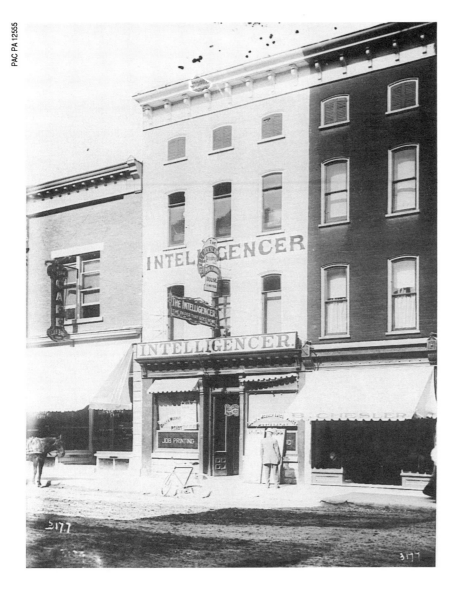

The Intelligencer *Printing and Publishing House, Belleville, c. 1923. One of Ontario's oldest "continuous" newspapers – first printed in Belleville by George Benjamin as* The Weekly Intelligencer *in 1834. The first daily issue of the* Intelligencer *was 1 May 1867. By the end of the First World War Ontario had nearly six hundred newspapers, mostly on a weekly basis but including forty-five dailies. The province's most successful paper was the mammoth* Toronto Star, *whose "razzle-dazzle" antics were gobbled up by avid readers. On one occasion a* Star *reporter telegraphed his scoop to Toronto and then, to jam up the wires for his competitors, shoved a copy of* The New Republic *at the operator and told him to start tapping. The line wasn't cleared until after the* Star *was on the streets.*

195

Sharon Temple, Sharon, 1925. The Temple of Peace was built between 1825 and 1831 by a religious sect known as the Davidites (after their leader David Willson) or "Children of Peace." Formerly Quakers, the Davidites constructed the temple with identical sides to symbolize their tenet that all men are equal before God. The lanterns at the corners of the three roofs held candles to represent the twelve Apostles.

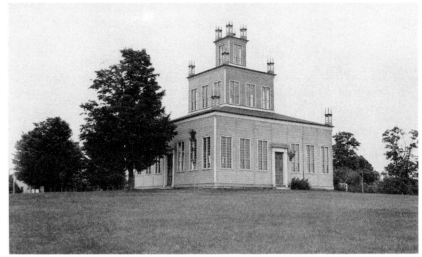

Loblaw's first self-service grocery store, 511 Yonge Street, Toronto, 1919. T.P. Loblaw opened his first grocery in 1900.

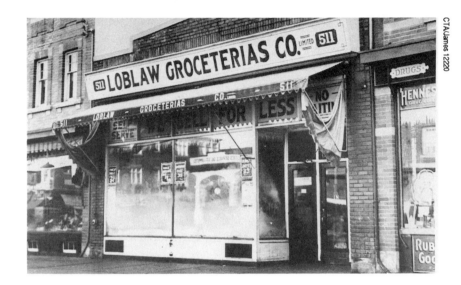

Men's furnishings department, the T. Eaton Company, Toronto, 1919.

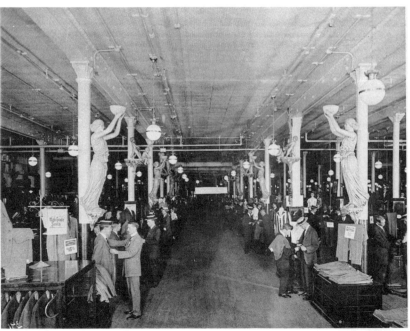

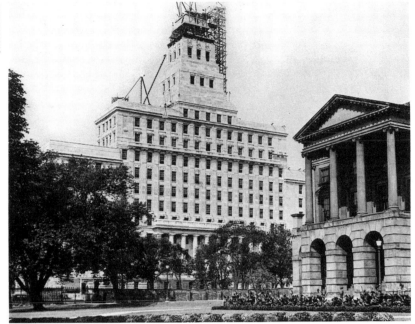

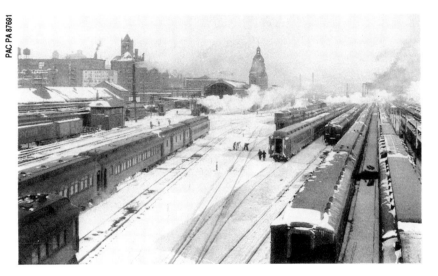

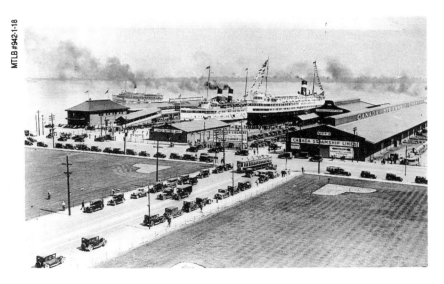

Left: *Canada Life building, University Avenue, Toronto, 1929. Osgoode Hall in foreground.*

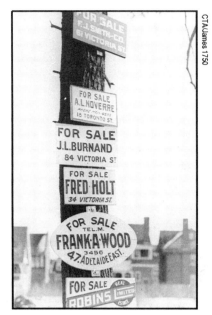

Above: *Before Multiple Listing, Toronto, 1919.*

Toronto Union Station and rail-yard, 1926.

Canada Steamship Lines pier, Toronto Harbour, 1924.

Works locomotives in the round-house of the International Nickel Co., Copper Cliff, Sudbury, pre-1928.

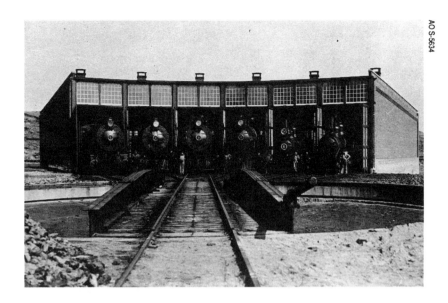

Mission school blaze, Albany House, 1924. Devastation by fire persisted in the Ontario north and remains an awesome hazard even yet despite modern air detection and control services.

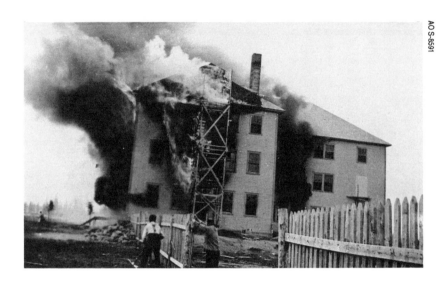

Toronto street-cars used for office and home, after the great fire, Haileybury, 1923.

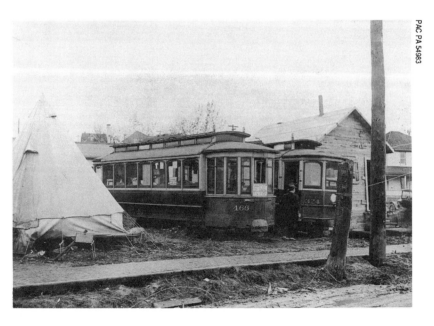

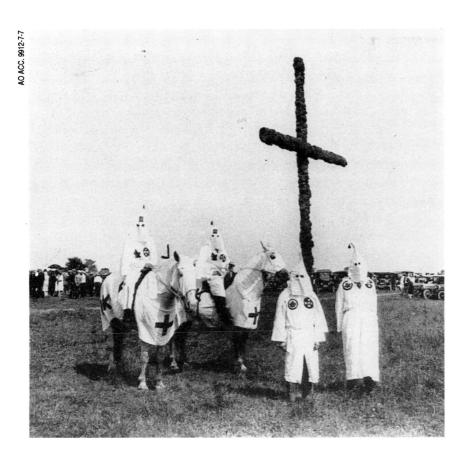

The Ku Klux Klan, hooded defenders of the white race, originated in Tennessee in 1866. They probably took their name from the Greek word *kuklos,* which means "circle." In the 1920s they moved into Canada and, finding blacks scarce, directed their venom towards Jews, Catholics, southern Europeans, and Communists. By 1925 it was widely reported that they were active in Ontario, and it is apparent that several "klaverns" were organized throughout the province, and that the U.S.-based Klan magazine, the *Kourier,* found a Canadian audience.

The most spectacular incident occurred at Oakville in February of 1930 when the Klan paraded boldly through the main street and burned a cross in protest against an impending white-black marriage. The crown attorney took swift action, and charged four of the local Klan leadership under an ancient law that decreed masks could not be worn at night. Only one Klan member was found guilty, however, and he was given a sentence of three months. Public opinion in Ontario and Canada ruled against the Klan and guaranteed it would never gain a substantial foothold. In 1955, however, crosses were burned and KKK signs erected in Amherstburg, but pranksters appear to have been the cause.

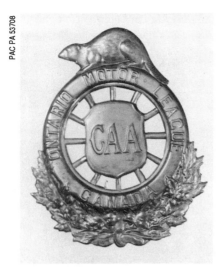

Ontario Motor League badge. The Ontario Motor League was organized in 1907 as an amalgamation of various city automobile clubs throughout the province. By 1915, fifty-four clubs were represented. The number soared in the 1920s. The Canadian Automobile Association was founded in 1911.

Prosperity in the 1920s was exhibited in a number of ways, but the most conspicuous example was the demand for the automobile. Before the war, with huge tariff walls ruling out foreign imports, Canada had a large automotive industry, and Ontario took the lion's share; over thirty-five different Ontario makes had been manufactured, from the graceful Tudhope (Orillia) to Woodstock's practical (and shortlived) Early Day. After the armistice, tariffs began dropping and continued to do so through the 1920s and 1930s. The Canadian automotive industry foundered, and by the mid-1930s all manufacturing was fully under American control.

Not that foreign ownership dissuaded Ontarians from buying cars. By 1929 over half-a-million were registered in the province; in 1918, the figure had been scarcely a hundred thousand. These cars choked ten thousand miles of roadway, only a quarter of which was paved. Maximum speed permitted in the country was 35 miles per hour; in cities, towns, and villages, 20 mph, and on curves and turns, 10 mph.

The automobile changed society. Country and city were drawn closer together, and some of the distinctions were blurred. The primacy of the automobile contributed to an upsurge of mobile crime; the privacy of the automobile changed sexual habits. Tourism was practically re-invented, and older modes of transport – cruise ships and the railroads – suffered a decline from which they never recovered.

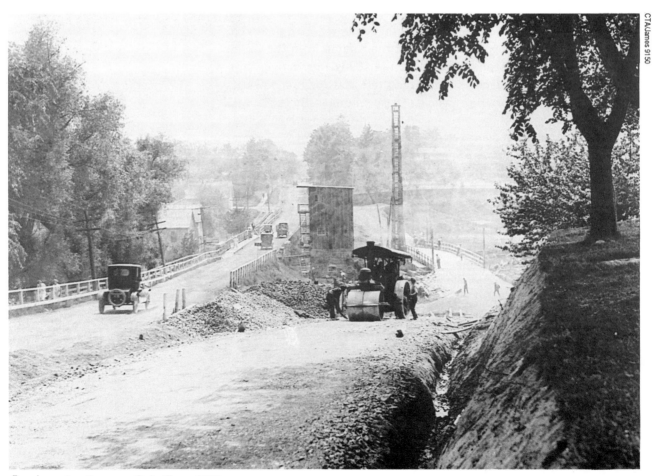

Road construction near Oakville, c. 1920.

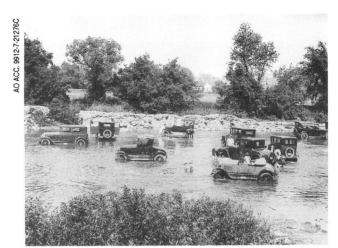

"Auto Laundry," Humber River, Lambton Mills 1927.

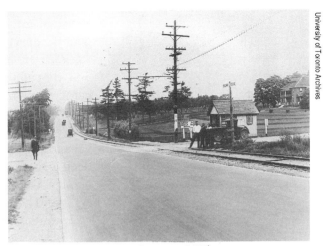

Yonge Street at Highway Seven, c. 1925.

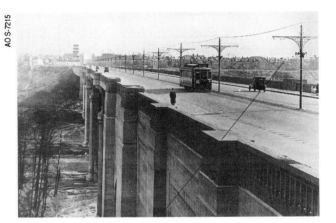

Bloor Street Viaduct, Toronto, c. 1920.

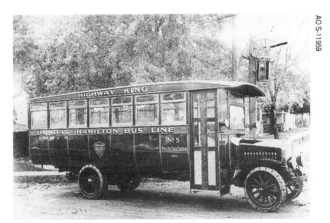

Associated Bus Lines coach, Dundas, c. 1920.

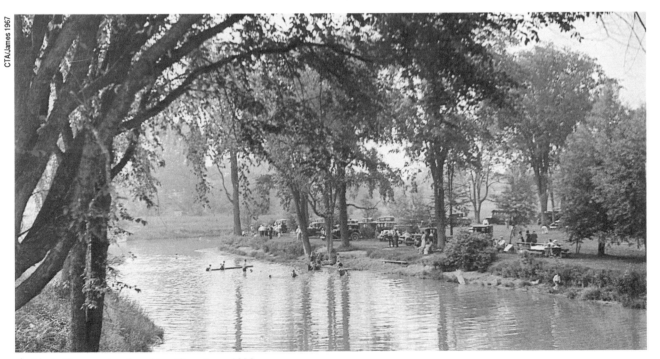

A ride in the country, Lambton County, c. 1928.

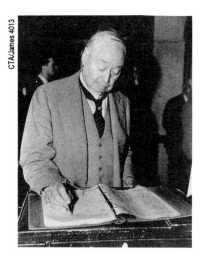

Sir Henry Pellatt visits the home that bankrupted him, Casa Loma, Toronto, 1930.

Depression

Ontario during the Depression was probably better off than most of the Prairies, Québec, or the Maritimes; but of course it depended who you were and where you were. John David Eaton believed that nobody cared about money because there was no money about – after all, he said, you could take out your girl for the evening for $10! He should have ridden the rods to Thunder Bay, or stood daily in lines facing "no vacancy" notices, or slogged in makeshift, makework relief camps deep in the Haliburton Highlands. Then the Depression was desperate enough. Out of it grew an attitude of mind which was fearful and cautious and which cut deeply into the relative gaiety of the 1920s. The government of lacklustre George Henry, who was more at home on his dairy farm at Oriole than at Queen's Park, was an enormous disappointment to those who had backed the bouncy Ferguson administration. Unable to provide enough work or halt rising prices, the government became a perfect target for two forces arising from the Depression and benefiting by it – one was Liberal Mitch Hepburn, the other the phenomenon of socialism seen in the CCF (Co-operative Commonwealth Federation).

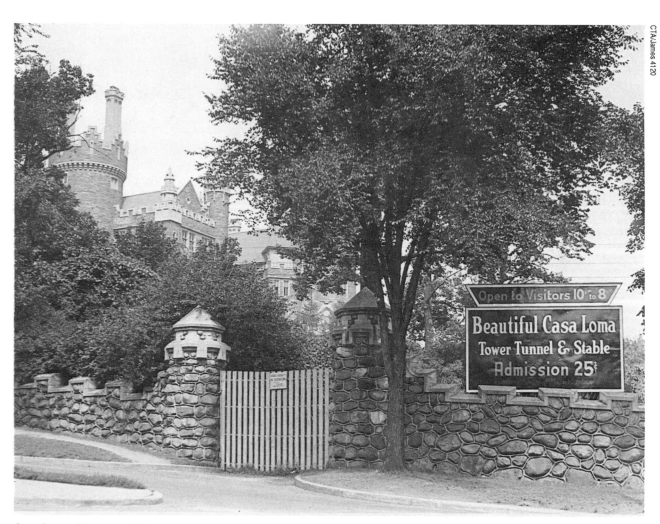

Casa Loma, Toronto, 1930.

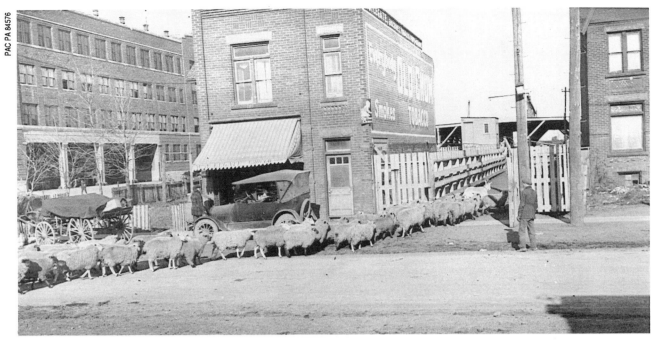

PAC PA 84576

Sheep to slaughter, Union Stock Yards, Toronto 1920.

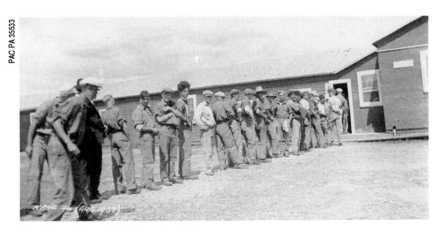

PAC PA 35533

Meal line, Barriefield, August 1933.

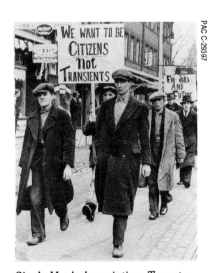

PAC C-29397

Single Men's Association, Toronto, 1930s.

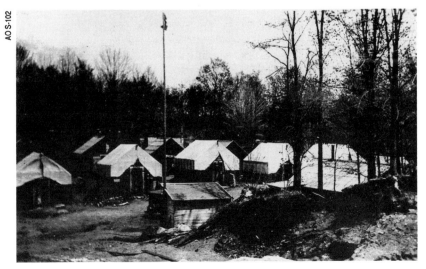

AO S-102

Haliburton Relief Road Camp, Hall's Lake, 1934.

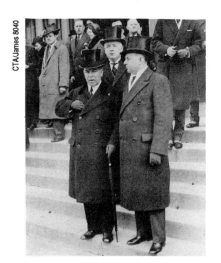

Hepburn with W.L. Mackenzie King, Ottawa, 1930.

Mitch

Mitch Hepburn spent his life talking-up the folk on the back concession lines and talking them into electing him Liberal party leader in December 1930. "I'll supply the pep and ginger and you people hold the brakes," he confidently told the adoring crowd at the King Edward Hotel in Toronto. The brakes were never applied by his rural supporters, because Mitch ran out of pep and ginger in a short time – first by alienating the urban labour vote, and second by trying to outflank the wily prime minister in Ottawa, William Lyon Mackenzie King. In June 1934, Hepburn became the first Liberal premier of Ontario for nearly thirty years and the youngest ever. He had ousted George Henry by promising "the little fellows" a clean, honest, and economic government at Queen's Park – and indeed made quite a show of auctioning off ministers' limousines at Varsity Stadium to prove his point. He offered the kind of mixture of caution and vigour, basically conservative, which Ontarians needed in the harsh, crimping times of the 1930s.

Hepburn had also been able to take advantage of the fissures within the ranks of the CCF, a party which had been welcomed by thousands in 1932 as the "new social order" – even initially by the discontented United Farmers of Ontario. The CCF honeymoon with Ontario barely lasted a year before socialism became too hard for Ontarians to swallow. CCF dogma and in-squabbling soon drove the electorate into the aggressively hospitable Liberal arms of Mitch Hepburn. In uncertain times, a balanced-budget promise appealed far more than an overthrow of the social and economic fabric.

As for labour, though Hepburn pushed through the legislature a progressive industrial Standards Act which did him some credit, he really knew and cared little about labour contracts and such novel ideas as collective bargaining. In this he reflected his rural conservative upbringing in Elgin County and, to be fair, much of the Ontario

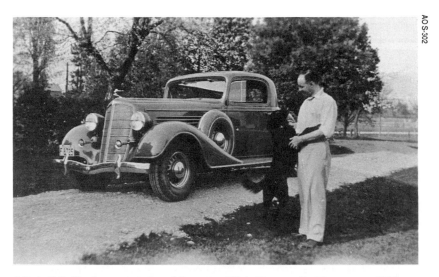

Mitchell F. Hepburn, premier of Ontario, 1934–43, near St. Thomas, c. 1935.

populace at large. Unions meant a threat to law and order in the collective mind, and the resulting higher wages were thought damaging to the province's economy. Nowhere is Hepburn's toryism seen more clearly than in his handling of the Oshawa auto-workers' strike of 1937, where fears of American and "red" infiltration were blown up into preposterous fears and reactionary behaviour. Using RCMP mounted constables and the Ontario Provincial Police augmented by a force of special constables (known as "Hepburn's Hussars" or more bitterly as "Sons of Mitch's"), Hepburn teamed up with the bosses to make sure things went nowhere. When it ended, in weak compromise, Hepburn was lauded across Ontario; but few people saw exactly how much of a demagogue he was and how he had sold out the "little fellow" after all.

It was his attacks, often vitriolic, on Prime Minister King that brought his downfall after 1938. Hepburn was in poor health, aggravated by his punishing pace and his increasing reliance on the bottle. The two tendencies together fed one upon the other during the early years of the war as his personal antipathies and animosities found their way into attacks on the Canadian war effort and connivance with Québec premier Maurice Duplessis against Ottawa. His championship of provincial rights led to excesses which did little to help national unity and Hepburn increasingly looked foolish with his accusations of Nazi-like government from the King administration. Hepburn always seemed to know who and what he was against, rather than what he was for. Even his home county newspaper the St. Thomas *Times Journal* reflected in 1942 that he had "reaped what he had sown." It was time to stand down, and he did, in ignominy.

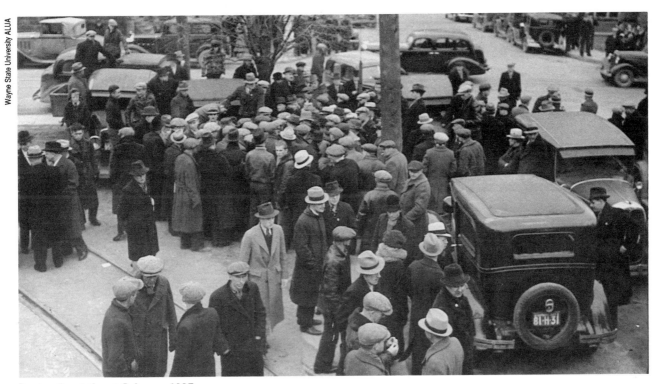

During the strike at Oshawa, 1937.

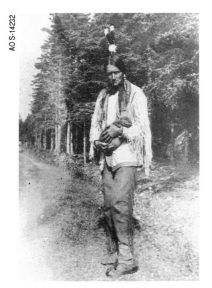

Grey Owl, n.d.

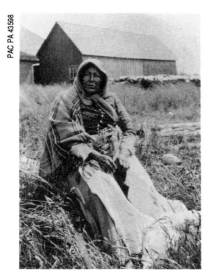

Mrs. Black. Missinaibi, n.d.

Natives – and an adopted Son

In 1938, Wa-Sha-Quon-Asin (He-Who-Flies-By-Night) died. Grey Owl, as he called himself in English, had been born Archie Belaney some fifty years previously in England. He came to Canada at 15 and soon identified himself with the Ojibway Indians around Temagami in Northern Ontario, learning trapping, woodcraft, and Indian lore. He adopted Indian dress and habits and acquired a reputation as a hunter and woodsman. But after falling in love with an Iroquois girl, Anahareo, he turned to protecting animals and wrote and lectured extensively in their defence. He gained a global reputation, and an audience with the King. Only at his death did the truth about Grey Owl begin to emerge. His publisher and biographer, Lovat Dickson, thus explained his impact on the world:

> He reached unerringly to the instinctive longing felt by nearly everybody at a time of crisis for a way of life uncomplicated by progress, unthreatened by war and poverty and hunger. The world depression of the Thirties was at its worst. No ray of hope showed on the gloomy horizon. There seemed no reason why unemployment, the dole, hunger and fear, and a bad conscience among people who did not suffer these things in the same degree, should not become a permanent feature of modern life. *Pilgrims of the Wild* told of the same economic forces desecrating a noble project elsewhere and driving not only people but animals to hunger and flight.
>
> *Wilderness Man*, 1973, p. 233.

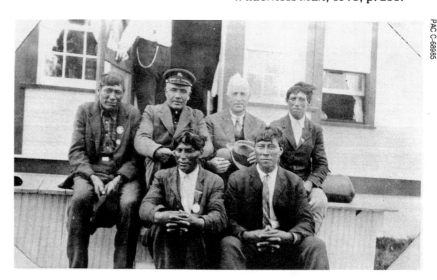

Chief and councillors, Fort Hope Indian Band, with interpreter (in cap) and commissioner, 1929.

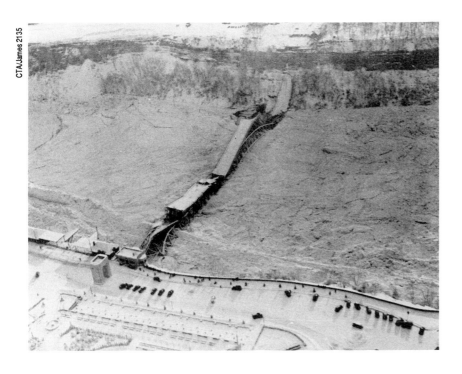

Wreck of the Honeymoon Bridge, destroyed by ice, Niagara Fails, 1938.

"When the giant Lockheed 14H twin-motor thunders out of Malton Monday morning to inaugurate Trans-Canada Airlines daily Montreal–Vancouver express service, a large bundle of copies of the Globe and Mail will lie among the freight. Cities from Winnipeg to Vancouver will receive a Toronto paper with the shortest interval in history between the roar of the presses down by Lake Ontario and the first crackle of the pages as the prairie reader spreads them out."

Toronto *Globe and Mail*, 15 October 1938.

Below: *The pilot of this first air express was Captain R.M. Smith whose career perfectly reflected the development of Ontario civil aviation. He first flew with the forestry division of the Ontario Department of Lands and Forests at Sault Ste. Marie, joined Dominion Airways flying mining supplies to northern fields, then moved on to British North American Airways at Sioux Lookout before joining Trans-Canada Airlines (the future Air Canada). It was fitting too that his plane should touch down en route to the west in 1938, not at the Sault or the Lakehead, but at Porquis Junction (on the T&NO railroad near the South Porcupine turn-off) and Wagaming, north of Superior.*

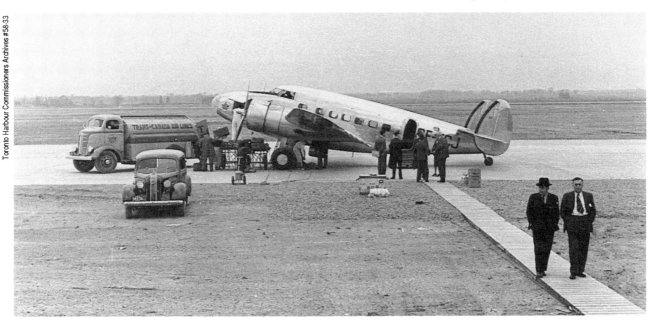

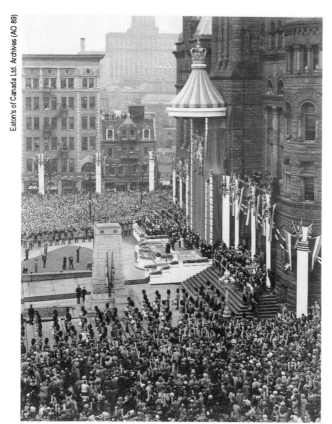

Royal Visit, Toronto City Hall, 1939.

Royal Tour

On the eve of a second world war the Royal Tour of North America in June 1939 was the occasion for tumultuous outpourings of loyalism. Everywhere the tour moved it was greeted by thousands of people waving British flags and cheering – even in Québec. King George VI summed it up in a speech at the Guildhall when he got home:

> I saw everywhere not only the mere symbol of the British Crown; I saw also, flourishing strongly as they do here, the institutions which have developed, century after century, beneath the aegis of that Crown; institutions British in origin, British in their slow and almost casual growth, which, because they are grounded root and branch on British faith in liberty and justice, mean more to us even than the splendour of our history or the glories of our English tongue.

Two months later, Canada was once again at war in defence of those institutions. The decision to go to war was not in doubt, but this time it was a Canadian decision.

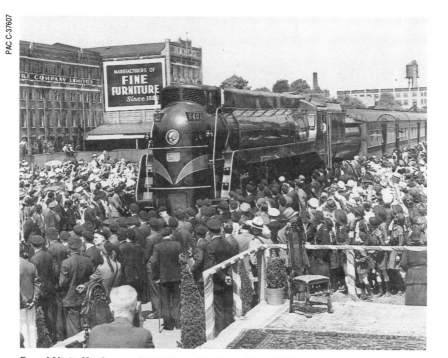

Royal Visit, Kitchener, 1939. Type Northern Class U-4A locomotive #6401 was the product of a special streamlined design tested in the wind-tunnels of the National Research Council and built by the Montreal Locomotive works in 1936. Regarded as one of the most modern of its kind, this massive engine was exhibited at the New York World's Fair just before the Royal Tour.

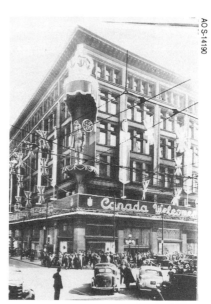

Royal Visit, Robert Simpson Company, Toronto, 1939.

War 1939–45

Ontario's role in the Second World War was no smaller than it had been in the First but by 1939 Canada was not so dominated by Ontario. Factories and railroads still worked to or over capacity as Britain's reliance on Canada as an arsenal of supply and training facilities increased, especially after the fall of France in 1940. The Commonwealth Air Training Plan, by which Canada made a major and expensive (over $5 million in three years) contribution to the war at home, was largely Ontarian in make-up. Nearly half the Canadian aircrew applicants and graduates came from Ontario and, not surprisingly, the epithet "Royal Ontario Air Force" was not far from the truth.

Inevitably conscription raised its head again, more so as the American example after 1941 pressed the issue. King had tried to avoid French-Canadian criticism by bringing in compulsory service only for home defence but in April 1942 a plebiscite was introduced to determine whether the government should be absolved from the pledge not to send conscripts overseas. The answer was a sharply divided English "yes" and French "no." Still King held back to prevent a recurrence of the 1917 crisis. When he was forced to surrender to pressure after casualties outran reinforcements in late 1944, to everyone's relief the racial storm did not break.

In the flailing strands of the Hepburn administration in Ontario, there emerged a rejuvenated Tory party and CCF – each with a new leader, George Drew and E.B. Jolliffe. As the fatigued Liberals

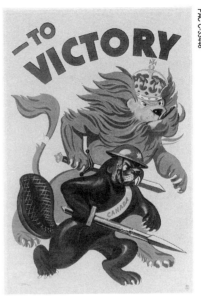

To Victory, National War Services poster, Ottawa, 1939.

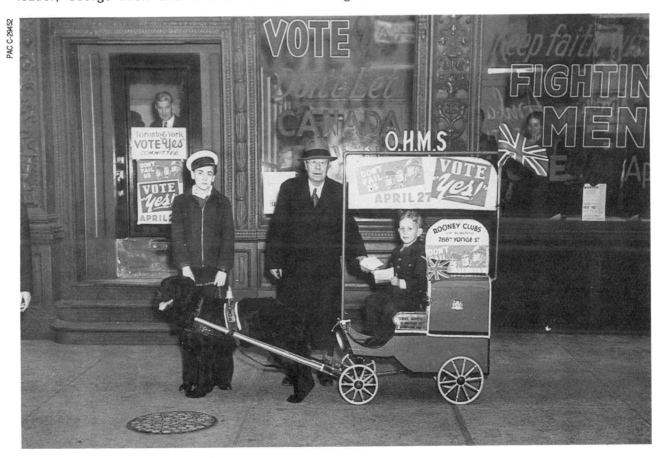

Conscription plebiscite, Toronto, 1942.

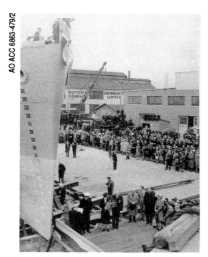

Construction of a minesweeper at a Great Lakes shipyard on Lake Huron, Goderich, 1941.

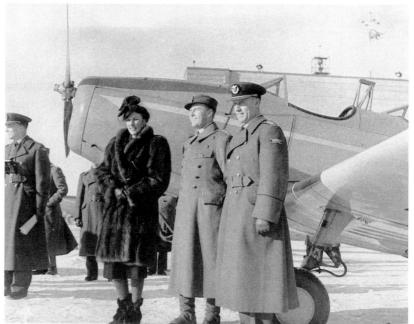

Visit by the Crown Prince and Princess of Norway to Toronto during the Second World War. Many Norwegians trained with the Royal Canadian Air Force as fighter pilots.

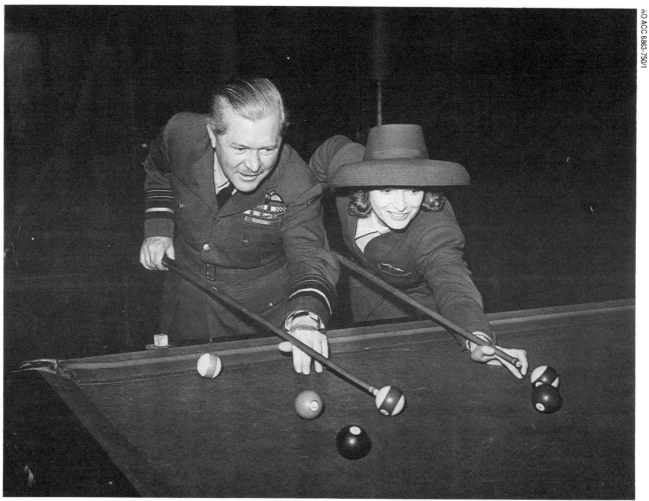

British film actress Anna Neagle and First World War Canadian air ace Billy Bishop appearing at a service canteen, Toronto, 1942.

subsided, Drew and Jolliffe fought it out at a 1943 general election on the kind of program that each could offer to bring Ontario safely through the war and into the expected light at the end. CCF socialism was narrowly beaten by Drew's new "Progressive Conservatism," but in fact they both embraced and advocated the basic tenets of the welfare state. Two years later when Drew took the government back to the polls, the Liberals shrank to a mere 11 seats at Queen's Park; the CCF (through Jolliffe's misjudgement) were reduced from their 34 seats (from scratch in 1943) to a paltry 8. George Drew romped home on the backs of 66 elected party members – a clear mandate to stay firm, cautious, and British.

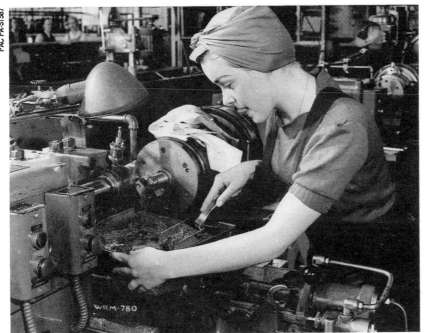

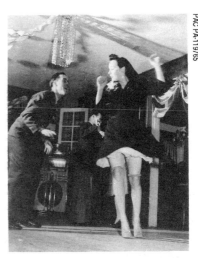

Veronica Foster jitterbugging at the Glen Eagles Country Club, Bolton, May 1941.

Veronica Foster, "The Bren-Gun Girl," at the John Inglis Company Bren-Gun plant, Toronto, 1941.

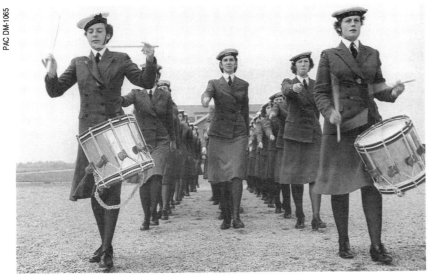

Wrens drilling, Conestoga, June 1944.

Fleet "Finch" II Aircraft of the RCAF, July 1940.

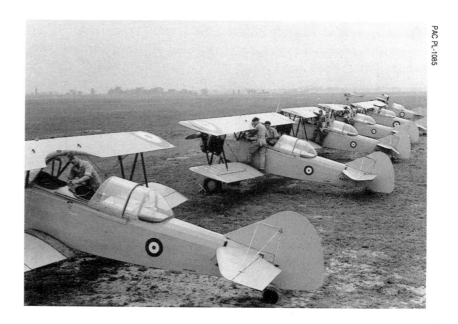

In 1945, Ontario reaffirmed that it wanted Progressive Conservative government by giving George Drew and his party a substantial majority. The Tories were to stay in power another four decades – until 1985 – and then it would take an alliance between the other two principal parties to lever them out. For Ontario the twentieth has largely been a Tory century: sixty-seven years of power to 1990!

Tory popularity was based on a superb party organization, visible leadership, and the general prosperity of the place. But where the Tories have really excelled was with their ability to change leaders while keeping the same government ticking on. Drew begat Frost begat Robarts begat Davis, with the NDP and the Liberals squabbling over the remains. Much of the credit must go to backroom organizers who kept internal divisions from erupting into raging public feuds, and who possessed a watchmaker's sense of timing. When a Tory premier seemed to have peaked in popularity, he resigned and was replaced, but he always retired an undefeated champion. This periodic rejuvenation gives a sense of continuity to government policies. But were they policies or simply postures in a media age?

Ideology has certainly not been a factor in Ontario's politics since the war, except of course with the NDP, whose record of electoral success was substantial but not stunning until the conclusive victory of September 1990. Since Oliver Mowat's day, Ontario's political life has been ruled by "brokerage" politics; that may not be true for the Farmers' government of 1919, nor for some of Mitch Hepburn's frantic interregnum, but it certainly held true for the Tories from 1943 to 1985. Moreover, brokerage politics formed David Peterson's early success and should be the basic path for Bob Rae.

But it is a special kind of brokerage, one that readily reflects the thinking of a great number of Ontarians. The characteristics are familiar – cautious, moderate, "progressive" legislation. The citizenry applauds each achievement at the polls without considering just how carefully contrived the plan really is. But that's good politics.

A case in point, perhaps *the* example, is the "22-point program" upon which the Tories first came to power in 1943. It was a blueprint for the post-war world that sketched in the society that everybody seemed to be fighting for. Among its highlights: number one (interestingly) was to maintain the British connection; then, win the war; safeguard Ontario's rights in Confederation; implement social-welfare schemes such as medical and dental protection; raise old-age pensions; create a provincial housing corporation and an independent Ontario Hydro; introduce municipal tax reform; stimulate the agricultural, forestry, and mining industries; sponsor better labour laws; revamp the educational system. Who would argue with these? Few, over the years, have.

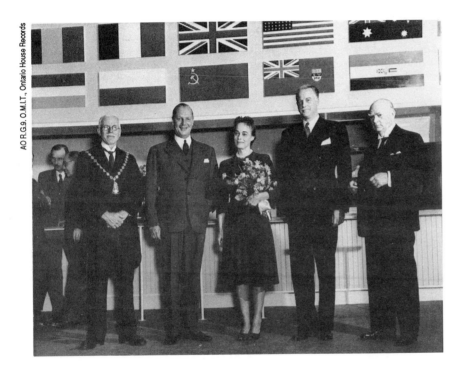

AO R.G.9. O.M.I.T., Ontario House Records

George Drew at the Ontario Services Club opening, London, England, 1944. Left to right, the Lord Mayor of Westminster, Drew, Mrs. Arthur B. Purvis, Major J.S.P. Armstrong, agent-general for Ontario, the Right Hon. Viscount Bennett, P.C., J.P., L.L.B., K.C., former prime minister of Canada.

Immigration, after 1945, continued to be of major importance to Ontario's economy and society. Between 1946 and 1971, 3,536,757 immigrants arrived in Canada – and 1,864,529 settled on Ontario as their destination, over fifty per cent. George Drew's Tory government in 1947 made a dramatic gesture by sponsoring a plan to fly seven thousand British skilled immigrants to resettlement in the province. At first, federal authorities were wary, but finally agreed, and a plan was initiated which eventually resulted in more than ten thousand air immigrants. Ontario labour's response was less than enthusiastic at the prospect of competition being brought in *en masse* and with government assistance. The airlift and the blast of publicity that accompanied it typified the attention-grabbing gimmickry of much of post-war Ontario's political history. The captions for the first three photographs on the following page are the originals prepared by the Ontario government.

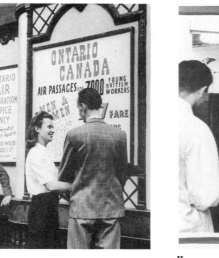

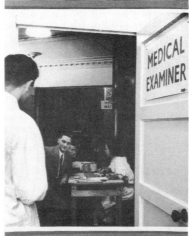

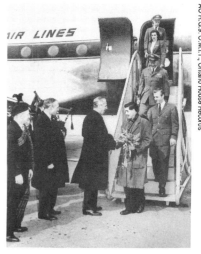

I

II

III

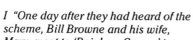

I "One day after they had heard of the scheme, Bill Browne and his wife, Mary, went to 'Rainbow Corner' to look into going to Canada by air. When Bill heard that it would mean leaving his wife and kiddies behind he didn't much like the idea but it was his wife,

Mary, who made the decision for she felt that it was necessary to make the start."

II "Everything is laid on at 'Rainbow Corner' to push the applicants through without delay. A medical examination

is given on the spot, for those in poor health are not wanted. Jim Pooley is next in the list to be examined."

III "The Premier of Ontario official[ly] welcomes Mr. Wm. McMullen, the 7000th Immigrant."*

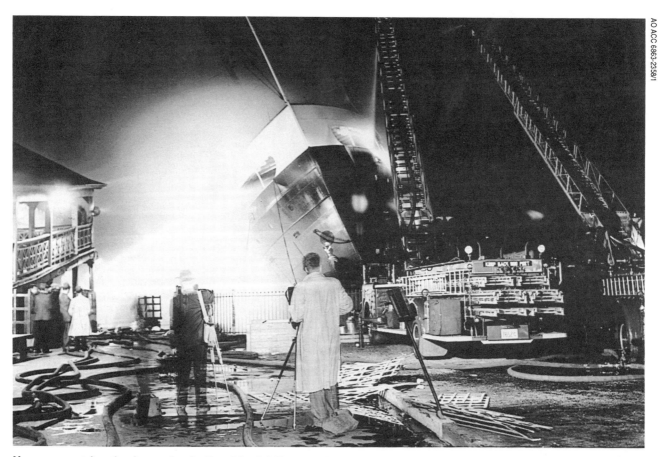

Newsman watches the destruction by fire of the S.S. Noronic, *Toronto, 1949. One hundred and eighteen people died in the dockside fire that consumed the* Noronic. *The tragedy contributed to the end of passenger services on the Great Lakes.*

"Old Man Ontario"

Leslie Frost, premier of Ontario from 1949 to 1961, is an ironic figure. In most ways he epitomized Old Ontario – British, loyal, Protestant, small-town Ontario. During the course of his premiership, however, much of that Old Ontario disappeared.

Frost's political platform was hardly outstanding. Basically he continued Drew's "22-points" program, and generally adhered to middle-of-the-road social policies, but his time in office also saw Ontario move into a wider world. Television, radio, jet aircraft, and modern highways finished off the job that industrialization, urbanization, and immigration had begun at the turn of the century. Ontario's old distinctive character was largely replaced by a new international style and scale.

Consumerism was the most conspicuous new feature of Ontario. And the definition was not simply economic; it stretched from automobiles to apartment blocks, from education to culture. Even Ontario's own history was shaped and fitted for easy digestion. The province's north, once exploited solely for minerals, was now invaded because of its solemn beauty; and its native inhabitants were urged to become part of the "culture package."

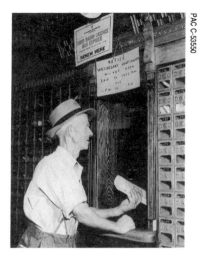

Collecting the daily paper, Merrickville, c. 1947.

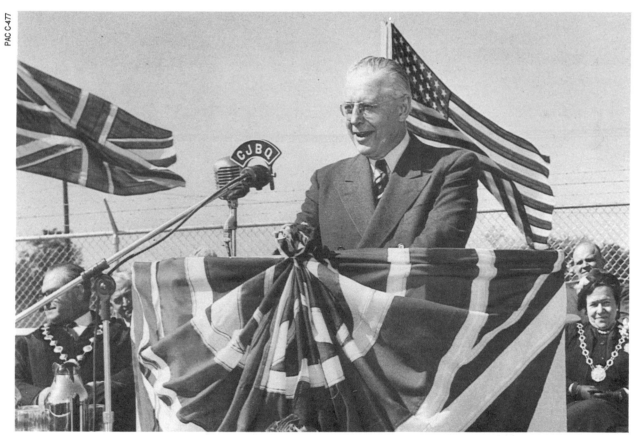

Leslie M. Frost, Premier of Ontario 1949–61, at the official opening of the Bethlehem Steel Corporation facilities, Picton, 11 May 1955.

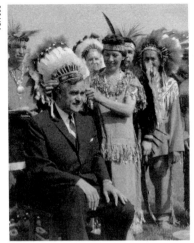

John Robarts receives "chief"
designation, Toronto, 1962.

Additionally, Ontario was beginning to look like everywhere else in North America. The automobile was largely responsible for this. Expressways, freeways, arterial roads, all appeared much the same; so did housing tracts, industrial plants, and shopping centres. Not only did Toronto look like everywhere else, much of Ontario took on a similar appearance – at least in the larger centres. Rural regions changed more slowly, but the intrusive neon sign and gas station were everywhere.

Leslie Frost believed that "government is business, the people's business," and he saw himself as discreet senior management in making Ontario into a modern and efficient industrial state. His personal image spoke of Old Ontario; his actions did not. In a genial way he steered his party through three substantial election victories balancing business growth with social progress; new health-care programs and expansion in education were particularly featured. That organizational caretaker image went further into the managerial boardroom with John Robarts and to some extent with William Davis.

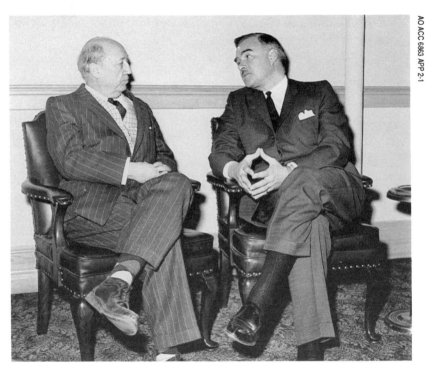

John Robarts, premier of Ontario, with veteran newsman and radio and TV
personality Gordon Sinclair, Toronto, 1961.

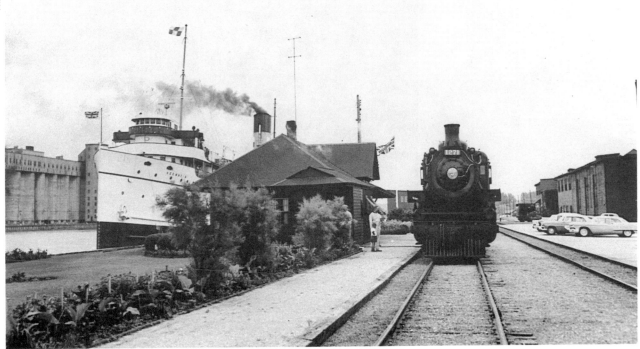

Port McNicoll, July 1957.

Robarts was cast in the role of chairman of the Board of Ontario Inc. He looked the part and frankly enjoyed it. But, significantly, he also fashioned a new role for Ontario in the Canadian confederation. It was Robarts' fate to be Ontario premier at the time of Québec's Quiet Revolution. The constitutional wrangles that characterized the 1960s saw Ontario under Robarts emerge as the nation's great pacifier. Sir Oliver Mowat's vigorous defence of provincial rights, although not entirely dropped, was submerged in new efforts typified by Robarts' optimistic 1967 Confederation of Tomorrow Conference. Ontario increasingly became the visible hinge between the centralized power of Ottawa and the energetic enthusiasms of growing provincial – and especially Québec – governments.

William Davis inherited all these tasks and functions – and, for most of his electoral reign – had the very good fortune to ride the twin steeds of prosperity and split opposition. Still, he came close to losing it more than once, as the Tories were forced from 1975 to 1981 to rule under minority government. Seen in retrospect, it is apparent that the old consensus was gradually breaking down. Ontario was becoming increasingly a multicultural society, regions in the province were finding new voices, serious technological challenges threatened the competitive nature of Ontario business, and, morever, the massive baby boom was at the ballot box, and this new and varied electorate would no longer accept vague bromides about everyone living happily under a shining Ontario sky.

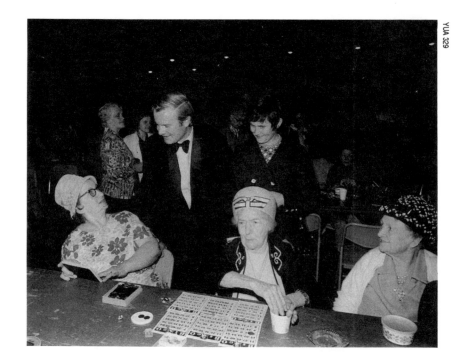

Premier William Davis at bingo, 1971.

The huge service state that had been created in the years after the war was a costly, complicated machine to run. Misguided attempts at sharing power through regional government plans were also proving expensive and unwieldy. William Davis had the good sense to realize that political solutions were as important as structural and bureaucratic ones. His minority governments were intensely sensitive politically and that paid off for him. The middle of the road again became the high road, and pipe-smoking, avuncular Bill Davis gained a national reputation and much respect for the stability of his government. "Bland works," he once proclaimed of governing Ontario. But was it the bland leading the bland?

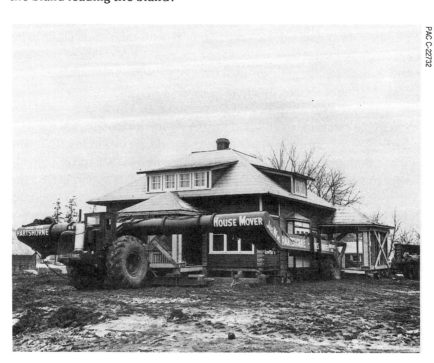

St. Lawrence Seaway construction, 1957. Last house moved from Wales, Ontario, now submerged.

If bland worked, plaid certainly didn't. The Tories stumbled and then fell badly after Davis's decision to step down in 1984. The new leader, pilloried for his personal taste in clothing among other things, was a man not of the familiar centre but of the right: Frank Miller, engineer turned automobile salesman from Bracebridge. This was not the small-town Ontario of old. And the image certainly didn't suit the image of a "world city" that puffed-up Toronto liked to cultivate. More significantly, Miller abandoned "the Big Blue Machine," the vote-getting apparatus that had so successfully propelled Davis' tenure. Most significantly, Miller left the centre of the political spectrum open to the Liberals. In the end, despite the advertisements to the contrary, it proved not to be "Miller Time" at all.

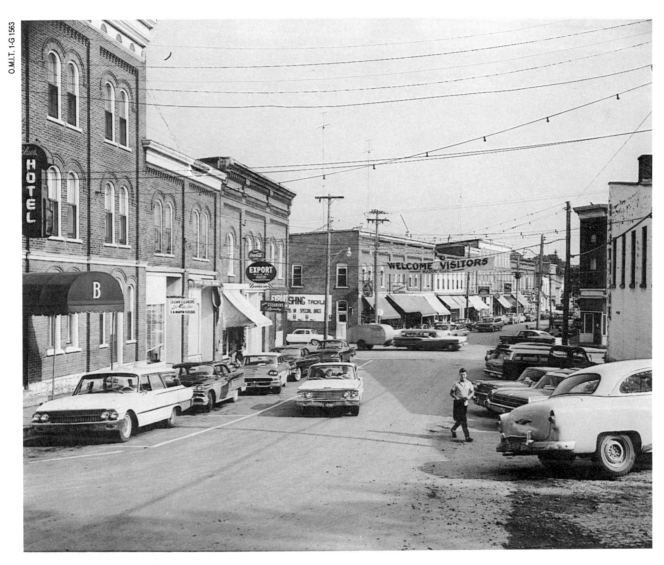

Main Street, Madoc, c. 1963.

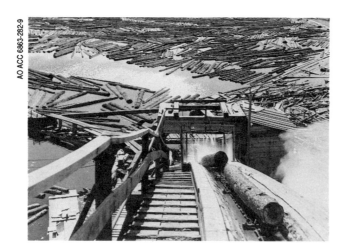

Timber chute, Temagami, c. 1950s.

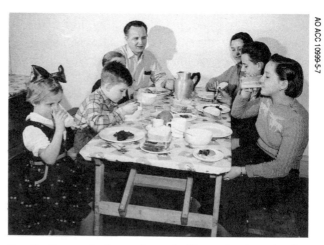

Family dinner of refugees from the Hungarian invasion by the USSR in 1956, Toronto, December 1956.

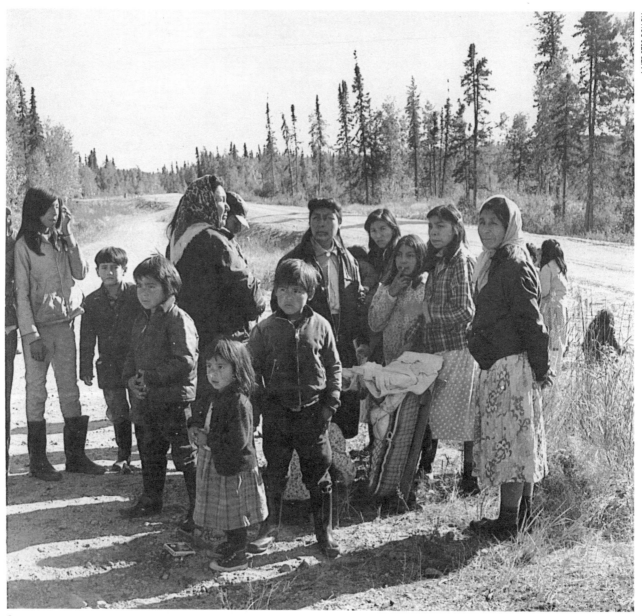

Spectators at historical plaque unveiling, near Pickle Lake, 1969.

220

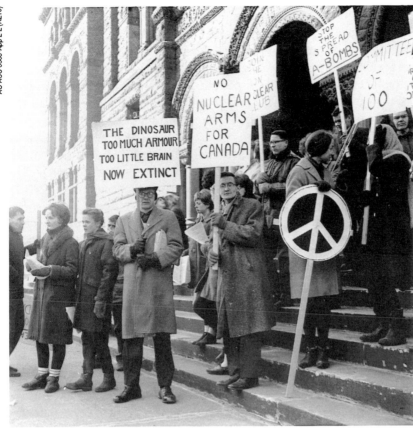

The "Committee of 100" outside City Hall, Toronto, c. 1961. The Canadian Campaign for Nuclear Disarmament was modelled on the British CND inspired by philosopher Bertrand Russell. It gained considerable public support, particularly amongst the young in the 1960s.

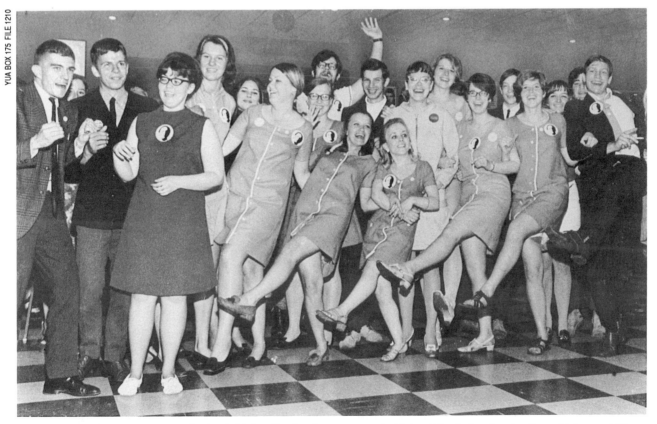

"Trudeaumania" – Toronto High Park MP Walter Deakon's supporters in high spirits during the election which swept Pierre Elliot Trudeau to power, 1968.

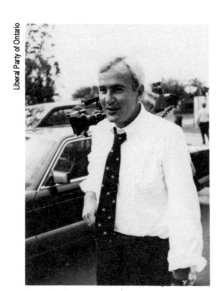

David Peterson.

The election of 1985 was not decisive in itself, but the events that followed it proved to be a watershed. Miller took 52 seats, Peterson's Liberals won 48, and Bob Rae's NDP cashed in with 25. The key was that the Liberals had done so very well. Clearly right-wing Tories could not expect unalloyed NDP support for their minority status. And so it was that an "accord" was worked out between the Liberals and the NDP. The purpose was to ring down the curtain on a near half-century of Tory rule – and even though the price for the NDP seemed a suicidally high one at the time it would eventually pay off for them.

David Peterson and Bob Rae agreed to work together for two years. Peterson was to be premier, and indeed his cabinet included no NDP members. The accord proved a sunshine period. Much popular social legislation was passed: the capping of doctors' charges under medicare, the extension of rent review to modern buildings, full separate school funding, and perhaps most significant of all – proactive pay equity legislation. At the same time the Ontario government stiffened opposition against the U.S.–Canada Free Trade Agreement and extended its role as national peacemaker by championing the accommodations of the Meech Lake accord, the ill-starred effort to restore Québec to a full place in the Canadian constitution. A "good-times" election in September of 1987 gave the Liberals a landslide.

The progressive legislative pace soon slackened. And Peterson's personal style increasingly struck many as being curiously like the Tories he had replaced: solid, centrist, reliable, and brokerage. The accent was more youthful and invigorated but the substance was the same. Ontario seemed once more to have found the dotted white line at the centre of the road and appeared ready to follow it into the future. Peterson additionally assumed Bill Davis's strong centrist position on the Canadian federation. Indeed, he was seen by many as the vital compromiser and it was argued that he was one of the few figures to emerge from the Meech Lake fiasco with some shreds of integrity.

But personal appeal apparently wasn't enough. Peterson's party always seemed less secure than he was. And that party had been

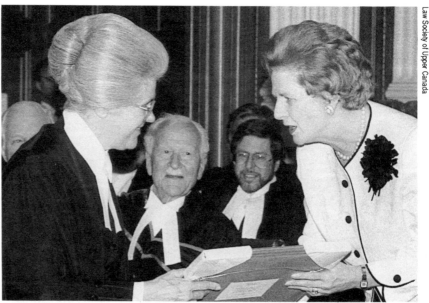

Former British prime minister Margaret Thatcher at her induction as a bencher at the Upper Canada Law Society, 1988.

scarred by a fund-raising scandal (the Patricia Starr affair), was embarrassed by links to Toronto land developers, and increasingly was seen by the lower and middle classes as a gigantic, uncaring engine squeezing more and more taxes. Many, in fact, saw the majority Liberals in cynical (and rather unfair) terms, identifying them directly with the excesses of the decade in which they took power – a group of self-seeking and opportunistic yuppies ignorant of the diversity of Ontario's interests.

Then, in that unhappy summer of 1990, David Peterson erred significantly. The province, the country, the world, were all tumbling into what would prove to be a significant economic recession. Abroad, the Middle East was aflame over the Iraqi invasion of Kuwait; at home, Meech Lake political wrangling had left a nasty taste in most mouths and national events were scarcely temporized by the subsequent dramatic confrontations at Oka and the Mercier Bridge in Québec among native peoples, police, governments, and finally the army. The Ontario electorate was in a cranky, testy mood and their anger against anyone "in charge" was seeking an outlet.

Peterson, after only three years of his mandate, unwisely called a snap summer election, assuming, as did most of the press, that the affair would be a Liberal coronation. In the end, it turned into a Liberal rout with even the Premier losing his own London seat (and resigning his leadership) and, for the first time in Ontario's history, the left-leaning NDP coming to power.

What had happened was both simple and profound. In short, the old tri-partite political model had been broken by the accord of 1985. The NDP was not seen universally any more as the black socialist bogeyman but rather as a party potentially capable of successfully governing all Ontarians, an honest, if untested, alternative that might stress Ontario's long-standing tradition of the use of state power for the public purpose.

Certainly it was clear that Ontario had not swayed towards a full embrace of socialism. Rather, a weighty protest vote had combined with old hard-core support to clinch victory. Upon examination, Bob Rae's majority (74 seats compared with 36 for the Liberals and 20 for the Conservatives under their new leader Michael Harris) rested on some very slender constituency victories and indeed only a scant 38 per cent of the popular vote, a circumstance reminiscent of some Tory minority victories in days past.

Many pundits suggested that a radical left turn loomed for Canada's biggest province. Cooler heads argued that Ontario had a way of temporizing political affairs and that the NDP to stay in power would have to exercise typical Ontario moderation and balance, and warned if they did not, they would be a one-term government.

Those with longer memories, or at least a better sense of the province's past, might have remembered other "dramatic" shifts – the first Whitney urban victory in 1905, or the farmer/labour triumph of 1919, or the Hepburn sweep – and recalled that those who swing too far from traditional Ontario centrist values inevitably do so at their peril. During its first few months of power, the inexperienced NDP government learned this lesson at the expense of several ministerial resignations.

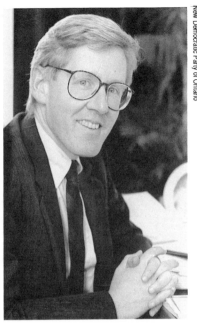

Premier Bob Rae.

223

And where is Old Ontario in all of this modern political hustle and bustle? It is there, certainly a shrunken presence, but still occasionally significant. It raises its hoary WASP head, for example, when issues like full separate school funding or continued allegiance to the monarch are discussed, or in opposition to beer and wine sales in corner stores, or Sunday shopping, or indeed, the thought that Ontario might be declared officially bilingual.

Naturally contemporary Ontario remains inescapably the distinctive product of its past and in many ways loyal to its past. The characteristics derived from its history, however, are getting harder to find. They are perhaps most obvious in forms of government and official procedures. They are also present, however, in what might be called Ontarian attitudes. And the most conspicuous barometer of attitudes in Ontario has always been the province's political life. Personalities and premiers will come and go, from stiff-back Tories to sandal-shod socialists, but moderation and cautious change remain the key to successful policies. The original Loyalists would be comfortable with that. That was what they wanted in the first place.

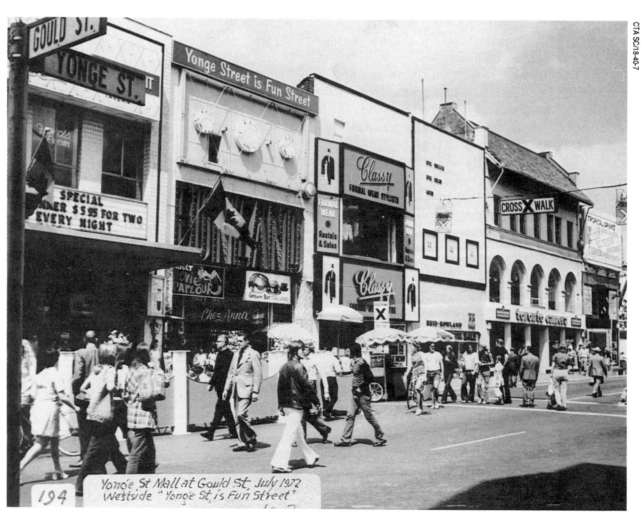

"Yonge Is Fun" – a street with a reputation, Toronto, 1972.

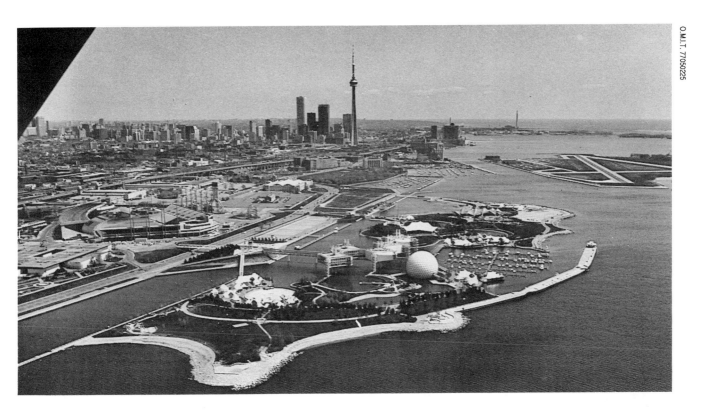

Toronto skyline, including Ontario Place (foreground) and Island Airport (middle right), 1977.

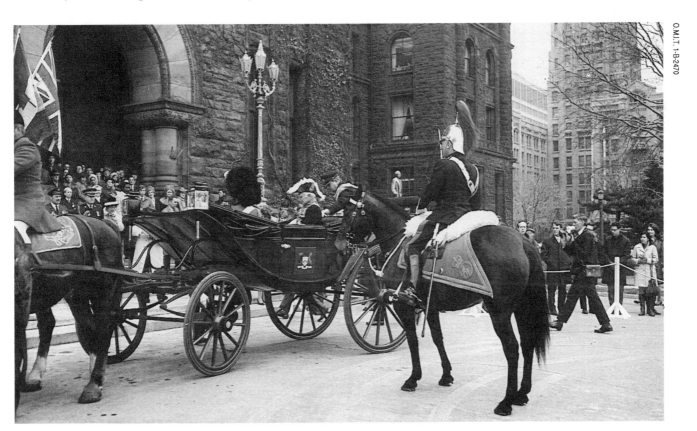

Lieutenant-Governor W. Ross Macdonald arriving to open the legislature, 1970.

Ontario or Anywhere at All?

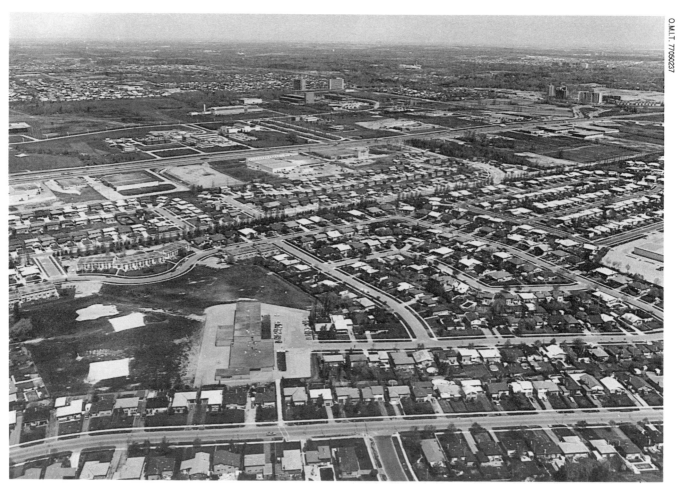

Sheridan Park, near Oakville.

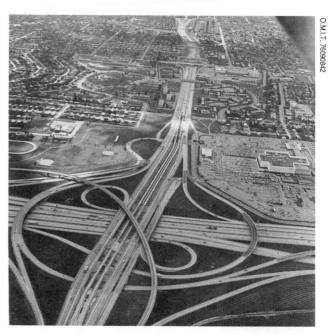

Highway 401 and Spadina Expressway with Yorkdale Shopping Centre, Toronto.

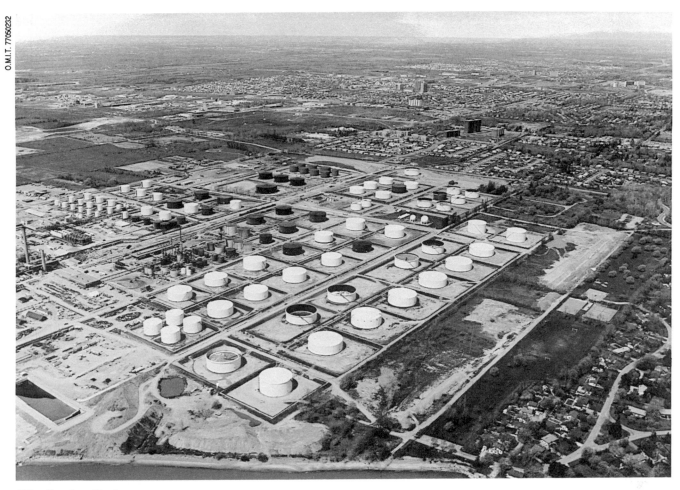

Oil refineries, Clarkson.

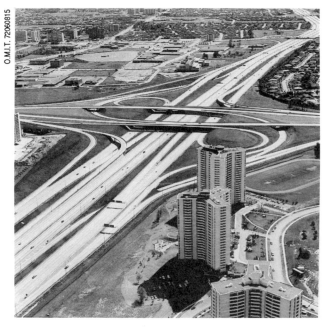

Freeway interchange – the Macdonald-Cartier at the Don Valley, Toronto, 1972.

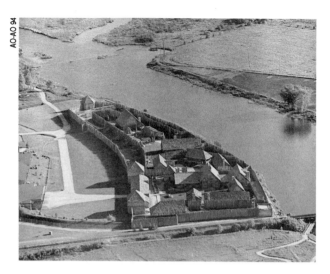

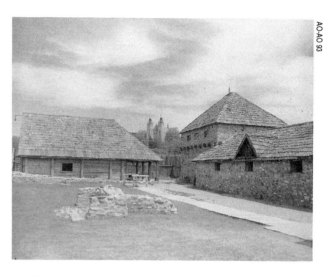

The restored seventeenth-century settlement of Jesuit missionaries on the shores of Georgian Bay, Ste. Marie Among the Hurons, Midland, 1967.

Ste. Marie Among the Hurons, Midland.

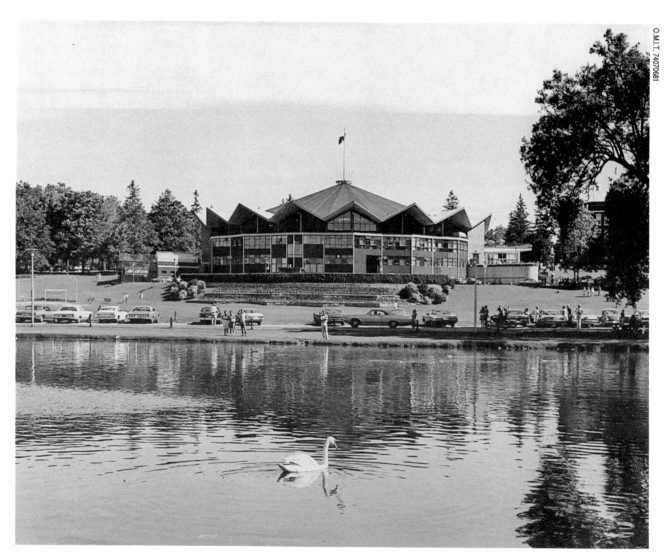

Festival Theatre, Stratford.

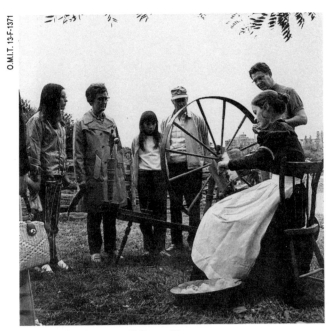

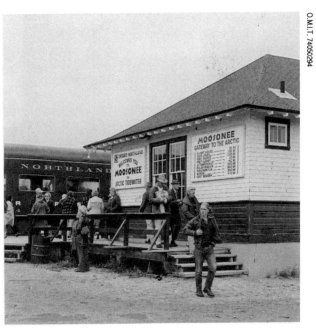

Black Creek Pioneer Village, Toronto.

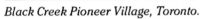

Railway station, Moosonee.

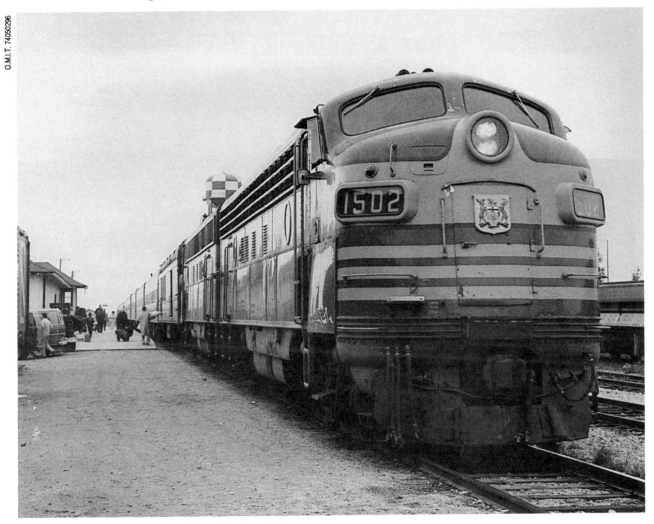

Polar Bear Express, Ontario Northland Railway, Moosonee.

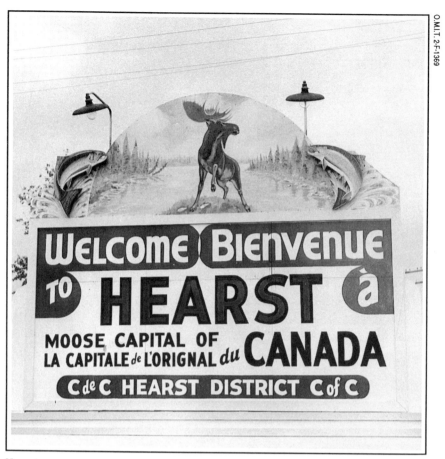

Hearst.

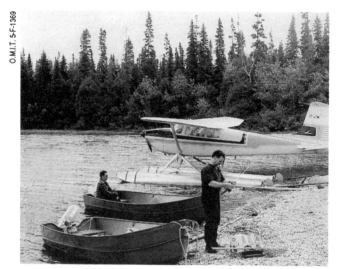

Near Hearst.

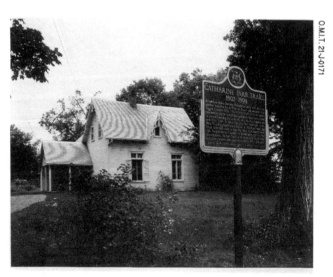

Traill House, Lakefield.

Opposite: *Eaton Centre, Toronto.*

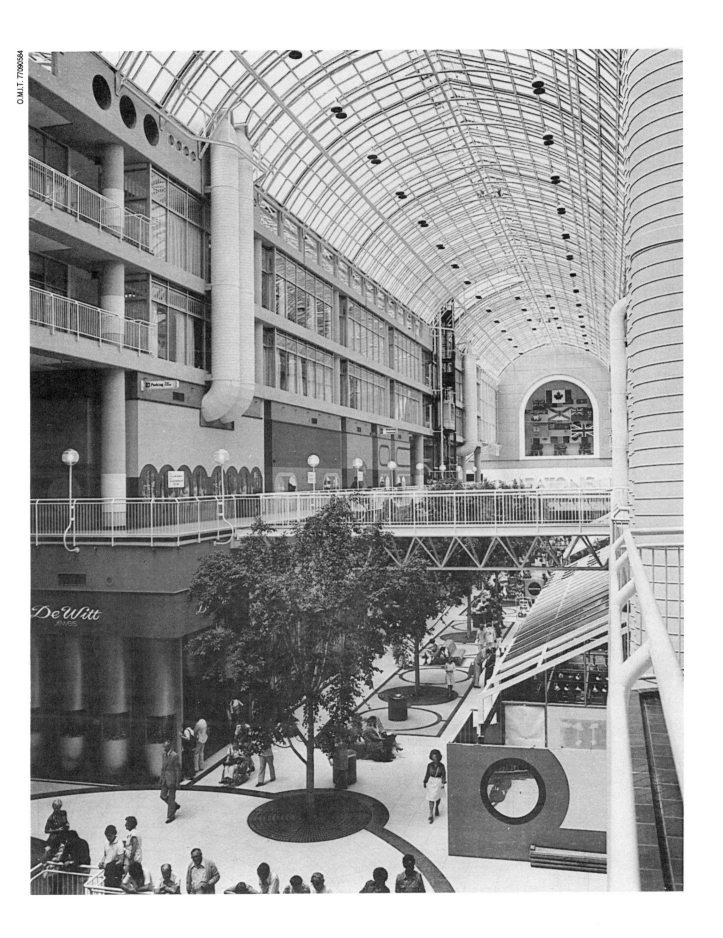

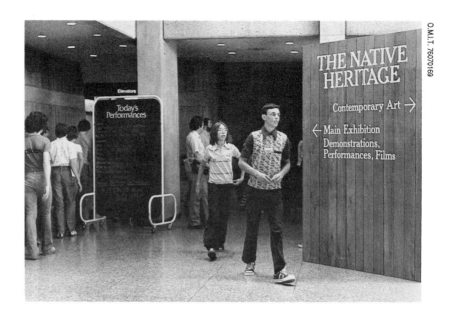

Ontario Science Centre, Toronto.

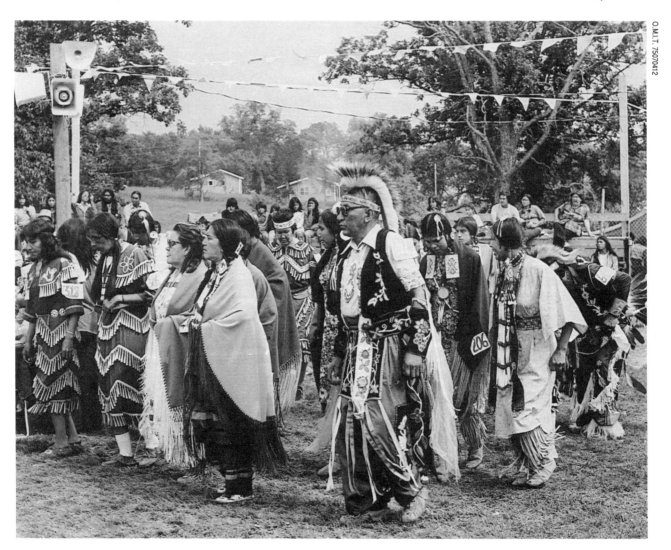

Native celebration at Sioux Narrows, 1975.

Further Reading on Ontario History

Ontario Historical Society. *Ontario History.* Quarterly journal.

Armstrong, Frederick H., ed. *Aspects of Nineteenth Century Ontario.* Toronto: University of Toronto Press, 1974.

Careless, J.M.S. *Brown of the Globe,* 2 vols., Toronto: Dundurn Press, 1989.

——. *The Union of the Canadas: The Growth of Canadian Institutions, 1841–1857.* Toronto: McClelland & Stewart, 1967.

Craig, Gerald M. *Upper Canada: The Formative Years, 1784–1841,* Toronto: McClelland & Stewart, 1963.

Hall, Roger, William Westfall, and Laurel Sefton MacDowell. *Patterns of the Past: Interpreting Ontario's History.* Toronto: Dundurn Press, 1988.

Johnson, J.K. and Bruce G. Wilson, ed. *Historical Essays on Upper Canada: New Perspectives.* Ottawa: Carleton University Press, 1989.

Manthorpe, Jonathan. *The Power and the Tories. Ontario Politics – 1943 to the Present.* Toronto: Macmillan, 1974.

Nelles, H.V. *The Politics of Development: Forests, Mines and Hydro-Electric Power in Ontario, 1849–1941.* Toronto: Macmillan, 1974.

Oliver, Peter. *Public and Private Persons: The Ontario Political Culture, 1914-1934.* Toronto: Clarke Irwin, 1975.

White, Graham, ed. *The Government and Politics of Ontario,* 4th ed. Toronto, Nelson Canada, 1990.

White, Randall. *Ontario 1610-1985.* Toronto: Dundurn Press, 1986.

Wilson, Barbara M. *Ontario and the First World War, 1914–1918.* Toronto: The Champlain Society, 1977.

The most noteworthy additions to this list since the last edition of this book have been the many volumes that comprise "The Ontario Historical Studies Series" supported by the Ontario government and published by the University of Toronto Press. The project, ongoing still, incorporates volumes that are biographical, geographical, and bibliographical plus a number of important thematic studies relating to diverse social, economic, and cultural issues. No student of either past or present Ontario should fail to consult them.

Credit Abbreviations

AO	Archives of Ontario
CTA/James	City of Toronto Archives/James Collection
ECA	Eaton's of Canada Archives (now at the Archives of Ontario)
MTLB	Metropolitan Toronto Library Board (JRR: John Ross Robertson Collection)
OLP	Ontario Liberal Party
O.M.I.T.	Ontario Ministry of Industry and Tourism (now at the Archives of Ontario)
PAC	Public (now National) Archives of Canada
THC	Toronto Harbour Commission
UCLS	Upper Canada Law Society Archives
UT	University of Toronto Archives
YUA	York University Archives

Index